D0824590

Armitage's
GARDEN ANNUALS

Armitage's GARDEN ANNUALS

A Color Encyclopedia

ALLAN M. ARMITAGE

TIMBER PRESS
Portland · Cambridge

All photographs, except those of Cleome
'Linde Armstrong' (page 118, by Linda Askey)
and Clitoria ternatea *(page 121, by Meg Green),*
are by Allan M. Armitage.

Copyright © 2004 by Allan M. Armitage
All rights reserved

Published in 2004 by

Timber Press, Inc.   Timber Press
The Haseltine Building   2 Station Road
133 S.W. Second Avenue, Suite 450   Swavesey
Portland, Oregon 97204, U.S.A.   Cambridge CB4 5QJ, U.K.

Designed by Susan Applegate
Printed in China

Library of Congress Cataloging-in-Publication Data

Armitage, A. M. (Allan M.)
[Garden annuals]
Armitage's garden annuals: a color encyclopedia/Allan M. Armitage
p.   cm.
Includes index
ISBN 0-88192-617-5
1. Annuals (Plants)—Encyclopedias.
2. Annuals (Plants)—Pictorial works.
I. Title.
SB422.A68 2004
635.9'312'03—dc21   2003056520

This book is dedicated
to all the plant breeders
I've met over the years.
It is your dedication and insights
that have allowed me to write
about the extraordinary diversity
of ornamental plants.
Thank you for enhancing
this thing we call gardening;
you are my heroes.

Contents

Part Two. Selected Plants for Specific Characteristics or Purposes 359

Preface

SOME THOUGHTS OF THE AUTHOR

Gardening is anything but staid and steady. When you talk with people who enjoy gardening, they are often so excited they can hardly stand still. They want to get out there and put a pond in their yard, or learn how to put in a stone wall, or build a path. They get dirty and downright exuberant when a particular plant or weed is discussed. Put gardeners together in a garden, and if they drink (which most do), they have to sip and walk at the same time. The most conservative people, who would never ask a stranger for the time of day, do not hesitate to ask a gardener for a piece of a plant they're lusting for. Vibrant, exciting, and changing—but hardly dignified.

On plant preferences

There are those who are collectors—their passions run to hydrangeas, daylilies, or iris. In general, they are in the minority, which is just as well; they are rather boring. I mean, how many daylilies can be described in a single sitting? (Answer: 67.) Most gardeners enjoy all plants if they perform well for them, although to be sure, we have many "woody camps" and an equal number of "herbaceous camps." As for me, I love them all. Annuals, perennials, shrubs, trees, bulbs, and ferns, who cares, as long as they look good.

On annuals

Nothing has changed faster in the last decade than the development, distribution, and use of annuals. In 1995, the predominant group of annuals were bedding plants such as petunias, marigolds, and alyssum. They were the engine that supplied most of the annual color in gardens. Today, those plants are still popular, but the volume of newcomers like angelonia, cuphea, verbena, and coleus has quadrupled as these genera become more available to the gardening public. Add bacopa, duranta, osteospermum, and stictocardia to the mix, and to be sure, we're not in Kansas anymore. However, while the genera keep appearing, the number of species of annuals within that category is often limited to one or two, and in many of these new genera, there may be only a handful of cultivars. The large number of cultivars of bedding plants like petunias and impatiens, by contrast, mirrors their longevity and popularity. Without doubt, some of the less common material shown in this book will be commonplace in five years, providing additional diversity each year.

On plant names

Most gardeners would be astonished at the amount of time and effort that goes into making a new cultivar of plant.

From hybridizing, selection, propagation, distribution, promotion, and marketing—not to mention the tedious jobs of removing viruses and the tissue culturing needed for some material—the outlay of time and money is significant. Yet isn't it amazing how many annuals (and perennials) are so poorly labeled? Labels are often missing, or too small for anyone over forty to read, or simply state "4-inch annual," and on and on. What is the point of going through such an expensive, time-consuming practice when retailers accept such shoddy labels? The losers, of course, are the gardeners, who seldom know what they are buying, and furthermore will be unable to purchase the same thing next year. And what a mess is created when the same plant is sold under two, three, or even four different names! We are a patient lot, we gardeners, but not stupid. Get your labels cleaned up, and we will come back for more. Make it simple to buy the product, and then get out of our way.

On new plants

A lady named Rachel walked into our greenhouse, which was overflowing with new and colorful exotic plants. She selected two plants and approached me to pay. I told her that they were research plants and not for sale, and, with great

8

disappointment, she turned to put them back. However, her selected plants caught my eye, and I was floored! Believing she had the entire contents of the greenhouse from which to choose, she had picked up a 4-inch pot of 'Better Boy' tomato and a 6-inch pot of Leyland cypress! Uncommonly common plants when surrounded by such beauty. I asked her why she had chosen these (after all, I figured I was making the world a better place), and she looked me straight in the eye and said, "That's all I recognized." Now, thanks to Rachel, I keep all this new stuff in perspective. They will soon be recognizable, but until then, there are some lovely new geraniums I'd be happy to share with you.

About the book

I wrote this book because people, including myself, love pictures. It is designed to provide well-researched and useful information, but in this book, the text supports the images shown. It was created as a complement to my larger annual book, *Armitage's Manual of Annuals, Biennials, and Half-Hardy Perennials*; in that book, the information is far more specific and in-depth, and the images support the text. Between the two, you'll learn everything you ever wanted to know about annuals but were afraid to ask.

It was also written to complement another wonderful color book, *Armitage's Garden Perennials*. With the two together, you can have your own photo-library of more than 2800 images, and some good reading to boot. I hope you enjoy yourself, enjoy your reading, and enjoy your garden.

ACKNOWLEDGMENTS

Thanks to Stephanie Anderson, who helped with the incredible job of image management, and to Judy Laushman, who read over the text and provided insightful comments. And without doubt, the book is far better because of my editor, Franni Bertolino Farrell.

PART ONE
Armitage's Garden Annuals
A to Z

Abelmoschus moschatus 'Pacific Scarlet'

Abelmoschus esculentus 'Little Lucy'

Abelmoschus

I first heard of *Abelmoschus* in a botany class in Canada, where we students were provided with various cooked vegetables to examine, identify, and taste. I looked at this long mucus-covered green thing in front of me and, after gagging on the taste, I was told it was a favorite vegetable for soups. It was called okra. No wonder there are so few tins of Campbell's in our pantry. And what kind of a name is abelmoschus anyway? If nobody can pronounce it, how in the world will anyone buy it for the garden?

Of course, the definition of conservative can generally be found in the dictionary under "Canadian cuisine," so when I moved to the South, I became far more tolerant of weird things like okra and grits. I tried okra again, and they . . . well, they were as slimy and awful as I remembered. However, when I had more opportunity to reexamine the ornamental members of the genus, I found some neat plants hidden in that long name (pronounced "a bel *mos* kus"). And, believe it or not, ornamental forms of okra are among my favorites.

While I can drive by a field of corn and hardly notice it, a field of okra (*Abelmoschus esculentus*) is another matter. At least I slow down, because the plants can be as tall as a man and the flowers are always ornamental. Fields

Abelmoschus esculentus 'Okrazilla'

Abelmoschus manihot

Abelmoschus manihot 'Cream Cup'

of okra are one thing, but who wants a 5' tall, prickly plant with slimy fruit in the garden anyway? Well, let me introduce you to the fat fruit of an ornamental form called 'Okrazilla', a name only its creator, Ralph Cramer, could think of. As hard as it was for me to get used to the idea, these are used in bouquets and floral arrangements. And I may add, people are always impressed once they learn what they are. Wouldn't you be? With the introduction of ornamental forms, the gardener now has some choice. A dwarf form such as 'Little Lucy' (only about 2' tall) has something for Canadians and Southerners alike, gorgeous cut-leaved bronze leaves, handsome flowers, and edible fruit. The genus belongs to the mallow family, so expect some damage from Japanese beetles and thrips. Full sun.

If the idea of ornamental vegetables is appealing, an even brighter member is aibika, *Abelmoschus manihot*. These are similar to okra and are cultivated extensively in the lowlands of Melanesia as nutritious leafy vegetables. The flowers are also beautiful, making it a candidate for both the flower garden or kitchen garden. Ornamental forms can be up to 3' tall; one such, 'Cream Cup', provides stunning creamy yellow flowers with a purple eye on spineless plants. Full sun.

If planting veggies is not up your alley and other colors are called for, why not try musk mallow (*Abelmoschus moschatus*)? The common name comes from the fact that the seeds smell somewhat musky. Other common names are musk-dana and ambrette, and plants are grown in India for seed exports, mainly to Europe, for use as an aromatic oil. Drug manufacturers are also introducing new herbal drugs containing ambrette for medicinal use. Odor and oil aside, the cultivated forms of the plant provide flowers in red and pink, and continue to bloom all season. As with all members of the genus, flowers persist only a day or two, but so many are formed, it does not seem to matter. Much shorter than *A. manihot*, they may be used as bedding plants or simply to provide some interest in containers or the front of the garden. Two of my favorites are 'Pacific Light Pink' and 'Pacific Scarlet'. Full sun.

Abutilon

FLOWERING MAPLE, CHINESE LANTERN

The flowering maple has been a favorite for a long time. It had its heyday in Great-grandmother's front hall or parlor, where it was much better known as the parlor maple (the maple name refers to the shape of the leaves). Sadly, as the parlor went the way of the smoking jacket, parlor maples all but disappeared from horticulture. They have come back,

Abutilon ×*hybridum* 'Bella Deep Coral'

MORE ☞

however, and showy abutilons can now be found in containers and gardens from Tampa to Toronto. Dozens of cultivars are sold, but mail order and the Internet are the best sources for flowering maples today. Availability in garden centers and nurseries is still limited.

Many species exist in this interesting group of plants, and the most common are generally listed under *Abutilon ×hybridum*, or common flowering maple. They come in an array of colors; if you find a good source of these plants, you may find them under their correct names, however, names like "Red" or "Yellow" are not infrequent. In general, the hybrids are 1–2½' tall and are better suited to containers or baskets than to the garden proper. I also enjoy some of

Abutilon ×hybridum Bella Hybrids

Abutilon theophrasti 'Salmon'

Abutilon ×hybridum 'Souvenir de Bonn'

Abutilon ×hybridum 'Savitzii'

Abutilon pictum 'Thompsonii', flowers

the newer flowering forms such as the Bella Hybrids, available in yellow and deep coral among other colors.

One likely parent of the hybrids is *Abutilon theophrasti*, known as velvet leaf. However, it is apparent that Tinkerbell has been spreading pixie dust over the leaves of some of the hybrids, and variegation patterns seem endless. Tall plants with exquisite eye-catching foliage may be found in 'Souvenir de Bonn', stunning almost-white foliage with green centers is seen in 'Savitzii', and leaves splashed with yellow are the norm in Thompson's flowering maple, *Abutilon pictum* 'Thompsonii'. The orange flowers on the variegated forms are handsome, but it is the foliage that catches the eye.

Not to be outdone are the pendulous forms, represented mainly by trailing maple, *Abutilon megapotamicum*. The flowers are tubular, pendulous, and generally in red and yellow. The most common form is 'Variegatum', in which the leaves are splashed with yellow, and I also enjoy 'Melon Delight', with its obvious trailing maple in its blood. Exceptional for containers and hanging baskets.

All abutilons tolerate full sun in the North; a little afternoon shade in the South is appreciated, especially with the highly variegated forms. Some of the larger-leaved forms will wilt in hot sun but come back fresh in the evening.

Abutilon pictum 'Thompsonii', foliage

Acalypha

Acalyphas are schizophrenic. The flowers of chenille plant (*Acalypha hispida*) are in long braids, whereas those of copperleaf (*A. wilkesiana*) are hardly noticed at all. Some plants bear large leaves in an array of incredible (some may say gaudy) colors, while others bear thin, twisted leaves in muted tones. Regardless, plants have found their way to the garden, and containers and baskets of acalyphas are seen more and more on porches and patios in North American gardens.

The prettiest of all is probably chenille plant, historically a gift plant, and its long-flowered relatives. Sold for the long tassels of pink to red flowers, plants are also grown for the attractive heart-shaped leaves. Try it in large hanging baskets in morning sun, afternoon shade. Trailing red tail, *Acalypha reptans*, has shorter flowers and is not quite as showy but may be tougher and can be used as a groundcover. The best is probably the pink-flowered 'Summer Love'.

Chenille plant may be the prettiest, but it is not the toughest for the long-

Abutilon megapotamicum 'Variegatum'

Abutilon megapotamicum 'Melon Delight'

MORE ☞

Acalypha hispida

Acalypha hispida, basket

Acalypha reptans

Acalypha reptans 'Summer Love'

Acalypha wilkesiana 'Copperleaf' with lantana

Acalypha wilkesiana 'Kona Coast'

Acalypha wilkesiana 'Bourbon Street'

Acalypha godseffiana 'Heterophylla'

Acalypha godseffiana 'Tricolor'

MORE ☞

season rigors of our gardens. My bet for tough goes to the foliage forms whose flowers are secondary. These are found mainly in the cultivars of copperleaf, whose splashes of color are eye-popping. They are dressed for the costume party, bedecked in colors that Ralph Lauren could not have dreamed up. In containers, they provide the pizzazz. 'Copperleaf' is a handsome plant well suited to containers, and 'Bourbon Street', with its copper and pink leaves, really made our containers at the University of Georgia look good. For simplicity, the bright green and yellow leaves of 'Kona Coast' are hard to beat.

While the leaves of some copperleaf plants are large and colorful, others are more like long pliant needles. I notice the expressions of people as I try to explain (unsuccessfully) the subtly variegated beauty of the plant known as 'Heterophylla', a selection of *Acalypha godseffiana*. The twisted leaves can be thought of as many things, but seldom is beautiful mentioned. However, the multicolored 'Tricolor', with similar ghoulish leaves and habit but far more colorful, evokes more sympathy, if not love. Of course, I think they are both must-have plants.

None of the cultivars is easy to find at your garden shop, however, many are available through mail-order sources. Full sun.

Acmella oleracea

TOOTHACHE PLANT, EYEBALL PLANT

Here is a plant with something for everyone. From the gardener's perspective, where else can you find eyeballs staring back at you as you putter around the place? From the herbalist's point of view, this plant is chock-full of medicinal goodies, and claims of its benefits can be found all over the Internet. It is best known for its numbing effect on the mouth and gums, and thus became known as toothache plant. In the event of a toothache, chew on the flower bud, and relief from pain will be almost instantaneous, probably lasting at least until you can get to the dentist. The flower buds are said to provide the most sensations, and in the name of learning, I make my students sample various plant parts. The sensation of numbness and the production of saliva occur within thirty seconds and, while not pretty, it is the only time I can get my students to salivate over my class. None of the literature I have read shows any danger from this sport, but by all means, try it first before introducing your neighbor to its medicinal virtues. By the way, slugs seem to like it as well—maybe that's where slug slime comes from.

Acmella oleracea

Acmella oleracea 'Peek-A-Boo'

Agastache foeniculum

Agastache foeniculum 'Honey Bee Blue'

Agastache foeniculum 'Honey Bee White'

The plant is now called *Acmella oleracea* (its original name was *Spilanthes acmella*). Seed is available through seed catalogs, but plants are finding their way to plant outlets as well. You might find a new cultivar called 'Peek-A-Boo', and although it is not significantly different from the species, it should be more available. Far prettier plants for sale, but few are more interesting. Full sun.

Agastache
GIANT HYSSOP

It may be argued that *Agastache* does not belong in a book about annuals, that many species can be grown as perennials at least to zone 5. However, plants grow rapidly and flower profusely in a single season (a characteristic unbefitting a self-respecting perennial), so that they can be enjoyed as annuals or perennials. In the Armitage garden (zone 7b), I find most agastaches persist for only two or three years. Regardless, these culinary herbs all provide a fragrance of anise, some gently fleeting and others highly pungent.

By the way, I don't want to get into plant pronunciation . . . however, people hesitate to say this genus because it doesn't seem to "sound right." Most Americans pronounce the name "*ah* ga

MORE ☞

stash," I prefer the British "ah *gas* ta key." I realize this makes me sound like a plant snob, but the real reason I prefer it is that it helps me spell the darn thing correctly. Both are just fine, and fulfill the Armitage Axiom of Plant Pronunciation, "Get the syllables in the right order, and fire away."

Many of the agastaches available to the gardener are hybrids, and offered as such. The nomenclature of some of the cultivars is either unknown or mixed up, so I will mention some of my favorites and attempt to put some parentage with them.

I think some of the best plants are associated with *Agastache foeniculum*, anise hyssop. These tough plants are easy to grow from seed but will be 3–4' tall. The cultivars 'Honey Bee Blue' and

Agastache foeniculum 'Golden Jubilee'

Agastache urticifolia 'Licorice Blue'

Agastache austromontana 'Pink Pop'

'Honey Bee White' are exceptional performers but grow no taller than 2½'. I am also most impressed with 'Golden Jubilee', whose golden yellow foliage looks good all season and contrasts well with the purple flowers. And if you can find some 'Licorice Blue', likely a selection of the nettle hyssop, *A. urticifolia*, you will be rewarded with an abundance of long-stemmed cut flowers for the vase.

If color is the goal, sit tight because breeders are really going to town.

Gardeners are still excited about one of the earlier ornamental forms of *Agastache barberi*, called 'Tutti Frutti', and while I have seen it look good here and there, I always thought the name was more exciting than the plant. However, I am really impressed with the endless flowers on 'Pink Pop' (probably a selection of *A. austromontana*) and the big rosy purple blooms of the hybrid 'Hazy Days'. But even those fine colors didn't prepare me for the wonderful golden

flowers found in the selections of *A. aurantiaca*. It is tough to walk by 'Navajo Sunset', which grows 2–3' tall and is covered with flowers all summer, without stopping for a moment. Its partner 'Apricot Sprite', which also causes knee-lock, differs by being a little shorter but is equally lovely.

Most of these plants are likely hardy to zone 6, but who cares? Enjoy them for a year or two. Full sun.

Agastache barberi 'Tutti Frutti'

Agastache 'Hazy Days'

Agastache aurantiaca 'Navajo Sunset'

Agastache aurantiaca 'Apricot Sprite'

Ageratum houstonianum, garden

Ageratum houstonianum 'Artist Blue'

Ageratum houstonianum 'Pacific Pink'

Ageratum houstonianum climbing stairs

Ageratum houstonianum 'Leilani'

Ageratum houstonianum

FLOSS FLOWER

Walkways, driveways, and garden paths have been lined with an abundance of floss flower for decades, and this old-fashioned bedding plant has really not changed a great deal over the years. Having said that, however, I can't think of a more beautiful use for this plant than the one I saw at the Isle of Mainau in southern Germany, where old stone stairs became so much more inviting in partnership with the floss flowers planted there. And the borders at the Butchart Gardens in British Columbia seemed to come into focus as the ageratum begged you to follow. Most of us can't reproduce such scenes, but they provide inspiration.

I tell my students that to help remember the name for *Ageratum houstoni-anum*, they should think about the city in Texas. However, while that is an effective mnemonic device, the species was named for a Scotsman, William Houston, who was a plant collector in South America.

A good deal of breeding has occurred in recent years. Ageratum is undergoing a transformation to include new colors for the garden and can also be highly useful as cut flowers, if the right cultivars are chosen. They occur in the common shade of lavender, but 'Artist Blue' is anything but common. Rose, pink ('Pacific Pink'), and white are quite popular. The best cultivar for the garden, as opposed to the garden edge, is 'Blue Horizon', which provides an upright habit, loads of flowers, and stems strong enough to be cut and brought inside. Professional cut flower growers thought it was so good that the plant was recognized as the Fresh Cut Flower of the Year by the Association of Specialty Cut Flower Growers in 2003. Compared to the standard edging form 'Blue Danube', the contrast is obvious. 'Leilani' is about halfway between the two in size and provides a choice between the tall and the short. Full sun in the North, afternoon shade in the South.

Alcea rosea

HOLLYHOCK

I can't seem to write about this species without dredging up bad memories of bad plants in a bad garden in Montreal where I grew up. That really isn't fair, because as I have gotten older, cultivars have gotten better, and heck, why should memories of a few Japanese beetles and a little rust disease ruin my youthful reminiscences? One thing that has not changed, however, is that people still love hollyhocks, warts and all.

MORE ☞

Ageratum houstonianum 'Blue Horizon' with *A. h.* 'Blue Danube' as edging

Alcea rosea 'Barnyard Red'

Alcea rosea, bicolor form

Alcea rosea 'Indian Spring'

Alcea rosea 'Nigrita'

Alcea rosea 'Nigra'

Alcea rosea 'Chaters Purple'

Most plants are simply raised by putting seeds in prepared soil, although started plants can be purchased and may be worth the extra dollars. Plants are technically biennials with plenty of cold tolerance, and although they may come back occasionally in the spring, or a few seeds may sprout, it is best to treat them as annuals. Many named cultivars have been selected; however, most people totally forget what the labels said and are really only interested in the flower color anyway. Plants produce a wide range of flowers, including singles in many colors, although old-fashioned reds, like 'Barnyard Red', and bicolors, in which the center is a different color than the rest of the flower, seem the easiest to find. One of the best single hollyhocks, 'Indian Spring', consists of flowers in a riot of color. They grow 4–6' tall on strong, stout stems. An "in" color that never seems to fade from a gardener's consciousness is black or deep purple, and both 'Nigrita' and 'Nigra' are "in."

Want a little weirder, try the doubles. Some excellent eye-poppers can be seen around gardens; I particularly like the Chaters series (a series is a group of similar plants that usually differ in flower color only), and 'Chaters Purple' is tough to beat. Of course, a little dose of reality

may be needed here. Most hollyhocks in most parts of the country are filet to bugs, beetles, and assorted fungi. The doubles are no better than the singles; in fact, the extra layers of petals simply seem to provide more meeting places for the beetles. If Japanese beetles are not a problem (careful of earwigs too), then plant a bunch of hollyhocks; if the pests arrive at the same time as the flowers open, get the bricks ready and start clapping. Certain chemicals are also quite useful, simply be careful. Full sun.

Alocasia

ELEPHANT EAR, TARO

Regardless of what the "experts" tell you, there are no easily visible differences between this genus, *Colocasia*, and *Xanthosoma*. I have visited taxonomists, studied books, and talked with aroidites (plants belong to the family Araceae), who say that simply looking at the plant, even if in flower, will not tell you if a certain cultivar is an alocasia or a colocasia. It drives me crazy not to be able to tell you to look at the petals, or stamens, or leaves to make a determination, but the only place these genera consistently differ is the ovary, and the way in which the

Alcea rosea with Japanese beetles

Alocasia macrorrhiza, Australia

MORE ☞

ovules are held there. In my book on annuals (*Armitage's Manual of Annuals, Biennials, and Half-Hardy Perennials*), I stated, "[Leaves] are always peltate in *Colocasia* but less so in *Alocasia*." In fact, leaves usually start out peltate in *Alocasia* but may change to normal attachment. The reason for this long-winded introduction is that the cultivars I mention probably belong to the genus listed, but then again they may not. The bottom line: as a gardener, it doesn't matter; if you want to be a taxonomist, meet me in the lab.

My, but how these plants have been embraced. Ten years ago, gardeners outside the Gulf States would have been hard-pressed to find any alocasias for sale. While they are surely not common today, they are no longer rare, and a few cultivars have become downright familiar. *Alocasia macrorrhiza*, with its enormous leaves, is one of those easier-to-find species. Some gardeners feel that these are "plants for the South," however, the large stand at the marvelous Allen Centennial Gardens on the Madison campus of the University of Wisconsin amply states the distance this tropical has traveled.

Alocasias are beautiful to behold, but holding is all you should do. All parts are poisonous, and eating is expressly forbidden. If you wish to test this statement, expect painful irritation of lips, mouth, tongue, and throat after chewing as well as difficulty in speaking. After that, probably nausea and diarrhea, delirium, and, finally, death. Ho hum, just another engaging plant for our gardens.

The choices of *Alocasia* are numerous, but only a few are easily found at the garden center. Alongside the big-leaved *Alocasia macrorrhiza*, you may find its variegated selection, *A. macrorrhiza* 'Variegata', with no two leaves seemingly the same. Both of these, but particularly the variegated form, tolerate some shade and still keep their color. Three or four extraordinary species may sometimes be found in the garden center, but mostly they reside in conservatories and botanical gardens. The leaves of copper alocasia, *A. cuprea*, remind me of burnished metal, the veins making a wonderful contrast to the rest of the wide leaf. The arrow-shaped dark purple leaves of the long-lobed alocasia, *A. longiloba*, are quite spectacular, while the big, bold shiny purple sheen of *A. plumbea* 'Metallica' makes the Armitage garden more exotic than ever. And the clean green and white lines of *A.* ×*amazonica*, usually known as green velvet, seem perfect in every way. However, do not fret if you cannot find such species for the garden; they are present in many of the hybrids, and these are becoming more readily available every year.

Alocasia macrorrhiza, University of Wisconsin

Alocasia macrorrhiza 'Variegata'

Alocasia longiloba

Alocasia cuprea

Alocasia 'African Mask'

Alocasia plumbea 'Metallica'

Alocasia 'Polly'

MORE ☞

I would not hazard a guess as to which hybrid I see the most, but 'African Mask' must be up there with the leaders. Plants go under a number of names; it's real name is *Alocasia micholitziana* var. *maxkowskii,* but I dare you to say that ten times. A few others have similar looks. I love the habit and leaf color of 'Polly', which is a dwarfer form with dark velvet leaves and obvious white to silver venation; it is quite spectacular. As a young or mature plant, it is my first choice. 'Frydek' is fabulous, with wonderfully velvety looking leaves; they are similar to those of 'Polly' but thinner, and with veins of light yellow rather than white. And how can you not enjoy the large smokey leaves of 'Corazon', the immense black foliage of 'Black Magic', or the white-veined dark leaves of 'Fantasy'? The only cultivar I have trouble falling in love with is the speckled thing known as 'Hilo Beauty', which is offered as an alocasia, a colocasia, and even as a caladium. I am alone, of course, as this is one of the best-selling tropicals on the market. To each his own.

In late fall, cut the foliage back when it starts to decline (around 40°F) and dig the tuberous rootstalk. If a heated cold

Alocasia ×*amazonica*

Alocasia 'Frydek'

Alocasia 'Corazon'

Alocasia 'Hilo Beauty'

Alocasia 'Black Magic'

Alocasia 'Fantasy'

frame or greenhouse is available, pot up the root and keep it around 40–50°F. If plants are to be enjoyed in a conservatory or greenhouse during the winter, be prepared to heat the structure to about 70°F. If no overwintering facility is available, enjoy their beauty during the season, and save your money for next year.

Full sun in the North, afternoon shade in the South, and reasonably good drainage: they are not bog plants like some species of *Colocasia*.

Alonsoa

MASK FLOWER

I first saw a diminutive plant of this genus in a greenhouse in Denmark, then a second species in a garden in England, where every plant seems to look its best. Small salmon to coral flowers were all over the 1' tall plants. They were cute, flowered heavily, and looked terrific in a container. I had to have some, and finally found some seeds, which I proceeded to sow. Not a month later, I spied the species I first encountered in England, in orange-red this time, in a container at North Hill, in southern Vermont, the extraordinary garden of Wayne Winterrowd and Joe Eck. If those fine gardeners were using it, well, then, maybe I wasn't so far off after all.

The plants were mask flowers, which is a simpler and far more user-friendly way of saying *Alonsoa meridionalis* or

MORE ☞

Alonsoa meridionalis, Denmark

Alonsoa warscewiczii, Vermont

Alonsoa warscewiczii, red form

Alonsoa warscewiczii, England

Alpinia zerumbet 'Variegata', Georgia

Alpinia zerumbet 'Variegata', University of Wisconsin

A. warscewiczii. The latter is perhaps a little easier to grow and may flower more profusely, but the former, although more shrubby, is also worth a try. There are not a lot of choices; plants come in pink, red, and salmon-coral, but probably others can be found with a little effort. They are not particularly happy in hot weather, but even if they melt out by July in the South or August in the North, they will have provided a few months of pleasure. Best in containers. Full sun in the North, afternoon shade in the South.

Alpinia zerumbet

GINGER LILY

The rise in popularity of tropical plants in the landscape should not be considered surprising when one understands that most annuals, such as impatiens and begonias, are from the tropics. However, the rise in demand for annuals like *Alocasia*, *Kaempferia*, and ginger lilies has been nothing short of remarkable. One of the first plants to be used by landscapers and gardeners was the variegated ginger lily, *Alpinia zerumbet* 'Variegata'.

I have always enjoyed ginger lily in my garden because it tolerates shade but grows well in full sun. The promise of flowers is an empty one in most temperate gardens; it simply is not warm enough for long enough, but temperatures that hover around 80°F are excellent for foliage growth. The big leaves all arise from the ground (no main stem) and are streaked in yellow and green. The amount of streaking differs on every leaf, and the leaves are brighter (i.e., more yellow) in the sun than in the shade.

They are particularly useful in areas of heavy foot or road traffic; they are tough, colorful, and essentially maintenance-free. Gardeners in the North and West tend to shy away from plants that have "ginger" as part of their name, in

MORE ☞

Alternanthera dentata 'Purple Knight'

Alternanthera 'Red Runner'

Alternanthera 'Red Threads'

Alternanthera 'Party Time'

it is not quite as dark as the other two, nor does it bear the same luster.

Two wonderful colorful but low-growing hybrids have been developed. 'Red Runner' is a bronzy red with relatively large leaves, but 'Red Threads' is even better, with its fabulous thin red leaves. The name joseph's coat refers to the fact that many colors were apparent on the leaves, but the demand for monochrome floral designs led growers to produce few of the old-fashioned multi-colored forms. However, with the appearance of 'Party Time' and its upright habit, three-colored leaves, and vigorous growth, gaudy is back! It differs from others in the genus by being more open in habit (not a great choice for a floral design), but it also performs better and is more colorful in shade. In sun, the pink fades, some damage occurs to the tips of the leaves, and the plant color is far more subdued. Full sun for most, partial shade for 'Party Time'.

Amaranthus

AMARANTH

If all the amaranths were put in a line, the genus would win the Halloween prize in the plant world, hands down! Perhaps that is why there is such a love-hate relationship with these wonderfully weird plants: you love to see them, just not in your own garden. I am the same way—I admire, I gush, I look twice—but always I am looking in public gardens, arboreta, or conservatories. Are we a little too timid?

Then again, maybe not. Fire-engine red has nothing on the color of some of the tall amaranths, and they can be seen from miles away. I always enjoy traveling to Ontario, and to the Royal Botanical Gardens, located between Hamilton and Burlington. Someone there has his or her act together and is not afraid of bright colors. I remember walking a path and spying large stoplights of color, beckoning me to come closer. They dominated everything around them and were perfectly sited to draw me like a magnet. They were plants of 'Early Splendor', and they were a warning of the brightness yet to come. As I rounded another corner, I had to shield my eyes as I came face to face with 'Molten Fire'. Their spectacular color made even the yellow celosias brighter. The color of 'Illumination' is a little more subdued but not much. Still a 55-mph plant, and still brightens up the flowers around it. But somebody really got into the sauce when they thought that 'Perfecta', sometimes known as 'Splendens Perfecta', would win a lot of

Amaranthus 'Illumination'

Amaranthus caudatus, British Columbia

Amaranthus caudatus, Ontario

MORE ☞

friends. Truly a clown at the circus, but impossible to ignore and even harder not to enjoy, the plant has been dubbed the summer poinsettia.

I admit to enjoying the show that amaranths provide. And, just when the red has strained the eyeballs a little too much, I find relief in one of my favorites, 'Aurora'. In Rastafarian dreadlocks of gold, these plants look like they just emerged from a good drenching at the end of the rainbow.

Most cultivars just mentioned probably belong to *Amaranthus tricolor*; however, the taxonomy of the genus is being debated, and species may be lumped or split in the future. The flowers of most are rather forgettable; it is the colored bracts that provide the show. But not all the amaranths are so endowed; a few, such as *A. hypochondriacus* (prince's feather) and *A. cruentus* have marvelously colored flowers. 'Prince's Feather' is used both as a cultivar and common name for the 4–6' tall plants, which seem to flow as they flower, while the wheat color of the thousands of small flowers on 'Hot Biscuits' proves that not all amaranths are red.

If plant people were to come up with their favorites, it is likely that the tassel flower (*Amaranthus caudatus*), also known by the macabre name of love-lies-bleeding, would be on a few lists. The flowers are similar to those of chenille plant (*Acalypha hispida*) but thinner and longer, and appear to be arranged in small knots down the tassels. In the Butchart Gardens in British Columbia, crowds were gathered, cameras were blazing, and people just wanted to know what it was. It was also impressive in mixed gardens in southern Germany and was on steroids in Hamilton, Ontario. For those with weaker constitutions, 'Viridis' is a far more subdued form of this bleeding plant, with green rather than red tassels. Quite excellent if

Amaranthus 'Perfecta'

Amaranthus 'Aurora'

Amaranthus 'Hot Biscuits'

Amaranthus caudatus Towers Mix

Amaranthus caudatus, Germany

Amaranthus caudatus 'Viridis'

Amaranthus 'Molten Fire'

MORE ☞

provided with a dark background: plants tend to get lost when placed with other greens. And last but not least in this group of amaranths, I came across Towers Mix, red and green weapons on stems, each of which would shame a good shillelagh. Awful, but like a car wreck, it is hard to ignore.

All amaranths have their great moments, but like the meteors they are, they crash and burn with regularity. Don't expect them to be spectacular all season, and although the flowers persist for a long time, once they have peaked, they are toast. Since all are raised from seed, replanting halfway through the season is a good way to keep the meteors coming. Fertilize heavily, as a tremendous amount of growth must be nurtured in a short period of time. Full sun.

Anagallis monellii
BLUE PIMPERNEL

I always enjoy a good planting of blue pimpernel (*Anagallis monellii*); the wonderful color always tickles my fancy.

Amaranthus 'Early Splendor'

Anagallis monellii 'Skylover' with pulmonaria

Amaranthus 'Prince's Feather'

Anagallis monellii 'Skylover', garden bed

Maybe because it is not the easiest plant to grow (at least not in the Armitage garden) or maybe it is simply supposed to make us smile. After all, the genus name comes from the Greek, *anagelao* ("to laugh") and was suggested as a tonic against sadness. This should be mandatory viewing on Monday mornings.

In the garden, blue pimpernel is best used in containers and baskets, although I have seen it peeking from beneath pulmonarias as well as growing vigorously in a landscape bed. Plants are far more suited to cooler summers than to hot, and do better for a longer period of time in a Duluth summer compared to an Athens summer. In hot weather, they look beautiful in May, okay in June, then struggle and proceed to the compost bin. They may end up in the same place in Seattle or Fargo, but they will take their own good time getting there.

Few cultivars have been selected. 'Skylover' and 'Blue Light' seem to be the most available; I believe that more purple is apparent in the former, but not a great deal of difference exists between them. Full sun in the North, afternoon shade in the South.

Anagallis monellii 'Blue Light'

Angelica

People always enjoy seeing angelica in gardens, but I am not sure why. It may be their sheer size (they pump themselves up to 6' in height), their great balls of flowers, their stately seed heads, or just that the name is so much fun to say. Regardless, they hold people's attention when they are in their glory, even though their glory is often short-lived. They are technically perennials, but they frequently disappear after flowering, or persist for no more than two years.

The best known of this group is wild parsnip, *Angelica archangelica*, whose

Angelica archangelica, stems

Angelica gigas

MORE ☞

very name conjures up images of a Raphael painting, or Michelangelo's frescoed ceiling in the Sistine Chapel. The stems and petioles of wild parsnip can be candied and eaten, and young shoots can be prepared like asparagus. However, most of us are more interested in the towering architectural plant than the vegetable. It looks rather like an interesting weed for a long time, until the huge globose heads of white flowers appear in late summer; then it is difficult to ignore. And even after flowering, the seed heads hold attention. However, if the seeds are allowed to form, there is little chance of the plant returning the next spring. Cut them off if you must, but you are missing a big part of the big show.

The other neat plant in this group has darker leaves and stems, gets up to a reasonable height, if not quite as tall as wild parsnip, and produces rosy purple flowers. This purple parsnip is *Angelica gigas*, and to many it is a better behaved and more civilized candidate for the garden. Quite lovely seed heads are also produced later in the season. But let's be honest, these plants are more than a little on the wild side, and they are not for the high-heeled gardener. In general, they will be making good compost after fruiting. And good compost is always in demand. Full sun.

Angelica archangelica

Angelica gigas, fruit

Angelonia angustifolia

ANGEL FLOWER, SUMMER SNAPDRAGON

A superb and highly popular plant, and a perfect choice for containers or the garden. Plants stand upright throughout most of the season, although in warm areas, they may need a little cutting back to keep them from falling over. In less than five years, this plant went from obscurity to sitting beside petunias on the retail bench. I like the name summer snapdragon because in most areas of the country, snapdragons look best when the weather is cool and decline in the heat. Not this one!

Angelonia angustifolia is available in

Angelonia angustifolia 'Purple'

Angelonia angustifolia 'Light Blue'

Angelonia angustifolia 'Blue Pacific'

Angelonia angustifolia 'Angel Face Bicolor'

Angelonia angustifolia 'Angel Mist Lavender Pink'

Angelonia angustifolia 'Carita Rose'

MORE ☞

Angelonia angustifolia 'Angel Mist Lavender Improved'   *Angelonia angustifolia* 'Carita Purple'

Anisodontea ×*hypomadara* 'Elegant Lady'

numerous solid colors as well as one or two bicolor forms. I love them in containers, where they can complement other plants, and I find that container planting results in shorter plants, often a good thing for today's vigorous cultivars. They are also prized as cut flowers because of their spike-like habit. Flowers will begin to fall off after a few days, but by then the party will be over and the guests will have gone home.

A number of cultivars have been bred, but from the gardener's perspective, there are only small differences in height and flower size. Older cultivars were simply named for the color, e.g. 'Light Blue' or 'Purple', but today look for cultivars with names like 'Blue Pacific' and series with names such as Angel Mist, Angel Face, and Carita. 'Angel Mist Lavender Pink' fills containers to overflowing, and 'Angel Mist Lavender Improved' is always a hit, particularly when planted in combination with

yellow everlastings. Larger-flowered forms like 'Angel Face Bicolor' are impressive, as is the newcomer, the Carita series, amply demonstrated by 'Carita Rose' and 'Carita Purple'.

All do well in full sun, and should be fed lightly. Overfertility results in too many leaves, weak stems, and few flowers. In general, a pinch when planted is helpful to make the plants branch, but if they become too tall later on, do not hesitate to cut them back. They will reflower in about two weeks.

Anisodontea

AFRICAN MALLOW

The mallow family is rich in ornamental members, including hibiscus and lavatera, not to mention functional crops like cotton and okra. The few gardenworthy members are essentially woody shrubs, and in a single season they will produce

woody stems with substantial girth. The stems, however, are not why we place them in the garden; rather it is the 1" wide, outward-facing bright rose to pink flowers that provide the charm. In their native habitat (Cape area of South Africa), they remain evergreen, flowering from early spring to fall.

Most plants available today are hybrids (*Anisodontea ×hypomadara*) and may go under such names as 'Elegant Lady'. Occasionally Cape mallow (*A. capensis*) can be found in garden centers; plants are similar, bearing smaller light lavender flowers, and are perfect as upright standards.

Plants should be pinched at least twice for best success: once when they are purchased, and again in early summer. This allows for better branching, reduced height, and additional flowers. At Athens we have been growing African mallow in containers for the last few years, and they do well until late summer, when they start falling apart. Since their native habitat is essentially Mediterranean, the combination of heat, water, and high humidity result in too much stress, but the early season growth is handsome. Northern gardeners will have fewer problems. Full sun; avoid wet feet but provide moisture as needed.

Antirrhinum

SNAPDRAGON

The snapdragon has long been a favorite, and its "snapping" flowers are common sights everywhere gardeners till the soil. The genus name comes from the

Anisodontea capensis, standard

Antirrhinum majus 'Liberty Bronze'

Antirrhinum majus 'Solstice Purple'

Antirrhinum majus 'Tahiti Mix'

Antirrhinum majus 'Tahiti Plum'

MORE ☞

Antirrhinum majus 'Sonnet Pink'

Antirrhinum majus Rocket series

Antirrhinum 'Chandelier Rose Pink'

Antirrhinum majus 'Liberty Yellow'

Antirrhinum 'Chandelier White'

Antirrhinum 'Chandelier Lemon' with bracteantha

Greek *anti* ("opposite") and *rhis* ("snout"), referring to the lopsided petals, which give the flower its common name. Next time you are in the midst of a few snapdragons, do what I do when I am teaching. Pull the flower off, align it so the "lip" of the flower is at the bottom, then hold the "cheeks" between your thumb and forefinger. Squeeze gently, and you will soon have the dragon snapping, not to mention the kids squealing. People age six to ninety-six love to see the dragon snap. Unfortunately for the snapper, some flowers on certain cultivars have been bred to be much wider, with a less obvious lip. This group of cultivars, referred to as butterfly types, are quite handsome, but they don't provide near the fun.

All snaps prefer cool weather and look their best in cool seasons. Where summers are cool, they may be a popular summer bedding plant, but where summers are hot, such as in the South, they are best planted in the fall and enjoyed as greenery in the winter and as early color the next season. In all areas, they are also effective if planted in mid to late summer and enjoyed until hard frosts reduce their beauty.

Tall forms are generally used as cut flowers and may be seen grown by the acre by commercial growers. These are mainly represented by the popular Rocket snapdragons, which may be bought in seed packages every spring. These may grow 4' in height, however; medium forms (2½–3' tall) do not topple nearly as easily and still give a bold upright look to the garden. Numerous medium forms have been bred, but one of the best is the Liberty group, available in many colors. 'Liberty Bronze' and 'Liberty Yellow' are tough to beat. The Sonnets are similar, and 'Sonnet Pink' is one of the best. A shorter group yet (2–2½') is seen in plants such as the Solstice group, also colorfully represented and a little earlier to flower than the Libertys. 'Solstice Purple' is but one

of the many colors of this popular garden plant. Finally, the shortest snaps (1–1½' tall) can be found when the Tahiti group is planted. They are still upright but are the most compact group and easy to use in mixed gardens. 'Tahiti Plum' is outstanding.

And more good news for snap lovers. In recent years, trailing snapdragons have been developed. These hybrids work particularly well in containers but also in the front of a garden. I have looked at dozens of these plants, and the Chandelier series is one of the prettiest. 'Chandelier Rose Pink' has done well in the garden, and 'Chandelier Lemon' and 'Chandelier White' are wonderful in mixed containers. As much as I am pleased with the ability of the trailing forms to tolerate hot weather, they are still snapdragons and flower well for only as long as the cool weather holds up. However, the trailing forms are a little more heat-tolerant and well worth searching out.

Full sun, cool weather for all selections; good drainage for the trailing forms is essential.

Arctotis

AFRICAN DAISY

Native to South Africa, this daisy is among the most beautiful and most underused flowers in American gardens. Hardly anyone has heard of it, let alone grows it! I have seen a beautiful planting of African daisies, deep rose in color, growing by a Long Island greenhouse, flowering away all summer, but hardly anyone knew what it was and fewer bought them. One can simply credit the paucity of plants to a lack of availability, or perhaps it is because the average American garden climate is not particularly conducive to the plants. Regardless, it is a waste of good garden space to put in marigolds when you could try some African daisies.

Arctotis ×hybrida 'Flame'

Arctotis ×hybrida 'China Rose'

Arctotis ×hybrida 'Silver Pink'

MORE ☞

If plants can be found in garden centers, they will be hybrids, often with related species, but also with related genera, such as *Venidium*. In general, plants will be labeled as *Arctotis* ×*hybrida*, with a melange of parents in their background. The hybrids have produced a magnificent array of hues, at least one of which will fit into any garden scheme. Some of the most colorful flowers belong to the Harlequin hybrids, which are usually sold by the flower color, such as 'Flame' and 'Mahogany'. All are compact with large colorful flowers. For a rose-colored flower, I search out 'China Rose', while 'Midnight Red' would satisfy my dark side, if I had one. But dark colors aren't always welcome in a garden, which is perhaps why my eye always goes to the

Arctotis ×*hybrida*, by greenhouse, Long Island

Arctotis ×*hybrida* 'Mahogany'

Arctotis ×*hybrida* 'Midnight Red'

Arctotis ×*hybrida* 'Sunset Gold'

Arctotis ×*hybrida* 'Zulu Prince'

Argemone

PRICKLY POPPY

Argemone platyceras

pastel of 'Silver Pink', the brightness of 'Sunset Gold', and the mysterious dark-centered white warrior, 'Zulu Prince'.

Plants prefer cool-temperate climes, and I have trouble growing them in the South. In the Northeast and upper Midwest plants grow far better, and in the Northwest, they are almost at home. If they are stressed, they will almost certainly go dormant and can perish, even before the onset of winter. They are all best placed in raised beds, on hillsides, or in containers, to enhance drainage. Full sun.

These plants are like kids' birthday parties: they are much better at other people's houses. In this case, other people's gardens. I include this group because sometimes ignorance is not bliss. The beautiful flowers, usually white in those that can be purchased, belie the true nature of the plant. The common name is not a misnomer, and even the species that are less prickly are not particularly user-friendly.

But to be fair, "One man's ceiling is another man's floor," and such plants will always have some followers. Having

grown the plant in Athens, I can vouch for a few things: The flowers are large and beautiful, and the plants, depending on species, aren't going to kill you. I admit to enjoying our western native, *Argemone polyanthemos*, as much for the blue-green foliage as for the flowers, but, if truth be told, any plant with a common name of cowboy's fried egg deserves to be grown somewhere. A more spiny cousin, with prickly fruit and foliage, is *A. platyceras*, the crested poppy, which grows 4–5' tall and can be quite intimidating.

Have fun with this group of poppies; they don't do well in gardens with high heat and humidity but are worth some pain in other parts of the country. Full sun.

Argyranthemum

MARGUERITE DAISY

What a taxonomic mess this group of plants has turned out to be. So many species, so much hybridization—it is a taxonomist's nightmare and a gardener's dream. The marguerites have long been cultivated, but in the last decade or so, breeders in Europe and Australia have crossed and recrossed the various

MORE ☞

Argemone platyceras, fruit

Argemone polyanthemos

species to obtain some rather spectacular, if confused, plants. Since most of us don't care what they are as long as they perform in our gardens, the "argys" have become quite popular.

The main species that make up this group include the yellow-flowering *Argyranthemum maderense,* which is seldom seen as a garden plant. Its single flowers are handsome, but its popularity is limited mainly to the plant breeder. The silver-leaved, white-flowered *A. foeniculaceum* is a beautiful species in its own right, and in containers or in the ground, it is tough to beat. I can think of no prettier plant when it is well grown. Unfortunately, most of the well-grown ones I have seen were on the West Coast or in Australia or England. A few cultivars are occasionally offered, but 'Vera' (with white flowers) and 'Roseum' (a pink form) are all I see.

Argyranthemum frutescens is the "original" marguerite daisy and is distinguished by the somewhat domed flowers available in many colors. Many forms have been bred, but their popularity is diminishing in direct proportion to

Argyranthemum maderense

Argyranthemum frutescens 'Sugar and Ice'

Argyranthemum frutescens 'Mary Wooten'

Argyranthemum foeniculaceum

Argyranthemum foeniculaceum 'Vera'

Argyranthemum foeniculaceum 'Roseum'

Argyranthemum frutescens 'Vancouver'

Argyranthemum hybrids, vista in California

Argyranthemum hybrids, Mainau, Germany

Argyranthemum hybrids, out of flower

Argyranthemum 'Summer Eyes'

MORE ☞

the rise in popularity of the hybrids. One of the cultivars I most enjoy is 'Sugar and Ice', whose domed white flowers were even whiter when I spied it growing through some zinnias. 'Mary Wooten' is not as clean a white as 'Sugar and Ice', but this old-fashioned selection throws out many flowers. For pink flowers, I would choose 'Vancouver'.

However, it is the hybrids, which possess a few genes of each of the species just mentioned, that people are growing. In coastal California, they are incredible most of the year, while containers of salmon-colored argys on an extraordinary railing at the garden at Mainau in southern Germany were fabulous. Argys are beautiful to be sure but not without some serious limitations. The limita-

Argyranthemum 'Butterfly'

Argyranthemum 'Midas Gold'

Argyranthemum 'Comet Pink'

Argyranthemum 'Summer Stars Pink'

tions are simply that they require relatively cool temperatures (45–55°F) to initiate flowers well. Since plants are produced in early spring in controlled temperature greenhouses, they are offered to the consumer in full flower. They will remain in flower in the spring; however, when temperatures start rising during the summer months, plants flower sparsely, and the result is a handsome, but not particularly welcome, small green shrub. Wonderful foliage, but no flowers! This is less a problem in areas of cool summer temperatures and high elevations.

Argyranthemum 'Comet White'

As is the case for all general statements, there are exceptions. Even in the heat of a Georgia summer, 'Butterfly' flowered its head off. An older cultivar, but still the best on the market for long term flowering in the heat. Almost as good in heat is 'Midas Gold', with its much lighter flowers; in combination with fan flower it can look good all season. Many cultivars have been developed, and some of those that have caught my eye include 'Summer Eyes' and 'Comet White' for good white flowers, but pink flowers also abound in this group. 'Comet Pink' is an outstanding plant, compact and with relatively good summer flowering; 'Summer Stars Pink' has beautiful foliage but is shy of flowering once the heat arrives. I have always enjoyed the form and flower color of 'Summer Melody', one of numerous argys bred in eastern Australia by Mal Morgan. Compact and handsome, perfect in a container. Many more cultivars have been bred, and many more are yet to appear; they are beautiful, simply be aware that for most of them, you will be enjoying more foliage than flowers during the summer. If the fall is sufficiently long before frost, flowers will reappear along with the cooler weather. Full sun.

Asarina

CLIMBING, CREEPING, TRAILING SNAPDRAGON

Several genera have borrowed the name snapdragon. The snapdragon is *Antirrhinum*, the summer snapdragon is *Angelonia*, and there is also a genus in which the flowers resemble snapdragons but whose habit is decidedly un-snapdragon-like. That genus is *Asarina*. At least these three all start with the same letter.

Although the flowers resemble those of the true snapdragon, all species are rather rangy, and some will climb if support is provided. However, the creeping snapdragon, *Asarina procumbens*, wants to scramble over rocks or out of containers and has no climbing tendencies at all. But it is a marvelous plant, with its gray foliage and creamy white flowers. Plants are hardy to about zone 6 and are particularly effective when drainage is excellent. The trailing snapdragon, *A. antirrhiniflora*, will climb but prefers to send out long stems that trail about the ground. The best choice for this species is 'Red Dragon', with deep red flowers on light green foliage.

The most fun, however, has to be with the climbers, which can scale tall

Argyranthemum 'Summer Melody'

Asarina procumbens

Asarina scandens 'Joan Lorraine'

Asarina scandens 'Mystic Pink'

Asarina antirrhiniflora 'Red Dragon'

Asarina scandens 'Jewel Purple'

vides many small deep purple flowers on a massive vine. The Mystic series is also grown; it seems that 'Mystic Pink' is one of the most prolific. They all want to flower in spring and, when summers are cool, will continue on and off throughout the season. In areas of hot summers, plants often grow rampantly, covering fences and trees, but flower again only as the weather cools down. Full sun.

Asclepias

MILKWEED

Ask a corn or wheat farmer about the ornamental value of milkweed, and he will think you are either crazy or just plain stupid. As a college student, I drove a large spray rig through the agricultural fields of southwestern Ontario, simply trying to keep the milkweed and other weeds under control. The cost for the equipment and the chemicals and the loss of production attributable to this weed did not endear it to anybody. So imagine my surprise when some-

buildings and jump wide canyons. Not really, but they do grow quite rapidly. The most common is the climbing snapdragon, *Asarina scandens*, which twines around the supporting trellis or netting. I place them at the base of a fence tacked with some woven wire. The wire is almost invisible when the plants are not

on it but is an easy structure for the stems to get around. Most cultivars are seed-propagated, and some people direct sow the seed into the ground once the soil warms up. Several seed selections are out there; one of the more common is Jewel Mix, the favorite being 'Jewel Purple', while 'Joan Lorraine' pro-

Asclepias curassavica, flowers

Asclepias linaria

Asclepias curassavica 'Silky Scarlet'

MORE ☞

body talked about an ornamental milkweed!

However, stupidity aside, several annual species truly are spectacular. Without a doubt, the colors of the flowers of blood flower, *Asclepias curassavica*, will make you stop for a second look, and maybe a third and fourth as well if you look closely at the flower structure. The flowers are orange and red and sit atop the green foliage. If a stem or flower is broken, they will exude a milky sap that is best kept off your skin, as some people are quite sensitive to it. In a grouping of a dozen or more plants, blood flower is difficult not to notice. Unfortunately, all members of the genus are magnets for aphids, so don't be upset if an aphid or two come to dinner: by planting asclepias, you opened a five-star restaurant and invited a few guests. A stream of water from the hose usually persuades them to find other fare. A number of cultivars are available, some, such as 'Deep Red' and 'Silky Scarlet', quite similar to the species. The Silky series also includes 'Silky Gold', a handsome golden-yellow form that people seem equally to enjoy. The fruit is upright, skinny, and also handsome. Open them up and have fun with silky seeds.

A few interesting species are grown more for the fruit than the flower. I found a stand of *Asclepias linaria* in Tucson, Arizona, with light green needle-like leaves and all sorts of bladder-like fruit. I thought that maybe this genus is special after all. However, it was while walking through Christchurch Botanical Garden in New Zealand that I first spied the swan plant, *A. physocarpa*. I looked at the weird inflated fruit, squinted a few times and yes, I could tell it was a swan dangling amidst the leaves. It is difficult to imagine that the rather nondescript clusters of green-white flowers could create such a strange seed

Asclepias curassavica

Asclepias curassavica 'Deep Red'

Asclepias curassavica with aphids

Asclepias curassavica 'Silky Gold'

Asclepias physocarpa, fruit

Asclepias physocarpa, flowers

Asystasia gangetica, flowers

vessel. Plants are native to South Africa, so I enjoyed the sight and doubted I would find them again. But I was not the only one to enjoy it, as I keep seeing it in gardens in America. The City of Swan Plants award probably goes to Washington, D.C., where great gardens, great plants, and great plantspeople abound. This plant can be found in the Smithsonian's wonderful Ripley Garden as well as in the expansive Green Spring Gardens Park, across the river in Alexandria, Virginia. It obviously reseeds, and the early start allows for 4–5' tall plants with many flowers and many swans. Perhaps it will soon be viewed as a noxious weed in the greater D.C. area, but I expect that it will be grown here and there for many years. Seed must be purchased, but if you are in and around our nation's capital, I suspect you can collect a few seeds there. Full sun.

Asystasia gangetica
GANGES PRIMROSE

Other than landscapers in Florida and the Gulf Coast, I would bet that ninety-nine people out of a hundred have never seen or heard of Ganges primrose, *Asystasia gangetica*. I rather enjoy this rampant, somewhat sprawling member of the acanthus family, which provides handsome rosy pink flowers with a white eye. Flowers can cover up the plant when conditions are right. However, therein lies the problem. The right conditions are not easy to provide in most parts of the country. Plants like it warm, no problem; reasonable drainage, again, no problem. However, plants flower only under conditions of warm temperatures and reasonably long nights (short days) likely more than twelve hours long. The beginning of long nights occurs in the fall, but in the North, temperatures are falling and are usually too chilly to sustain flowering

MORE ☞

Basella alba

'Rubra', with darker green leaves and red to rose flowers. In tropical countries, they are grown as a vegetable (like our pole beans) and used in the same way as spinach. Full sun.

Begonia

What an unbelievable genus: on the one hand dismissed as boring by gardeners who know of little except the wax begonia, on the other hand loved for the eye-catching flowers of the tuberous forms or the exciting foliage of the rex types. And begonias attract another segment of the gardening population: those who collect cultivars and species like stamps, a hobby that is fulfilling and frustrating at the same time. With a genus of over 900 species and an untold number of cultivars and varieties, begonia collectors will never reach the finish line, but what fun they will have trying to get there.

I have seen but a fraction of the known begonias; however, I must try to filter even those few to whittle the number down. This is, of course, impossible but necessary. I have cubbyholed the cultivated forms into four main groups, and then added an assortment of lesser known species that I feel have great potential for the bold gardener. The unfortunate reality, however, is that many of the finest forms are not easily available and must be aggressively sought out through plant associations or mail-order sources. But what else is new? Start with a few easy ones, and if the begonia bug starts to itch, enjoy the scratching. The four main groups, from a gardener's point of view, are angel wing begonias (*Begonia coccinea* and hybrids), rex begonias (*B. rex-cultorum*), tuberous begonias (*B. tuberhybrida*), and wax begonias (*B. sempervirens-cultorum*).

The angel wing begonias, among the oldest "parlor" plants in gardening, have been arching over plants on coffee tables and in conservatories and greenhouses for years. Only recently, however, has this group made inroads into the great "common folk" of the gardening public, and now the floodgates are open for

Begonia coccinea 'Maribel Pink Shades'

Begonia coccinea 'Torch'

Begonia coccinea 'Dragon Wing Red'

Begonia rex-cultorum 'Persian Swirl'

Begonia rex-cultorum 'Lalomie'

Begonia rex-cultorum 'Connie Boswell'

Begonia rex-cultorum 'Good and Plenty'

Begonia rex-cultorum 'Escargot'

Begonia tuberhybrida, red and orange mix

Begonia tuberhybrida 'Chanson'

MORE ☞

Begonia coccinea 'Dragon Wing Pink'

Begonia rex-cultorum 'New York'

Begonia sempervirens-cultorum 'Ambassador Rose'

Begonia sempervirens-cultorum Cocktail series

Begonia tuberhybrida 'Non-Stop'

Begonia tuberhybrida 'Illumination Salmon Pink'

Begonia tuberhybrida 'Spirit'

Begonia sempervirens-cultorum behind fence

garden experimentation. Most cultivars are hidden in mail-order nurseries and are not as easily accessible as they should be, but that will change as more are hybridized for general garden and container use. I have enjoyed the Maribel series, particularly 'Maribel Pink Shades', and other seed-propagated strains, such as the red-flowered 'Torch'. However, the angel wings became a mainstay of the public with the introduction of the now famous Dragon Wing series. 'Dragon Wing Red' was the original plant and was hanging about in greenhouses for years before some brilliant person at Ball Seed Company thought that the time was right for something other than a wax begonia. Plants performed well throughout the country, mainly in baskets, and became a highly sought-after item. This was followed by 'Dragon Wing Pink', a lovely plant but less in demand as it is not quite of the same vigor as the red. They are best for containers and baskets. Full sun or partial shade.

The rex group is where the gardening public has really made demands upon the begonia, pulling the beautiful "foliage" plants of the 1950s into the gardens of the twenty-first century. As I travel around public and private gardens, I see more of these plants appearing every year. It is the boom in container gardening that has been the impetus for the demand, and now I see marvelous plants like 'New York', 'Persian Swirl', 'Lalomie', and 'Fireworks' beautifying areas in the Missouri Botanical Garden, or the gorgeous 'Connie Boswell' flourishing in containers in Virginia's Green Spring Gardens Park. And who would have thought that a plant like 'Good and Plenty' would find itself plunged into a pot at the Chicago Botanic Garden? These old-fashioned plants have also spawned one of the neatest begonias in recent times, the nautilus-leaved 'Escargot'. People cannot help themselves—

MORE ☞

oohs and aahs are common language when this plant is on display. Partial shade, at least in the afternoon.

Planting the tubers of tuberous bego-nias in the small greenhouse at school was an annual event for me as a high school teacher in Montreal, accomplished on 1 March each year. With water and a little heat, these dried-up old things would expand into leaves and flowers in a couple of months' time, ready to be hung in baskets outdoors. I suppose there were many named cultivars, but we just called them red, yellow, etc. That was enough for me then and, to go by the tags of most tuberous begonias

Begonia rex-cultorum 'Fireworks'

Begonia sempervirens-cultorum, Michigan State University

Begonia sempervirens-cultorum 'Brandy' with purple fountain grass

sold today, still seems to be the case.

However, marvelous cultivars like 'Non-Stop' were developed from seed and became highly popular for landscapers and gardeners alike. Since then, 'Chanson', 'Illumination', and 'Spirit' have become available to the greenhouse operator. Tuberous begonias, however, differ from other forms in that they disdain hot weather and are seldom seen in the southern half of the country. Regardless of where they are grown,

they need consistent moisture and partial shade. They are at their best in the Northeast and Northwest, but gosh, they are still worth a try in other parts of the country, at least on 1 March.

I have been trialing and growing wax begonias for so many years I don't even know where to begin. One place I won't begin, however, is to make apologies for this bedding plant. Plants like wax begonias are so good, so diverse in color, so easy, and so carefree that their success

has bred a backlash. Perhaps they aren't new but neither are antiques, and nobody seems to tire of those. There are literally dozens of series and hundreds of named cultivars. Some have larger flowers than others; the leaves of some are bronze, while others are green. In the landscape, they are planted in mixes of colors, forming great mounds of colored cones; in public areas, they may be fenced off from curious dogs and gumwrappers. Although breeders have spent

Begonia sempervirens-cultorum 'Vodka'

Begonia sempervirens-cultorum 'Party Flair'

Begonia sempervirens-cultorum 'Espresso Rose'

Begonia sempervirens-cultorum 'Encore Light Pink'

Begonia sempervirens-cultorum 'Pink Avalanche'

MORE ☞

their lives improving the plants, providing subtle colors with fanciful names, all too often the gardener is facing a generic label that reads nothing more than "Red Begonia," and it is likely that named cultivars can be found more easily in good garden centers than in the box stores. Probably the only series that has reached the consciousness of the general public and one of the most popular is the Cocktail series, available by the drink. For example, 'Vodka' is a handsome rose-red begonia, 'Whiskey' is white, etc. One of the prettiest uses for 'Brandy' was at the East Lansing, Michigan, home of Will Carlson, one of this country's leading floriculturists, where he had interplanted clouds of purple fountain grass through great swaths of those pink flowers. Other rose-pink cultivars include 'Ambassador Rose', the large-flowered 'Party Flair', and one of the best per-

Begonia sempervirens-cultorum 'Olympic Light Pink'

Begonia sempervirens-cultorum 'Doublet Pink'

Begonia sempervirens-cultorum 'Kaylen'

Begonia fuchsioides

formers in the UGA Trial Gardens, 'Espresso Rose'. Pinks are everywhere; one of my favorites is 'Olympic Light Pink', although 'Encore Light Pink' and 'Pink Avalanche' are just as handsome. 'Senator White' provides hundreds of flowers to contrast with the reds, roses, pinks, and bicolors available in the spring. A number of researchers are looking for more cold-hardy forms of wax begonia; 'Kaylen' has wonderful bronze foliage and rosy pink flowers, hardy to zone 7b. All wax begonias are equally at home in full sun or partial shade. Double flowers have been bred in almost all ornamentals, so why not wax begonias? The Doublet series was so outstanding, it earned a Classic City Award from the UGA Trial Gardens. 'Doublet Pink' and 'Doublet Rose' are among the best.

The trend toward container gardening has allowed closer examination of the outdoor qualities of some little-known begonia species, and a few are leaving the obscurity of the greenhouse conser-vatory to find their way to gardens around the country. Some are best grown for the foliage, as flowers tend to be formed in winter conditions in the greenhouse; others have handsome flow-ers in the garden as well. Because of the huge number of species, there is no out-door testing program for begonia species anywhere; however, gardeners always try to stretch their plant horizons. I have seen some winners (and a few losers) as I travel, and in my own garden.

I think that the small-flowered fuchsia begonia, *Begonia fuchsioides*, has great potential to be a star. The flowers are somewhat similar to those of fuchsia, and the margins of the clean foliage are often flushed with red in the spring. Flowers come in rose-pink and red, and although they are less than 1" across, many are formed. Partial shade. I have also recently discovered the joys of the shield begonia, *B. popenoei*, whose large, light green rounded leaves look like shields advancing over an imaginary battlefield. I grew this under the shade of large trees in Athens, and although I never saw any flowers, the foliage was magnificent throughout the season. Apparently, the flowers are quite impres-sive in the greenhouse, but probably

MORE ☞

Begonia sempervirens-cultorum 'Senator White'

Begonia sempervirens-cultorum 'Doublet Rose'

Begonia popenoei

Begonia serratipetala

Begonia pedatifida

most gardeners won't see them. Who needs them? Partial shade.

One of the common greenhouse species that surprised me was the tooth-petaled *Begonia serratipetala,* whose deeply cut dark olive-green leaves, flushed with white or pink spots, are the main reason for including it. Occasionally, however, a few rose-pink to red flowers may also appear. Terrific in combination with other plants, in the garden or in a container. Heavy to partial shade. I was introduced to a new rhizotomous begonia, *B. pedatifida,* which has reveled in the dry, shady conditions of the Armitage garden. Plants just keep on growing and growing, with no concern for the abuse of a southeastern summer, finally discoloring a little in late fall. Supposedly, it produces white flowers, but it has not flowered for me. Its performance, vigor, and lack of insects and diseases have made me take notice anyway. Heavy to partial shade.

Bellis perennis

ENGLISH DAISY

A great deal of breeding of this English lawn weed has occurred, with the zenith of hybridization in the early to mid

Bellis perennis 'Pomponette White'

Bellis perennis 'Medicis White'

Bellis perennis 'Radar Rose'

Bellis perennis 'Chevreuse Rose'

1990s. They started out their lives as tiny but pretty weeds and in some cases have evolved into handsome colorful bedding plants available in a wide range of colors. The breeders have certainly left their mark; some of these poor little flowers appear as if they have been pumping iron. Single, fluffy, and doubled, they have been given no respite.

But to be honest, I still like these little guys. As do many other people. Pastel

Bellis perennis 'Carpet Rose'

Bellis perennis, Harrogate, England

Bellis perennis, Palmerston North, New Zealand

MORE ☞

which if planted in a cool area can make quite an impressive showing. Plants, however, may self-sow, and you might be cursing those beggar's ticks for a long time. Full sun.

Brachycome iberidifolia

SWAN RIVER DAISY

The Swan River runs through Perth, Australia, and empties into Fremantle on the Southern Indian Ocean. Flora in

the area include eucalyptus and fan flower (*Scaevola*), and rounding any corner on any spring day, one may come across beautiful plants of the ever-present Swan River daisy (*Brachycome iberidifolia*). Bringing the "brachys" out of the wilds of Australia and domesticating them for the containers of Chicago

Bidens ferulifolia 'Peter's Gold Carpet'

Brachycome iberidifolia, Perth, Australia

Bidens ferulifolia 'Smiley'

Brachycome 'Mini Yellow'

has been a challenge, but they have made a nice, if not eye-popping, addition to North American gardens. Plants generally grow no more than 1' in height and, if well grown, are covered with small single daisies. The common color in nature is lavender, but breeders have produced pink, rose, and yellow in small- and large-flowered forms. High temperatures are no problem, but they prefer areas of low humidity for best growth. Outstanding plantings are found in San Diego and high-altitude areas; more searching is needed to find picturesque plants in the Southeast and Midwest. Such areas may see poor flowering and disease problems, causing dieback and black leaves in the summer.

I see more and more hybrid brachys being used in combination with trailing snapdragons and pansies or other cool-loving plants. Hybridization has not only produced some beautiful material, but the additional hybrid vigor has

Brachycome 'Billabong Moonlight'

Brachycome 'Mauve Delight'

Brachycome 'Lilac Mist'

Brachycome 'Petite Delight', *B.* 'Mini Yellow'

MORE ☞

resulted in plants being successfully gardened in more areas of the country. I particularly enjoy the small-flowered forms such as 'Lilac Mist' and 'Petite Delight', both with lavender-blue flowers, and 'Lemon Drop', an excellent yellow-flowered cultivar. However, if bigger flowers are desirable, try the marvelous Billabong series, the best being 'Billabong Moonlight', with perfect light yellow flowers. 'Mini Yellow' provides some fine yellow hues but tends to fade later in the summer. In the world of retailing, bigger is perceived as better, and breeders went to work on creating larger flowers. The result was been plants with gaudy chrysanthemum-like blossoms such as 'Jumbo Mauve' and 'Mauve Delight', both beautiful on the retail bench but not as weather-tolerant in the garden as the small-flowered forms.

All brachys are better in containers than in the ground. Full sun or afternoon shade is recommended.

Brachycome 'Jumbo Mauve'

Bracteantha bracteata 'Nullabor Spectrum'

Bracteantha bracteata 'Bright Bikini'

Bracteantha bracteata

STRAWFLOWER

This fine Australian plant is experiencing a renaissance, and new cultivars are making significant inroads in North American gardens. It is a wonderful plant to put in the garden for no other reason than to enjoy the texture of the flowers; my goodness, they really do feel like straw. Kids love them, and so do people who want to cut flowers from their garden. The more established name for this everlasting plant was *Helichrysum*. Plants are still listed as such, so don't be confused when you can't find *Bracteantha* in the catalog index. Of course, if confusion is your thing, look up strawflower and you may find other genera as well, but this is the one you want.

The actual strawflower from eastern Australia does not reside in the garden centers or florists, but the hybrids are tougher and more weather-tolerant for North American gardens anyway. Plants such as 'Nullabor Spectrum' look quite at home beside lantana or other sun lovers, while 'Florabella Yellow' freely performed in a container, as witnessed one sunny morning in southern California.

The Chico series was one of the first compact groups of plants that provided a mixture of colors and good garden performance. The Bikini series was popular for many years, for the bright colors of cultivars like 'Bright Bikini', which stop people in their tracks, and the clean colors in 'Bikini White'. 'Golden Beauty' provided free-flowering plants, but the flowers were a little small and the plants a little big. But they certainly provided months of color. The big breakthrough for good garden strawflowers occurred with the Florabella series. Colors include bright yellow, brilliant gold, and a subdued lemon. Excellent flower size and good performance, although perhaps a little lanky and tall for some gardeners.

Dwarfer forms have been introduced,

Bracteantha bracteata 'Florabella Yellow'

Bracteantha bracteata 'Bikini White'

Bracteantha bracteata Chico series

Bracteantha bracteata 'Golden Beauty'

Bracteantha bracteata 'Dreamtime Antique Shades'

Bracteantha bracteata 'Sundaze Pink'

MORE ☞

providing good flower size, persistent flowering, and more compact plants. I have been impressed with the Sundaze series, particularly 'Sundaze Lemon Yellow' and 'Sundaze Pink', both of which garnered high grades in our

trials. As well, the Dreamtime series was impressive and a favorite of many passers-by, displaying unfettered growing and flowering. 'Dreamtime Antique Shades' was superb.

All the strawflowers are native to hot, dry areas, and while heat is not a problem, high humidity and summer rain

can be. Place in full sun in as well drained a location as possible. Hillsides, raised beds, or containers come to mind.

Brassica, Beta

If you live in an area of mild winters, you may miss the snowballs and the skating, but having flowers in the winter may help to stem your disappointment. In such areas, pansies, pinks, and snapdragons are often planted in the fall to provide color throughout the fall and winter and burst into even more color in early spring. And one of the plants that bursts the most is ornamental kale, *Brassica oleracea.*

Some people suggest that kale is rather boring, simply taking up space in an otherwise barren winter landscape. Not so, as witnessed by the scene in McDonough, Georgia, where kale became the presents under the Christmas tree, and when you see a bed of multi-colored foliage in the winter sun, that bed is hardly boring. Many fine series and cultivars of kale have been devel-

Bracteantha bracteata 'Sundaze Lemon Yellow'

Bracteantha bracteata 'Florabella Gold'

Bracteantha bracteata 'Florabella Lemon'

Brassica oleracea, Christmas in McDonough, Georgia

Brassica oleracea Tokyo series

Brassica oleracea 'White Sparrow', diseased centers

Brassica oleracea 'White Feather'

MORE ☞

Brassica oleracea var. *botrytis* (cauliflower)

Beta vulgaris 'Bright Lights'

Brassica ×*hybrida* (mustard) and *Petroselinum crispum* (parsley) in mixed bed

oped. The most common are the "cabbage" forms, which include the Tokyo series in a mixture of rose, red, and white, but some of the single colors are outstanding. Not all is perfect in kale paradise, however, and after particularly cold weather or heavy cold rains, the insides of white-centered plants often turn brown, such as was the case with 'White Sparrow'. If the cabbage forms are your choice, go with darker colors such as 'Rose Bouquet' and 'Red Chidori'. They do not show the damage and are unbeatable for weather tolerance; even when it snows or rains, the centers of the plants appear unblemished. But as bold as those incurled forms are, I am particularly impressed with the leafier kinds. I think the Peacock series is one of the most outstanding, and the Feather series also earns its name. 'White Feather' pro-

Brassica oleracea 'Peacock White'

Brassica oleracea in flower

Brassica oleracea 'Rose Bouquet'

Brassica oleracea 'Peacock Red'

MORE ☞

vides color, form, and creativity that all gardeners can count on.

One of the characteristics of any plant is that it wants to flower. When plants in the mustard family flower in the spring, it is referred to as bolting. Some people like the yellow flowers; I am not one of them. To me, they signify the end of the planting, and if I am not too lazy, I will remove them at that time. Research has shown that the leafy forms (Peacock, Feather series) bolt later than the cabbage forms. If you dislike the flowers, planting the leafy forms provides a few extra weeks of enjoyment.

Last thing: regardless of where one lives, if heavy snow cover is normal, these are useful only in the fall until several hard frosts. Perhaps in early spring, they may also provide some color prior to spring planting. Even in Athens, Georgia, if temperatures fall below 20°F for an extended length of time, plants turn into cabbage soup. Try a few, the worst that can happen is a few months of color where no color existed, regardless of how long they provide it. And if they die, you won't have to worry about those crummy flowers. Full sun.

There is no lack of creativity among gardeners in using other closely related veggies. Gardeners do not live by kale alone, so why not try some of the colorful chards (*Beta vulgaris*)? 'Ruby Red' is

Brassica oleracea 'Red Chidori'

Beta vulgaris 'Ruby Red'

Brassica ×*hybrida* 'Redbor'

Brassica ×*hybrida* 'Red Giant'

a favorite, but the winner in popularity among chards is 'Bright Lights', with stems of yellow, red, or orange. Not even mustard plants are immune from landscape beds, often incorporated in a winter bed with parsley as a companion. The ornamental mustards (*Brassica ×hybrida*) have been increasingly popular, I have always admired the frilled leaves of 'Redbor', growing from containers of lettuce. The biggest of them all is probably 'Red Giant', which towers over everything else in the winter garden in Georgia. And not to be left out or outdone, a creative vegetable gardener even puts cauliflower in hanging baskets. Nothing is sacred anymore.

Breynia nivosa

SNOW BUSH

Not a whole lot of snow bushes can be found in landscapes these days, although when I do see a planting or two, I wish availability was wider. Snow bush (*Breynia nivosa*) grows rapidly in its native environment and is often used as a hedge in some parts of the world. Passing by the hedge provides an insight as to its popularity, with deep hues of red, pink, white, and green all interspersed. However, where it is annual, which is most of this country, the length of the growing season provides insufficient time for such grandeur. We have to content ourselves with interesting specimen plants, which can be grown among other annuals or perennials. The plumage is brilliant in the spring but tends to fade a little in the heat.

I very much like what this plant can do in the landscape, but to be frank, I seldom see them for sale in the Midwest or Southeast, so it is difficult to run out and plant a specimen, let alone a hedge. All is not lost, however. Good growers like Denise Smith of GardenSmith in Jefferson, Georgia, and Mark Terkanian at Natchez Trace in Kosciusko, Mississippi, keep producing beautiful specimens in the hope that gardeners and landscapers will enjoy it as much as they do. I think we should give these people a break, and purchase some of these orphans. I have seen a few cultivars listed, but mostly it is the species that can be found. There are no flowers to speak of, plants are grown entirely for the zigzag stems and colorful foliage. Full sun.

Breynia nivosa, hedge

Breynia nivosa, flowers

Breynia nivosa with erigeron

Browallia

BUSH VIOLET

Browallia was a favorite in Grandmother's garden but is not grown very much in her granddaughter's garden. This is probably because this is truly an "old English" plant, having been brought over by the colonists and then benefitted by the huge popularity of English gardens and English garden literature in the 1950s and '60s. The common form (*Browallia speciosa*) produces abundant violet-blue flowers on 1' tall plants, and they combine well in containers with many plants, including 'Limelight' helichrysum. A number of cultivars are

MORE ☞

79

Browallia speciosa 'Daniella'

Browallia speciosa 'Blue Bells'

Browallia speciosa

Browallia speciosa 'Marine Bells'

available, mostly in the blue-lavender-violet spectrum. I have seen good-looking plants of 'Marine Bells' in the University of Minnesota arboretum, and 'Blue Bells' looked terrific in the Royal Botanical Gardens in Ontario. In Athens, plants seldom look good after 15 July, pointing out the lack of tolerance of warm temperatures. In containers at the Butchart Gardens in Victoria, British Columbia, 'Daniella' called for attention, but in Cincinnati, they needed to be put

out of their misery in early August. That plants do better in one area of the country than they do in another is true of almost all species, to deny it is to have never traveled. However, this is simply a problem of timing. In all areas, they look better in cool gardens, so southern gardeners should plant them early in the season and enjoy them for a few months, or place small plants out in early August to be enjoyed all fall. I hope this plant comes back in popularity, as I

enjoy seeing it; it simply won't get to the Armitage garden until later in the season. Full sun in the North, partial shade in the South.

Brugmansia
ANGEL'S TRUMPET

What was once a plant seen only in the tropics or in the tropical conservatory is now being sold across the country. What

Brugmansia sanguinea

Brugmansia arborea

Brugmansia ×candida 'Double White'

Brugmansia aurea

was once looked upon as a sloppy shrub is now being viewed as a magnificent architectural feature. I was fortunate to see natural groves in travels to South and Central America, and coming across maikoa, *Brugmansia arborea*, or red angel's trumpet, *B. sanguinea*, was indeed a rush! And, while they may not be 20' tall in our gardens, they can look equally impressive at home. Plants can be placed in the garden but will also look beautiful in large containers.

Angel's trumpet is a common name for plants in this genus as well as those in *Datura* (which see), but *Brugmansia* is certainly the more impressive of the

Brugmansia ×candida

MORE ☞

two. All the many species and cultivars residing under this name produce quite beautiful pendulous flowers, most single but a few doubles as well. Plants should be considered annuals in most places in the country, but that should not deter even cool-summer gardeners, as they can grow 4–5' in a single year. Some gardeners as far north as zone 7 may have them overwinter occasionally, but they should not be counted on as being perennial north of zone 8.

I have planted *Brugmansia versicolor,* the ever-changing angel's trumpet, in Athens, and people are always confused as they notice that the unopened flowers appear yellow then bloom into a rich salmon color and fade to white. But confused or not, they come back for a second look. And the golden angel's trumpet, *B. aurea,* with its large leaves and handsome yellow flowers, looks as good in Wisconsin as it does in Miami. Normally, the abundant flowers of *B.* ×*candida* open slightly yellow then turn white, but this hybrid also provides some double flowers, such as in 'Double White'. But most of the time, when you go shopping for these things at your local retailer, you will simply find the label stating "White" or "Orange," or other flower color. These are probably hybrids of *B* ×*insignis,* and they are perfectly fine plants to purchase. In specialty catalogs,

Brugmansia ×*insignis,* white form

Brugmansia versicolor

Brugmansia ×insignis, orange form

Brugmansia 'Charles Grimaldi'

Brugmansia 'Sunset'

Brugmansia 'Snowbank'

the correct names for the plants will be listed, and if possible, spend your money on a hybrid like 'Charles Grimaldi', with abundant and large salmon-pink flowers. Absolutely one of the best of these superlative plants.

And for those who belong to the ABG (Anything But Green) group, the variegated form, sometimes sold as 'Sunset', is all right, but you will go head over heels for 'Snowbank', a newer form with a much stronger variegation pattern.

Oh yes, I nearly forgot. These plants are poisonous. If you ingest large amounts of leaves, flowers, or fruits, you may suffer from hallucinations, dry mouth, muscle weakness, increased blood pressure and pulse, fever, dilated pupils, and paralysis. They are not as bad as chewing on datura, but try to restrain yourself. Full sun; take cuttings in the fall if you wish to overwinter a favorite form.

Caladium

I never used to be much of a fan of caladiums (either selections of or hybrids involving *Caladium bicolor*), but the more I see them, the more they grow on me. They come in many colors, from busy patterns of red to beautiful bright white forms. The key to caladium performance is not to plant the corms too early; they will simply sit in the ground until it

MORE ☞

warms up. The foliage will emerge eventually, but it is heat that these plants love, without which, forget it! Of course, buying plants already leafed out makes great sense if you want quicker success, and if

summers don't last long. I don't remember a lot of caladium tubers being planted where I grew up in Montreal; by the time it was warm enough for sprouting, fall was the next day.

Brilliant is a pretty good description for some of the cultivars out there. The

large pastel pink leaves of 'Fannie Munson' are outstanding, and the tricolor palette of 'Fire Chief' also catches the eye. However, perhaps because caladiums prefer shady conditions, the cooler white and off-white shades suit my fancy more. They simply seem to brighten up that

Caladium 'Fannie Munson'

Caladium bicolor 'Gingerbread'

Caladium bicolor 'White Queen'

Caladium bicolor 'Candidum'

shade a little, and I find myself drawn toward them. 'Gingerbread' is a little busy, but the smaller leaves and the flecking pattern on the off-white leaves are at least cute, if not handsome. I saw a planting of 'White Queen' at Longwood Gardens, towering over some red begonias, and the contrast was spectacular. However, I must be boring, as I would have the all-white foliage of 'Candidum' in the Armitage garden any day of the week. The leaves go with any color, and the shade in the garden almost disappears.

To overwinter caladiums, dig them out after the leaves begin to decline in the fall. Place the tubers in dry peat moss and place in an area that doesn't freeze. Replant in containers or in the ground when the soil warms up the next spring. Partial to heavy shade.

Calendula officinalis

POT MARIGOLD

In Montreal, pot marigolds (*Calendula officinalis*) were a summer staple; they were planted in the spring and contin-

ued to grow well throughout the summer. Often people tired of them before the calendulas tired of the people. However, the further south one moves, the more difficulty one has in growing this as a summer annual. Pot marigolds (so called because they were often brought into the house, and they looked like a marigold) flower in spring to early summer in much of the country and tend to struggle by mid July. Seed is easily purchased and can be started indoors so plants can go out early, even before the last frost occurs, assuming they have

Caladium bicolor 'Fire Chief'

Calendula officinalis 'Bon Bon Yellow'

Calendula officinalis 'Bon Bon Orange'

Calendula officinalis 'Mandarin Orange'

MORE ☞

been placed outside for a few days and nights to be hardened off. Otherwise start seed in the ground as temperatures warm up, or plant started material in April or May.

Many fine cultivars have been bred, some for bedding, some for cut flowers, and all quite colorful. Probably the dwarf forms, such as the Bon Bon series, have garnered the most attention; particularly striking are large drifts of 'Bon Bon Orange' and 'Bon Bon Yellow' in the landscape (honestly, I don't make these names up!). A planting of 'Mandarin Orange' often includes a few yellow flowers in the seed package, but that is not all bad. 'Indian Prince' is taller, with orange flowers with a distinct if not overwhelming red center. The undersides are also tinged red, making it a favorite with designers. Mixtures are popular; Gitano Mix provided a nice complement to plants of lavender at the Auckland Botanical Garden. Propagate from seed, full sun.

Calendula officinalis with sweet alyssum

Calendula officinalis 'Indian Prince'

Calendula officinalis Gitano Mix

Calibrachoa ×hybrida

TRAILING PETUNIA

Confusion reigned when the trailing petunia (*Calibrachoa ×hybrida*) was first introduced to the market in the early 1990s. Everybody thought it was a petunia: it looked like a petunia, smelled like a petunia, and even grew like a petunia, but no such luck, we all had to learn how to say calibrachoa instead. Actually when they are growing side by side, it is pretty easy to tell most "calis" from most petunias; calibrachoa's leaves and flowers are both significantly smaller. Regardless of their name, these plants with the petunia-like flowers grow rapidly, generally sitting about 4–6" tall and blanketing the ground like a groundcover. At Athens, we use them to complement the entrance to the UGA Trial Gardens. Flowers are plentiful in the spring and fall, and in areas such as the Midwest and Northeast, plants will flower well all season. They are exceptional for hanging baskets and quite at home spilling out of the base of mixed containers.

They are reliably hardy in zone 7 but should be treated as annuals elsewhere. In zone 7b and warmer, leaving plants in the ground over the winter provides unbelievable color in early spring. Some exceptional colors have been bred; five years ago nobody had even heard of this

Calibrachoa ×hybrida 'Million Bells Cherry Pink'

Calibrachoa ×hybrida 'Starlet Rose'

Calibrachoa ×hybrida 'Lirica Showers Blue'

Calibrachoa ×hybrida 'Terra Cotta'

MORE ☞

plant, and now there are almost too many out there to keep track of—all are starting to look the same. But here are a few you might want to experiment with in your basket, container, or garden.

The two most recognized series names are Million Bells and Lirica Showers, both of which offer numerous colors. I have been particularly impressed with the performance of 'Million Bells Cherry Red' and 'Million Bells Cherry Pink'. For blue flowers,

I would probably recommend 'Lirica Showers Blue', and for white, no doubt it would be 'Lirica Showers Pure White'; many more are available in the series and are equally good. Other hybrids continue to appear; we have trialed the Colorburst series, exempli-

Calibrachoa ×hybrida vs petunia

Calibrachoa ×hybrida 'Million Bells Cherry Red'

Calibrachoa ×hybrida 'Lirica Showers Pure White'

Calibrachoa ×hybrida 'Colorburst Violet'

fied by 'Colorburst Violet', as well as the Starlet series, nicely shown by the early spring flowering of 'Starlet Rose'. However, the color that has taken the garden world by storm is 'Terra Cotta'. I have seen it trialed from Georgia to California and photographed it across the country, but the overflowing basket in a garden on Long Island, New York, showed why it has become so popular. An outstanding color, used to perfection. Full sun.

Callistephus chinensis

CHINA ASTER

There need be no confusion about the aster name among gardeners. The China aster (*Callistephus chinensis*) is an annual, flowers all season, and generally produces one to three flowering stems. The genus *Aster* (*Aster* spp.) is perennial, flowers mainly in the fall, and produces dozens of flowering stems. That part of the common name is the same is simply because the flowers are similar. China asters are an important cut flower in the world's flower-producing countries. Rows upon rows of flowers in bud, such as the Matsumoto series shown here, are harvested every day. Flowers of the Meteor series and others provide good vase life after cutting and are used by arrangers to make vibrant statements on their own or as companions in a mixed bouquet.

Callistephus chinensis Matsumoto series, cut flower field

Callistephus chinensis 'Matador Salmon Pink'

Callistephus chinensis Meteor series, cut flowers

Callistephus chinensis 'Blue Ribbon'

MORE ☞

However, who said cut flowers cannot also make fine garden plants? People incorporate China asters in their gardens or containers to provide color and to cut a few flowers to bring in as needed. There are some disease problems with China asters, but for the most part, the flowering plants and the cut stems provide great pleasure. For flowers similar to those used by commercial growers, one of the Matador series, such as 'Matador Salmon Pink', provides good stem length but is not so tall as to flop over, a common problem with the large-flowered forms. Some mixes (Pommex series) provide pompon-like flowers and are easily grown in the flower garden. They can be purchased as seeds or as started plants and planted in the spring, then again in mid summer, for best succession of bloom. Recently, there has been greater garden demand for these flowers, and more dwarf material has steadily become available. 'Blue Ribbon' can be used in containers or the garden, and the small ball-like flowers of the Pompom series, like 'Pompom Red and White', are quite spectacular, if a little gaudy. I really am not a fan of "dog-eared" flowers like those in the Ballet series, but some gardeners really enjoy that frizzy look. As for me, I will take the Astoria series any day and plant them everywhere. The mix is awesome, and as

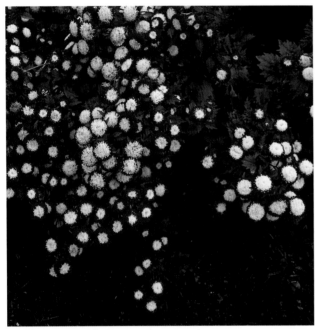

Callistephus chinensis 'Pompom Red and White'

Callistephus chinensis Ballet series

Callistephus chinensis Astoria series

Callistephus chinensis 'Astoria Deep Blue'

single colors, they are all lovely, my favorite being 'Astoria Deep Blue'.

Not everything is perfect in Camelot. China asters often look terrible by mid to late summer; if so, pull them out and replace with additional plantlets or seeds for fall enjoyment. This is not difficult to do but does take time and effort. They also have a history of being plagued by aster yellows. This virus is spread by aphids and other insects and results in leaves turning yellow and the general demise of the plant. Cut flower growers usually screen their plantings to eliminate the carriers, but we simple gardeners put up with these things only if we like the plant enough. Few other plants in the garden are susceptible to aster yellows, and if you see the problem, there is no cure. While I am no fan of yellows, that does not deter me from planting China asters every now and then. Full sun.

Callistephus chinensis Pommex series

Canavalia gladiata, seeds

Canavalia gladiata

SWORD BEAN

I learned long ago that there are two groups of people I will hear from when presenting a lecture: members of a hardy plant society (any state) and master gardeners (ditto). That is why I try to be prepared for anything, because as sure as day turns to night, I will get questions that people have gunnysacked for years, just waiting to ask the "expert." But always, I learn from them. And how I enjoy interacting with such enthusiasm.

One day, in such an interaction, Jose Tallent, a master gardener in Georgia, brought me a huge green pod from a vine and asked if I knew what it was. I did not, but I was intrigued: the thing could have been used as a lethal weapon in the wrong hands. The experts in tropical vines checked references, scratched their heads for a while, and then came up with sword bean, *Canavalia gladiata*, well known in Africa and Asia, where it is grown as a

legume for animal feed and human consumption. When Jose give me the pod, the pink-claret seeds within were just waiting to be sown. Like Jack, I tossed the seeds out, and once warm temperatures arrived, away my magical beanstalk climbed. Now, I don't want to tell you that this vine can in any way compete with the beauty of clematis or passion flower, but it was, well, neat. It climbed by tendrils and formed many heart-shaped leaves on a robust vine. In the summer, small rosy pink pea flowers occurred, which were handsome even if not particularly overwhelming. Even the fruit that Jose originally brought me was not particularly eye-catching, being as green as the leaves and hardly noticeable until pointed out.

Canavalia gladiata

MORE ☞

But oh my, once they were pointed out, their size became obvious, and whenever I toured people around the garden, I would scramble to the fence and harvest a pod. And just like Jose, I would ask, "Do you know what this is?"

The seeds mature in the fall and can be kept in a jar on your desk. Wait until the soil warms up, then sow them in the ground; doing so earlier will not gain any time. This is a plant for plantspeople; it will not excite those who have eyes only for the brightest. Full sun.

Canna ×generalis

CANNA LILY

Where did all these cannas come from? It used to be that canna lilies (*Canna ×generalis*) were fillers, green leaves and red flowers, maybe one or two with yellow blooms or with burnished leaf

Canavalia gladiata, flowers

Canna ×generalis, leaf in border

Canavalia gladiata, fruit

Canna ×generalis 'Tropicanna', in water

color. Those are becoming collectors' plants; today the choices of flower and foliage colors put cannas right up there with petunias and impatiens in their diversity. They have become popular because in zone 7 and warmer, most are comfortably hardy. And in the rest of the country, they grow vigorously enough that they can "strut their stuff" as far north as Nome. Every time I visit growers and breeders, I discover new cultivars of cannas, and it seems gardeners have also started to embrace these marvelous plants. And creativity is not dead—even if the plants don't flower, designers use the foliage alone as feature in a mixed border. And how many plants do you know that can grow in normal garden soils and be equally at home immersed in water? More and more water gardeners are using the handsome foliage of cannas to brighten up their wet spots, from bogs to ponds.

Canna ×generalis 'Erebus', in water

Canna ×generalis 'Tropical Red'

Canna ×generalis 'Tropical Yellow'

Canna ×generalis 'Bugle Boy'

MORE ☞

But like any other plant out there, they are not plastic and are bothered by some serious insect pests. Leaf rollers cause the leaf to roll around itself like a rolled tongue, but unfortunately, it can't unroll. The other bugaboo is Japanese beetles, who like to savor cannas as much as hibiscus, although some cultivars appear less susceptible than others. Both can cause severe disfigurement. One can spray chemicals, but that is generally a losing battle. The leaf rollers can be unrolled, and the beetles, depending on population density, can be picked off and disposed of. If you're defeated by dense populations, at least remove the flowers; they are the primary target. If they become too much of a frustration, don't plant any more cannas.

But if you do, what a choice you have! As wonderful as the big cannas are, breeders are also concentrating more on shorter forms. The Tropical series consists of relatively short cultivars and should not to be confused with 'Tropicanna', a much larger cultivar. 'Tropical Red' and 'Tropical Rose' are obviously shorter than "normal" cannas and have been excellent plants for containers and smaller gardens, but 'Tropical Yellow' is to die for. In Georgia, we placed it in a mixed container, and it flashed its bright smile all season. And while I still enjoy the flowers and functionality of green-

Canna ×generalis 'Tropical Rose'

Canna ×generalis 'King Humbert'

Canna ×generalis 'Liberty Scarlet'

Canna ×generalis 'Perkeo'

Canna ×generalis 'Cleopatra', flowers

leaved cultivars such as 'Bugle Boy' and 'Perkeo', they are taking a backseat to the multicolored foliage cultivars.

Dark foliage is always desirable, and there is nothing wrong with the old-fashioned 'King Humbert'; however, gardeners also have choices, from the Liberty series, like 'Liberty Scarlet', to the orange-flowered, almost black 'Australia'. If that is too much darkness, 'Cleopatra' provides some purple striping on the broad green leaves along with interesting speckled bicolor flowers. But for real brightness, the perennial favorite 'Bengal Tiger' brightens up landscapes regardless of where it is planted. Other variegated forms include 'Kansas City' and 'Stuttgart'. The former is difficult to find, and the latter is terrific if you want a canna where sunshine is limited. 'Stuttgart' performs far better with afternoon shade; it burns up in full-sun gardens.

The sight of 'Panache' always elicits differing opinions. The long sword-like leaves are different from most others, and while the flowers don't blow anyone away, a second look is always in order to appreciate the subtle color. I always include 'Pink Sunburst' in my recommendations because, like Baby Bear's bed, it is not too big and not too small, and has wonderful colored foliage and handsome flowers. It simply works, and works well. However, as I am always asked what canna brings the most com-

Canna ×*generalis* 'Kansas City'

Canna ×*generalis* 'Panache'

Canna ×*generalis* 'Cleopatra', foliage

Canna ×*generalis* 'Pink Sunburst'

MORE 🖙

ments in the garden, I must come clean and tell you more about 'Tropicanna'. Big, bold, and beautiful, the dark multicolored leaves simply radiate and become the center of attention. The flowers are orange—pretty enough, but absolutely unnecessary to complete this marvelous cultivar. Find it, buy it, grow it.

Full sun for all but 'Stuttgart'. Dig up roots after the first frost, cut off all foliage, and store in a 35–40°F place, like a garage area. If perennial, divide every three years or so. Wet soils are better than dry.

Canna ×generalis 'Bengal Tiger'

Canna ×generalis 'Australia'

Canna ×generalis 'Stuttgart'

Canna ×generalis 'Tropicanna'

Capsicum annuum

ORNAMENTAL PEPPER

I love it when high school students tour the UGA Trial Gardens, especially when both girls and boys are in the group. When I point out the ornamental peppers (*Capsicum annuum*), all I need to say is, "These are very hot, anybody want to try one?" Saying that is like putting a red cape in front of a bull, and these young bulls would probably be smart enough not to charge, except for the presence of the bull-ettes. Invariably, the girls elbow the boys a little, and soon one or two bulls will have to show the herd that they are up to the task. And the peppers are indeed hot! And how those bulls sweat. Between the girls, the peppers, and the *Acmella* (which see), these guys don't stand a chance.

Ornamental peppers are easy to use in the garden, seldom growing more than 1' tall. I have seen individual plants in a patio container to whole populations lining a walkway at Longwood Gardens. They bear white flowers, which give way

Capsicum annuum 'Holiday Flame'

Capsicum annuum 'Medusa'

Capsicum annuum 'Explosive Ember'

Capsicum annuum 'Treasures Red'

MORE ☞

to green or white fruit and usually mature to bright colors. Occasionally, plants with variegated leaves, such as 'Jigsaw', are chosen, but they don't have the vigor or joie de vivre of the others. The fruit are the best part, and they can be long and narrow, rounded, and might be purple, red, or orange. I am biased; I do not much like the squat rounded fruit of 'Fireworks' and other selections, or the fat stuff I see on cultivars like 'Korona'. Interesting but no subtlety. 'Treasures Red' provides lots of color, and the fruit are getting a little closer to my taste (although not to my tongue). My favorites have to be the long narrow forms, like the incredibly abundant 'Explosive Ignite', which matures to a bright red in the fall, and 'Holiday Flame', an older cultivar but still with excellent eye appeal.

Some recent releases to gardeners have made me a solid pepperite, particularly with 'Medusa' and 'Chilly Chili' (an All-America Selection in 2002); both provide abundant fruit and are easy to look at and ridiculously easy to grow. Along with the fruit, some purple-leaved

Capsicum annuum 'Korana'

Capsicum annuum 'Explosive Ignite'

Capsicum annuum 'Chilly Chili'

Capsicum annuum 'Masquerade'

forms have also emerged as winners. A favorite for many is 'Masquerade' with dark fruit and dark green leaves, but the winner of this beauty contest has to be 'Explosive Ember' with seemingly hundreds of purple peppers clothed in bronze foliage. Everybody loves this one. Full sun, eat at your own risk.

Cardiospermum halicacabum

LOVE-IN-A-PUFF

Love truly takes on many faces, but finding love inside a puffy fruit has to be one of the more creative forms. Some of the early names of flowers must have been coined by frustrated nearsighted old men—how else can you explain names like love-in-a-puff (*Cardiospermum*), love-in-a-mist (*Nigella*), and love-lies-bleeding (*Amaranthus*)? Talk about finding love in all the wrong places! But love-in-a-puff, at least, makes a little sense; break open the puffy fruit, and look at the seed. Each black seed has a white heart shape

MORE ☞

Capsicum annuum 'Jigsaw'

Capsicum annuum 'Fireworks'

Cardiospermum halicacabum, seeds

Cardiospermum halicacabum

Cardiospermum halicacabum, fruit

on the outside. Plants look best growing through other plants, although they are quite happy on arbors and fences.

The white flowers of *Cardiospermum halicacabum* are tiny and uninteresting, but the fruit inflates as it grows and after a while, puffs are all over the place. Later the fruit dries to an unattractive brown color, but then you know the seeds are ready to be studied or gathered for next year's crop. Simply a fun plant, and no other reason is needed to grow this vine. Full sun.

Caryopteris incana

BLUE MIST SPIREA

Ninety-five percent of the caryopteris plants in gardens are the perennial hybrid, *Caryopteris* ×*clandonensis*, but if you get lucky, you might find some seed or starters of the annual form, *C. incana*. This has been one of my favorite plants for years, but seeds and plants have almost disappeared because of the popularity of its perennial cousin. It differs from the common perennial by being more upright and single-stemmed, with clusters of blue flowers surrounding the stem. They are used as fresh flowers from the garden, combining well in the vase with other cuts.

Plants can be planted quite densely, and a fine display will be had by about late June. More flowers result in full sun, but afternoon shade is also tolerated, at least in the South.

Caryopteris incana, flowers

Caryopteris incana

Caryopteris incana, arrangement with celosia, statice, and white loosestrife

Catananche

CUPID'S DART

Only one species, *Catananche caerulea*, is common in gardens, although many are known. Plants prefer cool weather and are more often seen in the Northeast and Northwest than elsewhere. They produce thin stems topped with lavender flowers bearing a darker eye, the target of Cupid's dart. Supposedly, plants were used in those ubiquitous love potions of yesteryear, thus the common name. Quite beautiful, but they can become leggy and a little weedy at times, particularly in the heat of the summer.

Catananche caespitosa is a yellow-flowered species, best for rock gardens or containers. Both prefer full sun and good drainage.

Catananche caerulea, flowers

Catananche caespitosa

Catananche caerulea

Catharanthus roseus

VINCA

From an almost unrecognizable small flowering plant on the island of Madagascar, vinca (or Madagascar periwinkle) has been reinvented by plant breeders into a bigger, bolder, and more vigorous plant. Gardeners now can chose from dozens of cultivars, in an astonishing array of flower colors and flower sizes.

Most gardeners, when eyeing the sun-loving, heat-seeking flowers, refer to these plants (*Catharanthus roseus*) as vinca, but no one should get this mixed up with perennial vinca (*Vinca* spp.). This vinca is sold as a bedding plant and became popular when its tolerance to heat, humidity, and full sun were combined with outstanding new flower colors. Plants look good in the garden, in a container, and even as an edging to large beds and walkways. They seldom grow more than 1' tall and are covered with flowers from June to frost.

However, their popularity declined in recent years because of their susceptibility to root rots associated with overwatering. If you are overzealous in over-

Catharanthus roseus, edging

Catharanthus roseus 'Bourbon Street'

Catharanthus roseus 'Heat Wave White'

Catharanthus roseus 'Icy Pink Cooler'

Catharanthus roseus 'Caribbean Lavender'

head watering, or the bed is in a low area, these are not the plants for you. One of the few good things about times of drought is that many plants suffer far fewer fungal problems, and vinca is certainly one of them. It is unfortunate that a good plant suffered because of poor gardening practices, but this is not the first example, nor will it be the last.

Given a few brains, most gardeners can succeed easily with these plants, even under normal rainfall. Don't include them near the in-ground sprinkling system you use on your turf in the middle of the night. Don't plant them where the rain does not drain well, and provide full sun. Then get out of the way.

The change in flower size and shape over the past fifteen years has been nothing short of spectacular. Cultivars such as 'Bourbon Street' and 'Orchid Stardust' have obvious eyes in the flowers and are quite eye-catching themselves. White is always in fashion; 'Heat Wave White' provides clean color, while 'Icy Pink Cooler' adds that hint of pink. Pinks and lavenders are well represented in the land of vincas, and I have always enjoyed 'Pacifica Pink' and 'Tropicana

Catharanthus roseus 'Pacifica Pink'

Catharanthus roseus 'Tropicana Bright Eye'

Catharanthus roseus 'Tropicana Rose'

Catharanthus roseus 'Pacifica Red'

MORE ☞

Bright Eye', as well as 'Caribbean Lavender', all of which sport off-color centers. Some of the brightest flowers occur on 'Tropicana Rose', whose white eye con- tracts wonderfully with the rose petals. Years ago, I was struck by the true red of 'Pacifia Red', one of the very best red-colored flowers available to the gardener. Great then, still great today. Full sun, good drainage.

Celosia
COCKSCOMB

So much diversity in flower, habit, and use can be found in this genus that it will never go away. As a cut flower, plants are

Catharanthus roseus, UGA Trial Gardens

Celosia argentea var. *cristata* Jewel Box Mix

Catharanthus roseus 'Orchid Stardust'

Celosia argentea var. *cristata* 'Bicolor Chief'

Celosia argentea var. *spicata* 'Purple Flamingo' with sweet potato

Celosia argentea var. *spicata* 'Cramers' Amazon'

Celosia argentea, cut flower field

MORE ☞

Celosia argentea var. *cristata* 'Amigo Mahogany Red'

Celosia argentea var. *plumosa* Castle series

Celosia argentea var. *cristata* 'Prestige Scarlet'

Celosia argentea var. *plumosa* Sparkler series

Celosia argentea var. *cristata* 'Red Chief'

Celosia argentea var. *plumosa* 'Apricot Brandy'

rowed out like corn and appear in bouquets and as single stems throughout the country. Gardeners have never had a major love affair with *Celosia argentea* but not for lack of visibility of the plant. Although not as popular as petunias or geraniums, celosias have been aggressively hybridized to keep plants new and fresh, resulting in their continued visibility in public places and retail outlets. This is a good thing, because while bedding plants in general have lost some of their luster, celosia continues to reinvent itself. One of the ways the genus remains in the crosshairs of landscapers and gardeners is in its multitude of forms. Like begonias, they wear many different costumes, all of which can be welcome in the garden.

The cockscomb look (var. *cristata*) is the form easiest to hate. Colored brains always come to my mind when I teach these plants, but who is to account for taste? What had to have started out as a joke among breeders ("I can make a shorter, uglier celosia than you, wanna bet?") resulted in a startling transfiguration of quite a nice plant. I can think of many adjectives for 'Amigo Mahogany Red', but "subtle" would not be one of them. Each large colored brain squatting on the plants of Jewel Box Mix persists most of the summer, so one can relive *The Hunchback of Notre Dame* remakes every day. But to be fair, I am likely in the minority in my aversion to this group, because more just keep on coming. But at least they are getting better. I have come to enjoy the upright flowers of 'Prestige Scarlet' and believed they would also make fine cut flowers. But when I was introduced to the mother of all cut flowers in celosia, the Chief series, I realized the cut flower market had already been taken. In the garden, they really are awesome, producing large clubs so in case anyone attacks you in the garden, you have a ready-made defensive weapon. All sorts of colors may be had, but if a picture is worth a thousand words, looking at 'Red Chief' and 'Bicolor Chief' can substitute for an essay. When they are taken out of the garden and teamed with goldenrod or other bright flowers, put on your shades and duck for cover.

Celosia argentea var. *spicata* 'Purple Flamingo'

Celosia argentea var. *spicata* 'Venezuela'

Celosia argentea var. *cristata* 'Scarlet Chief', arrangement with goldenrod

Celosia argentea var. *plumosa* 'New Look'

A relatively recent group, wheat celosia (var. *spicata*), is often seen in parks and botanic gardens. Tall and stately, wheat celosias can be impressive in the background or surrounded by other plants at their legs. The purple-leaved, purple-flowered form 'Purple Flamingo', outstanding in its own right, is tough enough to anchor a corner of the UGA campus in concert with 'Margarita' sweet potato. The drawback of this cultivar is that it does not flower until fall and can reseed with gusto. Season-long flowering, however, is the norm for 'Flamingo Feather', and seeing it towering over other celosias puts its height in perspective. 'Cramers' Amazon' is a popular tall cut flower form and for those who like this form but don't have space for such

Celosia argentea var. *spicata* 'Flamingo Feather'

Celosia argentea var. *plumosa* 'Century Red'

Celosia 'Enterprise Dark Pink'

Celosia 'Punky Red'

monsters, 'Venezuela' can work in containers or in gardens.

Competing for the honor of best known is the plume celosia group (var. *plumosa*), whose flowers look like the plumes of gladiators. This is my favorite by far, and some outstanding breeding has been concentrated in this form. Gardeners can choose short plants, such as the 9–12" tall Castle series; 'Castle Yellow' is an outstanding performer. The ever-popular 'New Look' is a little taller. Plants are taller but the feathery look is a little muted in the Sparkler series; however, several fine colors are available in the mix. If the traditional feather look is important, it is impossible to overlook the knock-your-socks-off color of 'Century Red'. Its color combined with its compact habit makes it an easy choice when bright colors are demanded. And when taller forms are wanted, surely 'Apricot Brandy' should appear on a gardener's wish list. An All-America Selection in 1981, plants have stood the test of time. And still celosias change, exemplified by the mix of wheat and feather blood in such new hybrid cultivars as 'Enterprise Dark Pink' and 'Punky Red'. Never a dull moment! Full sun, deadhead in mid summer.

Centaurea

BACHELOR'S BUTTONS, CORNFLOWER

By placing a blue-flowered daisy in his label, the single Victorian gentleman signaled his marital status, and plants became known as bachelor's buttons. This same flower was also an inhabitant of cornfields, and cornflowers have become blue sentries at the edge of many of our roadways in this country. The sultan of Constantinople enjoyed the sweet smell of one species' flowers, and one of our lesser-known American natives is also a member of this fine genus of plants. However, not all species are appreciated and even fewer are grown consistently in our gardens.

The common blue of bachelor's buttons (*Centaurea cyanus*) is underappreciated, but flowers look right at home in gardens or containers. They are also useful as fillers in arrangements. There are some choices in colors; I am fond of Florence Mix, which sports a wide diversity of colors. 'Garnet' is one example of single colors becoming more available; this one provides dark colors for the garden plan.

Centaurea cyanus, flowers

Centaurea moschata 'The Bride'

The American basket flower (*Centaurea americana*) is hardly seen in North American gardens, although it is produced as a cut flower by growers around the world. The plants can grow to about 4' in height. The flower of the most common cultivar, 'Jolly Joker', starts out as long, thick hair-like strands, seemingly straining to get out of their case, and opens to a large, bushy pink flower. A great deal of fun to grow, but don't expect it to be well behaved.

Sweet sultan (*Centaurea moschata*) has an ephemeral sweet fragrance that requires nose-to-flower contact. The common Imperialis series produces a potpourri of colors on 2' tall plants and is especially useful for bouquets. I also enjoy the white form called 'The Bride'. Sweet sultans prefer cool summers and perform better in the North than in the South.

Centaurea cyanus 'Garnet'

Centaurea americana 'Jolly Joker', opening bud

Centaurea americana 'Jolly Joker'

Centaurea moschata Imperialis series, as cut flowers

Centaurea cyanus Florence Mix

All members of the genus are grown from seed, which can be sown after threat of frost. Deadhead for most persistent performance, and, if needed, sow again in mid summer for fall flowering. Full sun to afternoon shade.

Cerinthe major

HONEYWORT

Honeywort (*Cerinthe major*) has such a weird flower, it is small wonder that so few people grow it. It is difficult to describe the small pendent purple and black flower; I mean, come on, how many people really want purple and black as part of their floral display? But to those of you who must have the newest and the weirdest: this fascinating plant should definitely be on your short list.

The gray-green leaves are waxy and thick, and plants are relatively drought-tolerant; however, high humidity and wetness are not to their liking. The flowers lean over the foliage and don't really contrast well, and for me at least, tend to get lost. But believe it or not, some people think they make good cut stems. I have also tried the yellow form, 'Aurea', whose flowers are a lot more likeable and more reliable as well. Still a tough plant to keep alive throughout the sea-

MORE ☞

Cerinthe major

Cerinthe major

Cerinthe major 'Aurea'

son in areas of warm, humid summers, but I'd grow it again. A great plant to check out the plant knowledge of your know-it-all gardener friend. Full sun, good drainage.

Chrysanthemum

Only a few species remain in this once glorious genus, and the ones we are able to put our hands on are all annuals. Often, purchasing seeds from a good seed catalog is the sole means of finding plants. While they are not well known to gardeners in North America, many of the plants originated as European weeds. All these mums prefer cool summers, and in areas of warm, humid summers, it may be necessary to replant in mid summer for all-season performance.

Tricolor daisy (*Chrysanthemum carinatum*) seems to be the most difficult to

Chrysanthemum carinatum 'Polar Skies'

Chrysanthemum segetum

Chrysanthemum coronarium 'Primrose Gem'

Chrysanthemum segetum 'Prado'

Chrysanthemum segetum 'Eastern Star'

find, and this three-colored flower remains rather obscure. However, some cultivars are breaking through the garden ranks, and I find 'Polar Skies', a handsome white-flowered form, quite lovely. Crown daisy (*C. coronarium*) has ferny leaves and usually bears yellow flowers. The best selection is 'Primrose Gem', with dozens of small double light yellow flowers.

Lastly, in our search for the true chrysanthemum, let us not overlook the best one of all and discover what a corn marigold (*Chrysanthemum segetum*) really looks like. What it really looks like is a common yellow daisy with handsome dark green dissected leaves. The smaller darker center contrasts with the lighter yellow rays. However, there are enough boring yellows out there, and I prefer 'Prado' for its much more contrastive flower center. Excellent performer as well. 'Eastern Star' is the most unusual in that the only trace of yellow surrounds the center. Quite beautiful.

Full sun in the North, afternoon shade is tolerated in the South. All purchased from seed. Deadheading is beneficial. Reseed in the summer for fall flowers.

Chrysocephalum apiculatum

NULLABOR BUTTONS, GOLDEN BUTTONS

Here is a plant that definitely needs to be grown to be appreciated. To see this plant in a container at the garden store is to walk right past it, but that would be a mistake. Nullabor buttons (*Chrysocephalum apiculatum*) is native to the Nullabor Plain in Australia, indicating a tolerance for heat and drought. I was impressed with the plant when I first saw it growing in eastern Australia, so I brought some home and grew it out in Athens. I was not disappointed.

Buy it for a sunny, difficult spot; it will

Chrysocephalum apiculatum, Australia

reward you with aggressive, but not invasive, growth, and with dozens upon dozens of small button-like yellow flowers that just keep on appearing. Plants tolerate conditions from Minneapolis to Miami and are as at home in the ground

MORE ☞

as in a container, where they are not so tamed that they look like marigolds.

Hopefully, there will be a pot of this stuff at the garden center to walk by, and if there is, stop and buy. Full sun.

Cirsium japonicum

JAPANESE THISTLE

The very word "thistle" is a major turnoff to most gardeners; however, as thistles go, the Japanese thistle (*Cirsium japonicum*) isn't all bad. I am sure that such

a powerful endorsement may not result in everyone searching for seed, but for some of you, additional information may be useful.

Plants are prickly, to be sure, but not nearly as bad as most other thistles that come to mind, in particular Canada

Chrysocephalum apiculatum, UGA Trial Gardens

Cirsium japonicum 'White Beauty'

Cirsium japonicum 'Rose Beauty'

Cirsium japonicum 'Pink Beauty'

thistle or Scotch thistle. These grow only about 2' tall, and the long-lasting cut flowers are colorful and quite useful in arrangements. The only cultivars I am aware of are in the Beauty series, appearing in rose, pink, or white. 'Rose Beauty' is the best of the three; 'White Beauty' is fair at best. Full sun.

Clarkia amoena

SATIN FLOWER

Having wandered through landscapes and gardens all over this country and a few above the 45th parallel as well, I can honestly say that less than one percent of that buying public purchase satin flowers with the idea of enjoying them outdoors. That is not to say satin flowers are ugly— in fact, well over half the people who regularly purchase cut flowers in the grocery store or florist buy satin flowers. So they must be grown somewhere. And they are, in greenhouses around the country and in fields in the Northwest and occasionally in the Northeast. However, there are a few problems.

Satin flower (*Clarkia amoena*), also known as godetia, loves cool, dry conditions. In eastern gardens, heat usually gets to them by mid June to early July

and they tend to stretch and get floppy. I love their understated beauty but have come to terms with the fact that, outside coastal California and the Far North, I will have to enjoy them as amputees, not as the entire plant.

Of course, the more the challenge, the more we want the plant in the garden. Satin Mix contains a number of handsome pastel colors including 'Satin Pink' and is sometimes available in seed packets in the spring. The best series by far is the Grace series, used by cut flower growers because of the wonderful colors

and uniform habit. I especially enjoy 'Grace Rose Pink' and 'Grace Salmon Red'. Not particularly creative names, but quite spectacular plants. Full sun, excellent drainage.

Cleome

SPIDER FLOWER

Grandmother's garden would never have been without a few spider flowers (*Cleome hassleriana*) partly because they

MORE ☞

Clarkia amoena 'Grace Rose Pink'

Clarkia amoena 'Satin Pink'

Clarkia amoena 'Grace Salmon Red'

were so common at the time and also because they self-seeded everywhere and never disappeared. Plants were a bit of a nuisance, and kind of leggy, and okay, they fell apart halfway through the summer, and yes, they did self-sow, but still, the flowers were quite lovely in their detail, and Grandma did like them.

Some of the older cultivars are still around today. 'White Spider', a selection of *Cleome marshallii*, is still occasionally seen but never caught on in garden circles. It was the Queen series, among the first named cultivars of *C. hassleriana*, that people flocked to. The series included the muted 'Pink Queen', the violent 'Violet Queen', and the handsome 'Purple Queen'. These were the main-

stays along with 'Helen Campbell', a fine tall white form. All were grown from seed and were wonderfully simple plants to include in the garden. However, over the years, it seems people started tiring of them, and they became less noticeable in our gardens.

However, in the early 2000s, the interest in spider flower was reinvigorated by the introduction of two new cleomes. The

Cleome hassleriana, flower

Cleome marshallii 'White Spider'

Cleome hassleriana 'Pink Queen'

Cleome hassleriana 'Violet Queen'

Sparkler series is a hybrid that provides outstanding performance and colors. It is shorter than the common forms but certainly cannot be considered dwarf. 'Sparkler Blush' is my favorite, with its pink and white flowers, and in combination with 'Sparkler White' makes quite a show. 'Sparkler Rose' is among the most eye-catching; it is impossible to walk by it, in combination with other plants like mealy-cup sage (*Salvia farinacea*), without stopping. Plants produce few viable seed, and the self-sowing problems are of little concern. However, in warm-summer climates, plants still pooped out by mid summer.

At the same time, a new entry in the cleome game came to market under the name 'Linde Armstrong'. This dwarf (<18" tall) plant is named for two wonderful Charlotte gardeners, Linde Wilson and Ann Armstrong, who promoted its charms. The bright rose-colored flowers are beautiful, and plants look outstanding in the garden or in mixed containers. Plants begin blooming in May, and while most cleomes fall apart by mid to late summer, 'Linde Armstrong' continues to flower until frost. If needed, she can be

Cleome hassleriana 'Purple Queen'

Cleome 'Sparkler Blush', *C.* 'Sparkler White'

Cleome hassleriana 'Helen Campbell'

Cleome 'Linde Armstrong'

MORE ☞

Cleome 'Linde Armstrong', flowers

Cleome 'Linde Armstrong', container

Cleome 'Sparkler Rose'

given a haircut to rejuvenate the plants. This plant is grown from cuttings, seedlings will be similar but will not be 'Linde Armstrong'. All cleomes prefer full sun.

Clerodendrum

A large number of species reside in the genus, but all are on the periphery of gardeners' consciousness, unless, as one

or two are prone to do, they have become noxious weeds. The harlequin glory bower (*Clerodendrum trichotomum*) is hardy as far north as New York and as beautiful as the fruit can be, plants can

Clerodendrum trichotomum, calyces and fruit

Clerodendrum speciosissimum

Clerodendrum ugandense

MORE ☞

spread rapidly by underground suckers and soon get out of control. The same can be said for shrubby glory bower, *C. bungei,* which for some people is a treasure, for others a smelly obnoxious weed.

Most of the plants in this genus are interesting but usually disappointing in the garden. The only garden annuals worth trying, and even that is debatable, are the showy clerodendrum and the blue butterfly bush. I have seen the former, *Clerodendrum speciosissimum,* in full red regalia in outdoor containers, but plants are at their best if protected from the elements. The red flowers knock your socks off, and if you can find a pot or two, try them on a protected patio. The other plant I have long been fascinated with is the blue butterfly bush (*C. ugandense*), which grows reasonably

Clerodendrum bungei

Clerodendrum ugandense

quickly in the garden. The handsome blue and white flowers that are formed truly are beautiful, but unfortunately, the plant has a sprawling habit and doesn't flower consistently. Keep it within arm's reach: it is a plant for a container near where people gather, so the flowers can be admired, even though there may not be many of them. Certainly worth growing, but may not be worth the time or expense in subsequent years. Full sun.

Clitoria ternatea

BUTTERFLY PEA VINE

What a beautiful vine, how little used it is. It's common name needs to become far more common, for this is a terrific plant. The butterfly pea vine (*Clitoria ternatea*) hails from the island of Ternate, one of the Molucca Islands in Indonesia, an interesting but absolutely useless piece of plant trivia. Plants grow rapidly and climb by tendrils, which allow them to scramble up walls or through shrubs. The handsome foliage consists of five leaflets per leaf, but it is the dark blue flowers that are so outstanding. After flowering, long thin pods

form, which should be saved for next year's crop. Plant the seeds after the threat of frost, and sit back and enjoy this fine import from Ternate. Full sun.

Cobaea scandens

CUP AND SAUCER VINE

Another marvelous annual vine that can fill an arbor or clamber through a shrub.

Cobaea scandens

The cup and saucer vine (*Cobaea scandens*) is well named, with a well-defined cup and saucer dancing on the vine. Soak the seeds overnight, then sow them in the ground after frost is no longer a problem; starting any earlier is simply a waste of time. Otherwise start them in containers about two weeks before the last frost-free date. Plants grow quickly and can easily reach 10–15′ in a season.

In general, the lavender-flowered

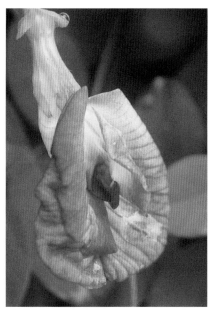
Clitoria ternatea, flower

Clitoria ternatea

MORE ☞

Coleus 'Dip't in Wine'

Cobaea scandens 'Alba'

Coleus 'Alabama Sunset'

species itself is as good as any cultivar, and cultivars are few and far between anyway. The only other choice I have seen is 'Alba', whose white flowers tend to discolor as they age. Collect seeds in the fall. Full sun.

Coleus

Coleus, coleus everywhere, and more on their way: if one plant exemplifies the explosion of specialty annuals in North America, it has to be coleus. Actually, the real name for coleus is *Solenostemon*

Coleus 'Aurora'

Coleus 'Copper'

Coleus 'Velvet Lime'

Coleus, container

MORE ☞

Coleus 'Solar Morning Mist'

Coleus 'Solar Flare'

Coleus Stained Glass series

Coleus 'Kiwi Fern'

Coleus 'Flirting Skirts'

Coleus 'Ducksfoot'

scutellarioides, but no self-respecting gardeners are going to allow the whims of taxonomists to tongue-tie them, so *Solenostemon* will be bandied about the hallways of herbaria but seldom heard in the real world.

It wasn't so long ago that everyone believed that shade was a necessity for successful coleus garden performance; however, in the last ten years that myth has been soundly put to rest. Plants tolerate shade to be sure, but with the myriad of new cultivars, most selections do better in full sun. Coleus were born to be in containers, the larger and more chaotic

the better. A row of containers containing red canna lilies embraced with 'Dip't in Wine' is impressive in Madison, Wisconsin, while a planting of 'Copper' is set off wonderfully by the base of creeping zinnia in Athens, Georgia. I can picture 'Alabama Sunset', one of the most popular coleus throughout the country, dominating a pendulous planting of perennial vinca, and I relish the memory of datura at the base of a wild planting of random colei. One of my favorite combinations was a container of 'Aurora' and ageratum interplanted in the garden, but the blend of verbena with the new 'Velvet Lime' was

equally stunning. What fun these containers are, and how easy.

So many cultivars have been released lately that a coffeetable book of coleus images could easily be produced, but I'll contain myself and offer just a few. The Solar series, introduced by George Griffith of Gainesville, Florida, has to be one of my favorites, including such breakthrough plants as the deeply colored 'Solar Eclipse', and the bright 'Solar Flare', which is one of the few cultivars I recommend for the shade (it grows in a shady bed in the Armitage garden). And some of the largest most eye-popping

Coleus 'Solar Eclipse'

Coleus 'Diane's Gold'

Coleus 'Pineapple'

Coleus 'Amazon'

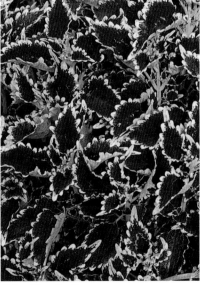

Coleus 'Daredevil'

MORE ☞

leaves were introduced with 'Solar Morning Mist'. You can't go too far wrong in bringing some Solar power home to the garden.

For plain fun, you might want to try the beautiful Stained Glass series, all of which provide vibrant colors, and for no other reason than plain fun, try the multicolored rounded leaves of 'Flirting Skirts'(aka 'Hurricane Jenni') and 'Diane's Gold', or the sensational 'Kiwi Fern'. All are novelties, all will bring many smiles and many comments, good and bad.

For more muted colors in the yellow and green hues, I have always found 'Pineapple' and 'Amazon' to be very effective. They are used en masse in many landscapes. Many coleus such as 'Daredevil' are big and bodacious (>3' tall and wide); others have a wonderful mounded habit. Many compact forms can be found, but probably the most popular of these medicine balls is the Ducksfoot series, with duckfoot-like foliage. 'Ducksfoot' makes a wonderful hanging basket in the Missouri Botanical Garden, but its cousin, 'Ducksfoot Purple', is equally beautiful in the landscape in Georgia. Another dark-leaved form that continues to impress is 'Merlot', almost as good as the wine and far better for you.

The series that helped start the coleus revolution was selected over ten years ago and named the Sunlover series. If available, they provide wonderful colors and a little history as well. Some you may still find are the chartreuse 'Gay's Delight', the muted orange of 'Rustic

Coleus 'Ducksfoot Purple'

Coleus 'Gay's Delight', *C.* 'Rustic Orange'

Coleus 'Merlot'

Coleus 'Rustic Orange'

Orange', the strikingly beautiful variegation of 'Collin's Gold', and the large yet handsome 'Freckles'. Part of the beginning, certainly not the end of the coleus phenomenon. Full sun for most; shade is tolerated for all, but colors will not be as vibrant.

Colocasia

ELEPHANT EAR

This introductory sentence is nearly identical to the one you read under the genus *Alocasia*: regardless of what the "experts" tell you, there are no easily vis-

ible differences between this genus, *Alocasia*, and *Xanthosoma* (see further discussion under *Alocasia*). The reason for mentioning this again is that the cultivars I cite probably belong to *Colocasia*, but then again they may not.

The common elephant ear (*Colocasia*

Coleus 'Collin's Gold'

Colocasia esculenta

Coleus 'Freckles'

Colocasia esculenta 'Nancy's Revenge' (top)

MORE ☞

Colocasia esculenta with bananas

Colocasia esculenta 'Black Magic', landscape

esculenta) is well known in the South. The immense fluted leaves provide an architectural feature that is difficult to ignore. Plants are highly tolerant of different soil conditions; they put up well with drought but also can be planted in a bog. They are used in containers, where they behave themselves reasonably well, but I have seen them locked in battle for supremacy with tropical bananas in a residential neighborhood. It was a violent sight.

The gardener has numerous choices, not all easily found but obtainable through reputable mail-order sources. I occasionally see the white and green leaves of 'Chicago Harlequin', which seems to be less stuck in conservatories and public gardens than it once was. The petioles are magnificent as well. Another interesting form is 'Nancy's Revenge'; it too is difficult to describe, but I have little doubt that Nancy McDaniels of Florida, after whom the plant was

named, is often asked just what she was avenging. The form I see the most, however, is 'Black Magic' (aka 'Jet Black Wonder') and for good reason. Although the leaves may unfold green, they mature to jet black and remain that way throughout the season. In bold landscapes or at the top of the Armitage driveway, this is a winner. Another handsome form is *Colocasia antiquorum* 'Illustris', whose purple and green pointed leaves look good in

MORE ☞

Colocasia esculenta 'Chicago Harlequin'

Colocasia esculenta 'Black Magic'

Colocasia antiquorum 'Illustris'

Colocasia antiquorum 'Illustris', foliage

containers or in the ground. It contrasts yet blends in with many ornamental annuals and perennials.

Overwinter *Colocasia* by digging the large tuber after temperatures dip into the mid 30s; remove the foliage, and put the tuber in sphagnum moss in a garage or other area that stays above freezing. Full sun for the species, afternoon shade for the cultivars.

Consolida

LARKSPUR

Larkspur is a mainstay for cut flower growers, particularly in the West, where it is grown by the acre for fresh and dried stems. Most larkspurs grown today are hybrids of two or three species. The characteristics that make it so appealing to growers can be taken advantage of by gardeners as well. Larkspurs are easy to grow: simply throw some seed out in the spring in the North, in the fall in the South, and get out of the way. Viewed as a single stem, one can see that the flowers are similar to those of delphinium, right to the spur, and plants are thus known as the annual delphinium. Seldom, however, do larkspurs grow as a single stem; rather, they reseed and crowd each other for attention. Double-flowered forms in pastels and pinks, lavender-purple flowers, and pastel pinks to white flowers are all possible from a single seed package picked up at the garden center. Larkspurs are cool lovers, and in the heat and humidity of the summer, they can decline rapidly. Replant in late June or early July if flowers are desired all season. If reseeding is a problem, cut down the plants before they produce fruit. But I bet you have a neighbor or two who would love to receive some of those seeds, so they too can bring in cut flowers next spring. Full sun, cool season.

Consolida 'Alba'

Consolida, flowers

Consolida, double-flowered forms

Convolvulus

BINDWEED

Say the words "morning glory" and "bindweed" in the same sentence, and many gardeners will run away in fear. Fear of reseeding, fear of rapacious weeds, and fear of the unknown are the reasons for turning tail. With the true morning glory (*Ipomoea*, which see), plants can become a terrible nuisance, but not so with ornamentals of this genus. While bindweed is a member of this genus, nobody in their right mind would plant it in a garden. A number of species are considered perennial, mainly the very silvery silverbush, *Convolvulus cneorum*, although hardiness south of zone 7 is questionable.

The popularity of some of the excellent annuals is not large, but they are gaining ground little by little. I think the prettiest is a selection of trailing morning glory, *Convolvulus sabatius*. 'Baby Moon' produces dozens of light blue flowers and can fill a container or brighten up the edges of a walkway. Its cousin 'Full Moon' is similar in habit but has darker flowers. Both are superb plants during the cooler days of spring and fall but may have difficulties in mid summer.

Some of the showiest plants are known as the annual morning glory, *Convolvulus tricolor*. The tricolor refers to the wild coloration of the flowers on

Convolvulus cneorum

Convolvulus sabatius 'Baby Moon', container

Convolvulus sabatius 'Baby Moon', garden

Convolvulus sabatius 'Full Moon'

MORE ☞

the short sprawling stems. The Ensign series includes two of the showiest plants, 'Blue Ensign' and 'Red Ensign'. The flashy flowers have one color in the outside and another in the eye, with a contrasting hue in the middle. They are excellent in containers or sprawling through the garden. Full sun.

Coreopsis

TICKSEED, CALLIOPSIS

Only one species in this large genus is worthy of being tucked into this annual book, and it is the colorful annual tickseed, *Coreopsis tinctoria*. All the other perennial species are much better known by gardeners, and as a result this wonderful plant from the south and central United States has been ignored. But a comeback has occurred with the greater interest in natives, meadow gardening, and lawn-free gardens. Meadows throughout the land feature calliopsis and other meadow-type plants like cosmos. There, as in other "wild" gardens, calliopsis seems most at home, romping around hand in hand with other fancy-free flowers. The footloose characteristic

Convolvulus tricolor 'Blue Ensign'

Coreopsis tinctoria with nasturtiums

Convolvulus tricolor 'Red Ensign'

Coreopsis tinctoria, narrow petals

is nowhere more wonderful than in the helter-skelter garden once tended by Monet at Giverny, which today is historically correct and a perfect study in chaotic brilliance. Because this plant is most at home in a meadow garden or

MORE ☞

Coreopsis tinctoria, red centers

Coreopsis tinctoria, wildflower mix

Coreopsis tinctoria, Giverny

where it can do its own thing, it is often found in native flower mixtures or from meadow-in-a-can companies. They are at their best when temperatures are cooler and are often found in the company of cosmos and nasturtiums.

All plants are raised from seed, and the diversity, even in a single seed package, is startling. The common golden color, often with a dark center, can give way to rounded flowers with a much larger red center and to wild, weird, and wonderful narrow-petaled red forms, a

wonderful surprise one year in the Armitage garden. Full sun; ignore them until they need to be cut back. Allow them to seed and plants will come back the next year.

Cosmos

This underappreciated plant does most anything most anywhere for most any-

body. Why it is not in everyone's garden is beyond me, it simply works. As a meadow and "wild" plant, tall cosmos (*Cosmos bipinnatus*) is easy on the eyes and cavorts with plants of all descriptions. The sulphur cosmos (*C. sulphureus*) is outstanding in the garden, and what more can I say about a flower that smells just like chocolate, which is a fact when you stick your nose in the flower of *C. atrosanguineus*?

Cosmos bipinnatus 'Versailles Pink'

Cosmos bipinnatus 'Sonata Pink'

Cosmos bipinnatus, wildflower mix

Cosmos bipinnatus 'Versailles White'

Cosmos bipinnatus 'Sonata White'

Cosmos bipinnatus 'Seashell'

Cosmos bipinnatus Early Sensation Mix

Cosmos bipinnatus 'Loveliness'

Cosmos bipinnatus 'Daydream'

Cosmos sulphureus 'Cosmic Orange'

MORE ☞

Tall cosmos, native to the southern United States and Mexico, dominates wildflower mixes, and in trials, its performance dwarfs that of others in the row. Wildflower plantings are fine, but the plant has been significantly improved to provide even more colorful flowers and lower maintenance. The Versailles series is a mainstay, and my goodness, was I blown away at the white garden outside Giverny, where 'Versailles White' and white flowering tobacco made people literally stop and stare. 'Versailles Pink' is no slouch either, and the combination of the two immediately elevates one to "professional designer." An equally beautiful group is the Sonata series, slightly shorter than the Versailles but just as useful. In combination with a light green background such as a cutleaf sambucus, 'Sonata White' is even whiter and lights up the shrub as well. 'Sonata Pink' is almost ball-shaped, with dozens of clear pink flowers top-

Cosmos atrosanguineus

Cosmos sulphureus 'Polidor'

Cosmos sulphureus 'Diablo'

ping the ferny foliage. Both series are no-brainers.

Other choices are available in this species. Early Sensation Mix is taller and a bit more weedy but excellent as cut flowers from the garden. And for novelty, gardeners can choose from the beautiful bicolored 'Daydream' and the different and statuesque 'Seashell' with its fluted petals. And wouldn't you know it, breeders just couldn't leave well enough alone, they created a double form. And even I, the curmudgeon of double flowers, have to admit that 'Loveliness' is just that.

The sulphur cosmos may not be quite as beautiful, but the number of flowers on a plant is astounding. The flowers of 'Cosmic Orange' are almost double and sit on compact plants that don't fall over. I recall coming across an entire bed of 'Diablo' in a landscape in Georgia, and the flowers just went on and on. As impressive as that was, I also loved approaching a bright planting of 'Polidor' lining a path, and then as I was beside them, admiring the contrast in combination with other plantings. Excellent.

And for the sheer hell of it, plant some chocolate cosmos one year. The somber dark purple flowers are quite different from the happy-face flowers of the previous species, and although performance doesn't come close to those, who cares when you can go to the candy store every time you put your nose near it? Non-fattening as well. Plant them in a container where you don't have to bend too far to inhale.

Full sun, good drainage. If plants begin to decline in the summer, resow the seeds directly into the beds, in and among plants already there. The second planting will keep you in color the rest of the year.

Cuphea

This group of plants is fast becoming a garden mainstay, for several reasons, not the least of which is the wonderful diversity exhibited in the genus. The purple cuphea (*Cuphea pallida*) has not really caught on yet but is quite marvelous, with its purple flowers filling the plant. Unlike most members of this genus, it is better in the cool Northwest than the warm Southeast. While we may not be cuphea connoisseurs, most of us have tried a plant or two of Mexican heather (*C. hyssopifolia*). The mounding plants with their pastel flowers have been attractive if not memorable. However, plants of 'Charmar Pink' are always full of flowers, even in the brutal heat of a southern summer, and the shrubby 'Allyson' still enjoys popularity. They are tough and resilient.

Those adjectives could describe most of the species because all work well under rather stressful conditions. Small-flowered but floriferous hybrids are also appearing, such as 'Twinkle Pink', which has filled containers all summer. Most of us are also well aware of the toughness of the cigar flower (*Cuphea ignea*), and they are available in a slightly bigger-flowered form, 'Dynamite', as well as in white, 'Kona White'. But if you like that smoking flower, you simply have to try the mammoth cigar plant, *C. micropetala*. Good grief, where has this been hiding all this time? In a single year, plants

Cosmos sulphureus 'Polidor' with white sweet alyssum

Cuphea pallida

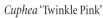

Cuphea 'Twinkle Pink'

Cuphea ignea 'Dynamite'

Cuphea ignea 'Kona White'

Cuphea hyssopifolia 'Charmar Pink'

Cuphea hyssopifolia 'Allyson'

Cuphea micropetala

Cuphea 'Firecracker'

Cuphea 'Firecracker', flower

will grow 3–5' tall, and when it flowers in September and October, it will be the dominant plant in the garden. The fact that it does not flower until the fall is looked upon too often as a detriment rather than a benefit. We need more autumn flowers, and this one is outstanding. Perhaps a balance between the duel-

ing cigars is a plant that I like even more. Similar in shape to the cigar flower, 'David Verity' flowers all season long on 2–3' tall plants. When the smoke clears, this hybrid will be left in the cuphea arena. There is nothing bad about it.

Two other plants have really caught my attention and are likely included in

the hybrid *Cuphea ×purpurea* group. I watched as a somewhat upright form with fire-engine-red flowers grew and thrived in hot, humid areas. The flowers form all summer and are relatively large for a cuphea. The plant is 'Firefly', and it looked outstanding in the ground and

MORE ☞

Cuphea micropetala, flowers

Cuphea 'Firefly', container

Cuphea 'David Verity'

Cuphea 'Firefly'

even more so when it fell out of one of our ginger containers. Plants grew all the way to the ground and then bent back up to greet passers-by. And then a year or so ago, we planted a low-growing free-flowering cuphea in the UGA Trial Gardens which turned out to be a hit for everyone passing by. The plant was called 'Firecracker', and it was fantastic. However, I recognized the plant from years past: it was first developed in Tifton, Georgia, under the name 'Georgia Scarlet'. A few years later I saw it in Australia called 'Tiny Mice', and then in America as 'Batface'; I love that name because if you pull a flower off and stare at it, that is what it looks like! Names notwithstanding, the plant by itself is a fabulous choice, but when it is put with other bright flowers like rudbeckias, you might consider sunglasses. Both 'Firefly' and 'Firecracker' are highly recommended. Full sun.

Curcuma

HIDDEN GINGER

Gardeners attach the name ginger to a number of genera, including *Asarum*, false ginger, and *Zingiber*, the true culinary ginger. The former is simple to find; the latter is available in specialty shops but mainly for eating, not for planting. The genus *Curcuma* is seldom seen in the local garden center, particularly in the North, but that may change as people discover its diversity and ease of growing. Warm temperatures are beneficial, but nowhere is it written that people in Michigan or Wisconsin cannot be successful with gingers. They may not be as dominant in the landscape in the North as in the South, but they will do just fine. Curcumas are increasingly produced as garden plants through tissue culture labs and are gaining a larger following in the landscape trade, so there is hope for us simple gardeners.

In choosing which gingers to include, I considered only a few whose garden attributes I had trialed as well as those that might be available, with some looking. There are dozens more, especially if you live in areas near the Gulf Coast or further south. I first tried a few tubers of the Siam tulip (*Curcuma alismatifolia*) many years ago and learned that buying the tubers might not be a good idea because

Curcuma zedoaria

Curcuma alismatifolia

Curcuma roscoeana

they need a good deal of heat to emerge. However, if germinated tubers are available, they quickly grow into upright plants with pink bracts, somewhat similar to a tulip. Place them close together as, like tulips, they do not branch. Flowers persist for months. Bigger gingers give more bang for the buck, however, and I enjoyed the habit, leaves, and the somewhat concealed flowers of the hidden ginger, *C. petiolata*. Plants are 3–5' tall and produce the pink flowers in the base of all those leaves. Quite stunning.

In many cases, certainly in the North, plants may not attain sufficient maturity to flower in a single season. We worked with *Curcuma roscoeana*, wonderfully named the jewel of Burma; its flowers are fabulous, but the foliage is also handsome, so this one is worth planting even if the flowers don't appear. If they can be flowered, inside or out, they will produce some of the neatest blossoms you have ever seen. The waxy basal flowers consist of shingled orange bracts surrounding the actual small flowers, and if picked, persist for weeks in a floral arrangement. It takes some bending to see those flowers, but it is well worth it. If I were to recommend one ginger to try, I would prob-ably choose zedoary, *C. zedoaria*. The plant does have lovely basal flowers, almost as pretty as the previous species, but the foliage and habit are always outstanding. Plants are upright and statuesque, but the foliage, with the obvious purple midrib on each leaf, is what makes it number one in my book. We have placed it in containers and in the garden, and regardless, they look good. And as a potential bonus, they are winter hardy to zone 7b, perhaps a little colder. Bring in like caladiums if you want to save them for next spring. Full sun.

Curcuma petiolata

Curcuma roscoeana, flowers

Dahlia

While some people in some places can consider dahlias perennial, most of us must dig, store, and replant. For me, dahlias are one of the most difficult plants to love: too much heat, too many bugs, too many diseases, and far too much staking. But while I don't love them in my garden, I love them in other places where they put on their show. And what a show a good planting provides: short ones, tall ones, singles, doubles, pastels and flashy colors—no end to what a crazy person can plant. Like a number of other large plant groups (daylilies, roses,

Dahlia 'Caruso White'

MORE ☞

Dahlia, Swan Island Dahlias

Dahlia, staking at Anglesey Abbey

peonies), a garden "collection" is fairly common, and while such plantings are extremely impressive, as seen at Anglesey Abbey just outside Cambridge, England, or Swan Island Dahlias in Canby, Oregon, after a while dahlias are kind of boring. Like roses, they are at their best complementing, and being complemented by, other plants.

There are literally hundreds of registered cultivars, so where to start? Think about categories, then find cultivars you can't do without. Most dahlias are quite tall, hence the staking, but several dwarf ones that have been bred are similar in habit to bedding plants. Most of the smaller forms bear single flowers, and when I want a white, I search for 'Caruso White', and when I think of a mix, I first look for the clean singles of 'Bon Esperance', or the semi-double flowers of Figaro Mix.

Dahlia 'Bon Esperance'

Dahlia 'White Queen'

Dahlia 'Rebecca Lynn'

Dahlia Figaro Mix

MORE ☞

With taller plants, there is a world of diversity out there. 'White Queen' is but one example of single flowers, and in the category of fully double flowers, lots of choice is available. I have always been impressed with 'Rebecca Lynn'; however, flower forms are like masks at Halloween: you never know what you will see next. Large bicolor flowers, such as 'Rutland Water' are common and eye-catching, but bicolor means different things to different people. 'Wheels' and 'Pooh' (what a great name!) are simply fun plants to have in the garden, with their semi-double multicolored flowers. More fun can be gained with examples of "spidery" flowers, such as 'Herbert Smith' and 'Red Devil'; such forms are wonderful in good weather but look like wet dogs after rain or high humidity.

Interest in flower color and form are not all that the genus can offer; foliar

Dahlia 'Rutland Water'

Dahlia 'Pooh'

Dahlia 'Wheels'

Dahlia 'Herbert Smith'

Dahlia 'Red Devil'

color too is important, and in particular, dahlias with purple leaves have gained a significant following. The best known is 'Bishop of Llandaff', with bright red flowers and handsome purple leaves, but many others, like 'Rumby', are also available to North American gardeners.

So many cultivars, so much to choose from, have fun. Dig and clean tubers in the fall; store in peat or sphagnum moss in an unheated garage or other area that does not consistently freeze. Full sun.

Datura

THORN APPLE

Here is a great genus with great stories. A weed in Virginia was responsible for all sorts of headaches, as well as hallucinations, when native Indians fed its leaves to the colonists at Jamestown. This plant became known as jimson weed. And even though that species (*Datura stramonium*) is not used in gardening, it seems a shame to waste the story, so who has to know?

The daturas that are available for gardeners are also poisonous if eaten in sufficient quantity, but that is no reason not to grow them. Don't worry about pets, they are smart enough to avoid them. Plants are shrubby and usually no more than 2' tall, and mostly carry white upright or outward-facing trumpet flowers, which are wonderfully fragrant. They are sometimes called angel's trumpet, the same as for *Brugmansia*, but the flowers of *Brugmansia* point down, those of *Datura* point up.

Dahlia 'Bishop of Llandaff'

Datura 'Ballerina Purple'

Datura 'Ballerina White'

Dahlia 'Rumby'

Datura 'Grand Marnier'

MORE ☞

Datura metel, garden

Datura metel

Datura, fruit

I have seen daturas used in many settings, and the gray-green color of the foliage and the white flowers complement most other flowers well. At Blue Meadow Farm in Massachusetts, they are simply part of the handsome mixed garden; at the Butchart Gardens in Victoria, they provide a nice background for variegated geraniums. Most gardeners grow the common white single-flowered datura, *Datura metel*, which is uncomplicated and as good as any other choice. The hybrid Ballerina series has thick flowers, often with a purple throat and purple underside to the flowers; 'Ballerina White' has semi-double clean white flowers. Most people like the singles better, and if I had my choice and I could find it, I would grow 'Grand Marnier' in a heartbeat. Her single soft yellow flowers are outstanding in every way. The common name, thorn apple, comes from the look of the fruit, which are covered in bristles and look somewhat like small green apples. Ornamental in their own right. Full sun.

Dianella caerulea

Dianella

FLAX LILY

I am including these plants (*Dianella tasmanica*, *D. caerulea*) because I have noticed that they are being sold in the American market, and most people have no idea what they even look like. They are annuals for most of us, perhaps hardy with good mulching to zone 7b. Plants have leaves much like an iris, rather forgettable, somewhat messy, and not much to write home about. The flowers are about 1" across at best, blue and yellow and quite disappointing if you are waiting for an iris flower. In and of themselves, they are handsome but can be overlooked if you walk by too quickly. However, the plant does have a nice habit, and its claim to fame, if you are lucky, is the dark blue berries that follow the flowers. They make a striking

Dianella caerulea, fruit

MORE ☞

Dianella tasmanica

Dianthus barbatus 'Cinderella Pink'

showing, and the fruit alone are worth the time. Best in containers. Overwinter in a warm area; they are too difficult to find to allow them to freeze. Full sun.

Dianthus

PINK

Annual China pink (*Dianthus chinensis*) and its hybrids, as well as the biennial sweet william (*D. barbatus*), are almost as popular as the perennial species. Sweet william doesn't fit neatly into categories like annual or perennial and, in general, requires a winter to provide the cold needed for flowering. Supposedly, it should be replaced after it flowers, but many biennial forms need replacing simply because they tire out, not because of their life cycle. Numerous cultivars have been selected; some like 'Cinderella Pink' are used exclusively for

cut flowers because of their strong, lengthy stems. Plants in the Messenger series are also strong of stem and useful for cut flowers, but the shorter plants fit into a garden setting a little easier. Most sweet williams simply come as mixes and provide pastels and bright colors all spring. Cultivars can be located, but if you are going to the effort of searching, you might want to search for the dark flowered 'Sooty', one of the favorite stopping points at the Missouri Botanical Garden and also in Athens. A persistent, unique performer in both places.

China pinks are hardly seen at all in North American gardens because, in most parts of the country, they are wimpy and seldom live up to the picture found on the seed package. Let it not be said that they are not beautiful: I have trialed and seen beautiful examples, such as 'Parfait' and 'Rosemarie'; however, they simply didn't stay beautiful

long enough. I think 'Snowfire', although old (it was an All-America Selection in 1978!), is the best of the China pinks, and it is still available.

The hybridization of sweet williams and China pinks, with the idea of combining the weather tolerance of the former with the long-flowering tendencies of the latter, has been accomplished, and the resulting hybrids (*Dianthus ×heddewigii*), such as 'Ideal Peace', have become immensely popular, being heartily embraced by gardeners and landscapers alike. In the South, combinations of white dianthus and purple pansies are planted in the fall, flower their heads off in March, and continue throughout the spring and into the summer. In the North, they can be planted in the fall as well, but most wait until early spring. In cool summers, they flower all summer. They look equally at home in large containers

Dianthus barbatus Messenger series

Dianthus chinensis 'Parfait'

Dianthus barbatus, garden

Dianthus chinensis 'Rosemarie'

Dianthus barbatus 'Sooty'

Dianthus chinensis 'Snowfire'

MORE ☞

showing off the architectural beauty of a fan palm, setting off the base of cold stonework, or showing off a warm picket fence. Colors and named forms are abundant, some of the better known being the Ideal series ('Ideal Red' makes a fine base to evergreen hedges on Sea Island, Georgia), and the timeless Telstar series, including 'Telstar Picotee', seen growing opposite in a garden in Swarthmore, Pennsylvania. We have conducted countless row trials of the hybrids in Georgia, and as uncreative as they are, 'Princess White', 'Festival Picotee', and others certainly illustrate the ample choices. The Diamond series

Dianthus hybrids with fan palm

Dianthus 'Ideal Red'

Dianthus hybrids with pansies

has become a favorite because of excellent performance throughout the country, and 'Diamond Purple' falling out of a bed is as good as any. So many of the hybrids have become available, it is difficult to find one that stands out from others, but 'First Love' probably fits that moniker. Flowers are of different colors and perform brilliantly almost everywhere I have seen them. In the Deep South (zone 8 and warmer), perhaps plants may need removal to make way for more heat-tolerant species, but in most of the country, they can remain and will flower well most of the season. They do prefer cool to hot, however. Full sun.

Dianthus hybrids with stonework

Dianthus 'Telstar Picotee'

Dianthus hybrids with picket fence

Dianthus 'Ideal Peace'

Dianthus 'Diamond Purple'

Dianthus 'Princess White', *D.* 'Festival Picotee'

Dianthus 'First Love'

Diascia

TWINSPUR

I enjoy teaching plant identification to students of all ages, and I especially love to show them how to teach a plant to someone else. The common name for this genus comes from the two append- ages or spurs on the back of the petals, and once you point them out, nobody forgets the name twinspur. They may not remember the name diascia, but who cares?

Twinspurs have long been a fixture in the British Isles, and when I traveled to that area, I was blown away with the confident indifference twinspurs demonstrated in that climate. I saw many species, including the spectacular rigid diascia, *Diascia rigescens*. I came home eager to experiment, and even yelled at our breeders to get some diascias in the country so we could trial them! They are doing just that, and

Diascia rigescens

Diascia hybrid, basket

Diascia 'Kate'

Diascia 'Rupert Lambert'

Diascia 'Emma'

Diascia 'Lilac Mist'

MORE ☞

Diascia 'Little Charmer'

Diascia 'Ruby Field'

Diascia 'Sun Chimes Red'

Diascia 'Coral Belle'

Diascia 'Red Ace', flowers

Diascia 'Whisper Dark Apricot'

Diascia 'Sun Chimes Coral' with bacopa

diascias in this country just keep getting better. North American companies are making a slow but concentrated effort to make twinspur a mainstream annual, and although it has a way to catch up to petunias and begonias, progress is being made. In Athens, hardly a hotspot for twinspurs, we row out these hybrids and enjoy flowers in the spring, then let them fill in so we can enjoy them again in the fall. We put 'Rupert Lambert' by the brick walkway and other hybrids in hanging baskets around the gazebo. Who said research had to boring?

The problem for much of the country is that the heat in the summer sucks the flower power out of many diascias. None have the weather tolerance of a begonia, but if they don't have to be perfect, there are some wonderful forms out there right now, and they're getting better every year. I planted a couple of ladies some years ago, and both 'Kate' and

MORE ☞

Diascia 'Red Ace'

'Emma' provided strong colors on short stems. Red and rose are common colors, but 'Lilac Mist' has proven to be a favorite because of its upright habit and unique color. 'Little Charmer' also provided handsome color but grew only 3–4" tall. One of the oldest of available twinspurs is 'Ruby Field', a so-so cultivar that looks far better in Portland than in Cincinnati; she doesn't have the weather tolerance needed for inclement places. Equally old but a marvelous performer in all weather is 'Coral Belle', number one in our cultivar trials a few years ago in Athens. Tough, available, and beautiful to boot.

When pots of 'Sun Chimes Red' first appeared on the scene, they made people's heads turn. In the garden, they lose that "flash" but still do well. A combination of 'Sun Chimes Coral' and white bacopa is pleasing to the eyes and can stay looking good for a long time. Outdoors, I have been most impressed with the performance of the Whisper series, and 'Whisper Dark Apricot' takes a backseat to none. One of the problems with twinspurs has been their relative lack of vigor. The cultivars I have included here, for the most part, perform with sufficient vigor to overcome the difficulties of warm, humid summers; however, if you decide to plant 'Red Ace', do it quickly and get out of the way. This thing grows and grows, swallowing up all other poor diascias in its path. Plants flower well in the spring, grow all summer, and kick butt again in the fall. Most twinspurs show reasonable cold tolerance as well, often overwintering if sufficient snow cover is received but usually hardy to zone 7b. Full sun.

Duranta erecta

GOLDEN DEWDROP

I have admired golden dewdrop (*Duranta erecta*) ever since somebody pointed out the verbena-like blue flowers many years ago. And there I was in Perth, Australia, minding my own business when I rounded a corner and was greeted by a 30' high specimen; it blew me away! Of course, under cover of the darkness of night, I clipped a few branches, rooted them, and brought them back to Athens. The plant is pretty impressive even in Georgia; though it is only about 5' tall, it bears hundreds of flowers and fruits.

In Florida and the Gulf Coast, plants are considered shrubs and will be perennial perhaps as far north as zone 7, but the rest of us should think of them as annuals. The species itself is the most

Duranta erecta, flowers

common, bearing many small but handsome blue flowers all summer. If you have a long summer, or if you have a hot season, clusters of round golden fruit will begin to form in late summer; and if frost does not come too early, the plant will be laden with these golden clusters of grapes. Unfortunately, the fruit doesn't want to form until August, and many northern gardeners may not enjoy the late color. Still, the plant, even without the fruit, is well worth growing.

Several interesting cultivars have hit the marketplace in the last few years. Probably the one that has elicited the most interest is 'Sapphire Showers', a wonderful upright form with dark blue flowers bearing a white stripe. This should become quite popular. A couple of variegated forms provide a wonderful contrast of colors, depending on which form you can find. 'Variegata' brings a riot of green and white leaves. This form remains more prostrate and looks particularly good falling over itself, falling out of a container. 'Gold Edge' is very striking with its green and yellow foliage and upright habit. Neither are as large as the species, nor do they produce signifi-

MORE ☞

Duranta erecta, fruit

Duranta erecta, Australia

Duranta erecta 'Variegata'

Duranta erecta var. *aurea*

Duranta erecta 'Gold Edge'

cant flowers or fruit. Another new form, with golden foliage and a dwarf habit (var. *aurea*), should become quite popular, perhaps even as an edging plant.

A word of warning. Depending on where the plants came from, they may bear some serious thorns. In nature, the species has a long thorn at each node, but cultivated forms are often thornless and should be sought out. The variegated forms are also armed and dangerous, but 'Sapphire Showers' is not. Don't poke your head in the middle of any of them. Full sun.

Echium

BUGLOSS

The echiums are most famous for the rocketship-looking plants with such wonderful names as pride of Tenerife (*Echium simplex*) or pride of Madeira (*E. candicans*), which you may discover on your fantasy trip to the Canary Islands or in gardens in southwest England. But not here, at least not outside conservatories. Great fun to visit,

see them in such exotic places, but not a snowball's chance in hell that they would be gardened here. However, that doesn't mean we have to ignore the whole genus, because there is at least one terrific plant, and another may be worth a try.

Finding started plants of annual bugloss, *Echium vulgare*, will be difficult, but seeds are easily available. The grow only about 1' tall but are full of flowers. They are categorized as bienni-

als, and the first year they may flower a little but won't be terribly exciting. Next year, however, they will be chock-full of blue to violet flowers, particularly in the spring and early summer. They are tough and provide a nice show with little effort.

We planted the species to greet visitors as they walked into the garden, but if I had it to do again, I would choose its much nicer selection, 'Blue Bedder'. They will tolerate full sun but have no

Echium vulgare 'Blue Bedder'

Echium candicans

Echium vulgare

problem in the midst of shade lovers like hostas. Another form I have tried, although for the most part quite unsuccessfully, is the red bugloss, *Echium amoenum*. I first saw it at Kew Gardens in England and was determined to find some seeds (which I did) and then revel in its beauty, which I did not because it was not. Probably Georgia was not to its liking. But that is no excuse for you: try some so you can do some reveling. Full sun to partial shade.

Emilia

TASSEL FLOWER

A little-known wildflower of India, Polynesia, and tropical Africa, tassel flower finds its way to gardens here and there

MORE ☞

Echium amoenum

Emilia javanica, flowers

Emilia sonchifolia

Emilia javanica, UGA Trial Gardens

for its flowers, which are useful as fillers in the garden and in the vase. The common species are the scarlet-flowered *Emilia javanica* and its closely related cousin, *E. sonchifolia*, better known for its orange flowers. They are similar in habit and ease of gardening. We grew what seemed like a ton of them in our cut flower trials, but maybe it seemed like that because we cut every stem and those we missed reseeded to make more, and more and more. It took us less than four weeks to fuel a major dislike of this weed; however, it was impossible not to admire its tenacity and color. And plants do make wonderful additions to the garden. The golden yellow forms were much more beloved than the red. They will reseed, so finding the seed should only be a one-time necessity. Full sun.

Erysimum

WALLFLOWER

The genus is probably best known for short-lived perennials, but without doubt the best and most colorful of the group are the wallflowers, all now classified under *Erysimum*, which used to be part of the genus *Cheiranthus*. Plants are technically biennials, although some flowering may occur the first year from seed. Nothing is brighter and fresher in the spring than a well-grown planting of wallflowers, either overwintered in a cool greenhouse prior to being sold at the garden center or overwintered in the garden. Unfortunately, for many gardeners the former is necessary, because plants don't overwinter much above zone 6.

When gardeners think of wallflowers, mostly they think of orange or yellow flowers, and hybrids (*Erysimum* ×*marshallii*) like 'Orange Bedder' and 'Yellow Bedder' are popular for good reason, whether complementing spring iris or planted on a wall for passers-by. 'Gold Bedder' provides softer color but with similar habit and vigor, and the flowers of 'Golden Gem' are equally handsome but on much shorter stems. A number of rainbow cultivars have also been developed, and while I am partial to the soft mauve of 'Constant Cheer', which only grows about 9" tall, I welcome the brighter, feistier colors of 'Warlock Beauty' as well. Not for the faint of heart, but they sure make spring more interesting.

In hot-summer climates, they should be removed after flowering. If the seeds are allowed to fall, they will germinate in late summer, and, if seeds are not killed by the cold, the plants should reappear next spring. Full sun.

Erysimum, United Kingdom

Erysimum 'Orange Bedder'

Erysimum 'Golden Gem'

Erysimum 'Yellow Bedder'

Erysimum 'Constant Cheer'

Erysimum 'Gold Bedder'

Erysimum 'Warlock Beauty'

Eschscholzia

CALIFORNIA POPPY

The name of this genus is a good example of why gardeners don't always embrace the joy of learning botanical nomenclature. Where did all those sch's come from and why? Well, turns out the plant was named for German physician and naturalist Johann Friedrich Eschscholtz, whose family had settled in Russia and whose original name "Escholtz" picked up another "sch" on the retranslation, back from Cyrillic to German. So now you know the rest of the story. By the way, the genus is pronounced "esh *olts* ee a."

The stunning orange flowers of California poppies (*Eschscholzia californica*) have became extraordinarily popular all over the country, not only for their brilliant color, but also because they seed

Eschscholzia californica with wallflowers

Eschscholzia californica, naturalized

Eschscholzia californica 'Lilac Gleam'

easily into naturalistic plantings. They are tough enough to be planted by busy roadways but also look at home in gardens, complementing wallflowers. Where they are allowed to naturalize, the orange flowers and the ferny foliage truly make an eye-catching vista in May.

Although most of the California poppies are flaming orange, other colors have been selected. 'Lilac Gleam' bears flowers in shades of lilac and purple, and one of my favorites has to be the simple white-flowered 'Alba'. Not as brilliant—perhaps that is why I enjoy it so.

Euphorbia

SPURGE

The most popular member of this genus, by far, is the Christmas poinsettia, and although many gardeners are either too attached or too cheap to get

Eschscholzia californica, roadside

Euphorbia milii

Eschscholzia californica 'Alba'

Euphorbia cyathophora

MORE ☞

rid of them, they will never become a garden plant. However, several annual euphorbs are sufficiently interesting or beautiful to include in the garden. Some are classically handsome, others can be said to be weird, which means that we will see more of it in the future. One such weird member that is sneaking into gardens is *Euphorbia milii,* which cannot be said to be shy.

Some gardeners, yours truly not included, find fire-on-the-mountain, *Euphorbia cyathophora,* interesting. Perhaps it is the name, because the name is probably the best part. Like a poinsettia, bracts turn red in late summer and fall, but there is very little va-va-voom to the plant. Interesting is the best thing I can say. However, if it is interest you want, you have to love gopher spurge, *E. lathyris.* A biennial, this plant supposedly releases chemicals that repel your hungry gophers, moles, and voles. I have not tested the theory, but gopher spurge has always remained standing in the Armitage garden, so it must work. Regardless of its properties, gopher spurge is a fascinating plant in its own right. The plant has handsome gray-green foliage, and where the stems branch near the top of the plant you may find the small white flowers. They are nothing to get excited about, but they give way to lovely purple fruit in the summer. If allowed to ripen, the seeds will germinate, assuring the continued presence of plants in the garden.

Euphorbia lathyris, flowers

Euphorbia lathyris, fruit

Euphorbia marginata 'Kilimanjaro'

Euphorbia marginata, cut flowers

I have seen it growing in the middle of gardens or by rock walls; I am never sure just where it will appear next.

The best known of the garden annuals is snow-on-the-mountain, *Euphorbia marginata*. Planted in early spring, plants will grow rapidly, showing off variegated foliage as they mature. With sufficient heat, plants can grow 3–4' tall, and when they flower, they produce clean white bracts. The flowers are white as well, but it is the bracts and the leaves that provide the show. 'Kilimanjaro' is a handsome compact selection with many clean white bracts. Where heat is less prevalent, such as in the Portland area, plants are equally beautiful but not as tall. This snowy plant is also useful for its cut stems; after cutting put the stem in boiling water or sear it on a hot plate to stop the flow of latex. Remember, all euphorbs have milky sap, and it can be quite irritating, so keep it away from your face, particularly your eyes. Full sun to partial shade.

Eustoma grandiflorum

LISIANTHUS, PRAIRIE GENTIAN

Prairie gentians are, as one might surmise, native to the American prairies, yet the actual wildflower is nowhere to be seen in North American gardens. But plant breeders around the world have discovered its marvelous properties as a cut flower, and flowers have been bred into a myriad of colors, occurring as

Euphorbia marginata

Eustoma grandiflorum 'Blue Liza'

Eustoma grandiflorum 'Avila Purple'

Eustoma grandiflorum 'Yodel Lilac'

MORE ☞

Eustoma grandiflorum 'Forever White'

Eustoma grandiflorum 'Avila Deep Rose'

Eustoma grandiflorum 'Echo White'

Eustoma grandiflorum 'Sapphire Pink Rim'

Eustoma grandiflorum 'Sapphire Blue Chip'

Eustoma grandiflorum 'Florida Blue'

singles or doubles in florists' coolers across the country. Sad to say, the majority of our native plants come back home from production facilities overseas. Cultivars for cut flower use abound, and they are beautiful. Just look at the Avila series, sold throughout the world and including 'Avila Deep Rose' and 'Avila Purple'. Some of the tougher cut flower cultivars are also at home in the garden, particularly the Yodel series (single flowers) and the Echo series (double). 'Yodel Lilac' and 'Echo White' have performed quite well in outdoor beds in Athens.

Most cut flower forms are too expensive, too tall, or too scarce to ever use them in the garden, and breeders have come up with dwarfer forms that make more sense for smaller areas. An excellent choice is 'Blue Liza', with dozens of flowers covering a compact habit, but 'Florida Blue' is almost as good, and with a little more heat tolerance. I have always enjoyed the white-flowered forms of lisianthus in the garden, and 'Forever White' makes a nice clean selection. But look what they have done to our flower! I stared in awe or perhaps morbid fascination at the meatballing of our prairie flower. The Sapphire series is impossible to ignore, and 'Sapphire Blue Chip' and 'Sapphire Pink Rim' may be abominations for purists but are wildly fascinating to those who admire detail.

Most areas of the country will be successful with lisianthus in the spring and early summer. They tend to decline in the heat and humidity of a warm summer, never to be seen again. Enjoy them while you can, indoors and out. Full sun.

Evolvulus pilosus

BLUE DAZE

Blue daze (*Evolvulus pilosus*) is one of those plants you can pass by one day, then stop the next and wonder why you

MORE ☞

Evolvulus pilosus 'Blue Daze', groundcover, with lantana

Evolvulus pilosus 'Blue Daze'

Evolvulus pilosus, garden

hadn't noticed it before. The plants are excellent in baskets and containers and as a low-growing groundcover.

They are only about 6–9" tall and flower most of the season. From a distance or on miserable overcast days, the flowers may not be terribly noticeable, but they make a terrific show most of the time. At the University of Georgia, plants are often used with 'New Gold' lantana, and while they work together from a distance, the blue flowers must be seen close-up to be appreciated. In small beds, they stay low, peeking out from their neighbors, to provide months of white-centered blue flowers to enjoy. Full sun to partial shade.

Felicia amelloides

BLUE MARGUERITE

I have always admired the wonderful blue flower of *Felicia amelloides*, espe-

cially on the West Coast or in Europe, but it does not get a fair shake in the East. True enough, plants prefer cooler nights and less humid conditions than those found in parts of the East, but not to try this at least once is to overlook a great offering. Even in the South, they

will look terrific until temperatures refuse to budge out of the 90s.

They stand only about 15" tall, and they can vary from the lightest to the darkest blue. In the Butchart Gardens, they were so pale that they were almost white, whereas in Santa Barbara, Cali-

Felicia amelloides, Butchart Gardens

Felicia amelloides, California

Felicia amelloides 'Santa Anita'

Felicia amelloides 'Variegata'

Felicia amelloides 'Read's Blue'

fornia, the bold blue flowers showed off their yellow centers to busy passers-by. They make excellent container plants or will color up the front of a garden without trouble and continue to flower for months on end.

A few cultivars have been selected, but a thorough search may be needed to procure them. I believe the dwarfer form, 'Read's Blue', is well worth the effort as plants can cavort with sages or reside in rock gardens with equal ease. 'Santa Anita' has larger flowers and is coarser than other forms, not particularly attractive where I have seen it. The most common, and by far the least handsome, is 'Variegata', whose yellow and white and blue all seem to get jumbled together. But there are so many people who love variegation of any kind—there is no reasoning with them. Full sun to partial shade.

Fuchsia

My grandmother loved her fuchsias. Living in a small house in Montreal, she drank tea under her catalpa tree, where she could admire her baskets of fuchsias. When I travel to Europe, especially Germany, there does not seem to be a bare piece of ground or empty container that half a dozen fuchsias have not been thrust into. California and the Northwest are hotbeds for the cool-loving plant, but Long Island and the Northeast also have their fair share of fuchsites. Living in the

Fuchsia corymbiflora

Fuchsia ×*hybrida* 'Annabelle'

Fuchsia ×*hybrida* 'Sonata'

MORE ☞

Fuchsia magellanica

Fuchsia ×hybrida 'Checkerboard'

Fuchsia magellanica 'Rosea'

Fuchsia ×hybrida 'Cascading Angel Earrings'

Fuchsia ×hybrida 'Beacon'

Fuchsia ×hybrida 'Golden Marinka'

South, I am able to grow only a few of these plants, and while I can grow countless other things, I still miss them when I see them in their glory.

Over 8000 cultivars of fuchsia have been listed, yet few of them ever see the light of day in our gardens. For the species and many of the cultivars, mail-order sources, specialty nurseries, and Internet garden rooms are your best bet. But then again, who needs 8000 when most of us are happy when we can select from half a dozen? For the hard-core fuchsite, a few species are sold, and if you can nurture them, have a go. The long pendulous flowers of *Fuchsia corymbiflora* are awesome, but you may die of old age looking for it in "normal" outlets. Magellan's fuchsia, *F. magellanica*, is quite common in Europe and South America, and is an important hybrid in the long-flowered hybrids. By themselves, the normal red type and the pink 'Rosea' are vigorous and handsome, and used as hedges where they are hardy. Many gardeners feel that the species is as cold hardy and heat-tolerant as any of the hybrids. Most of the fuchsias sold today are hybrids (*F. ×hybrida*), with a myriad of different parents. These are the selections you will find crammed into a 12" basket at your local garden center. They all start out beautifully, but they require attention to watering and feeding when you get them home. The more heat in the summer, the more attention must be paid.

Where to start for cultivars? 'Dark Ice' is nearly always used in baskets (many outlets offer all cultivars that way). I can heartily recommend 'Cascading Angel Earrings' as the most heat-tolerant

Fuchsia ×hybrida 'Dark Ice'

Fuchsia ×hybrida 'Mrs Lovell Swisher'

Fuchsia ×hybrida 'Thalia'

Fuchsia ×hybrida 'Gartenmeister Bonstedt', container

MORE ☞

172 *Fuchsia,* continued

selection we have trialed. Nothing fancy, but it works. There is no end to colors and shapes that breeders have created, and it is a losing argument to proclaim one more beautiful than the other; like politics and religion, there is no correct answer. Pinkish and plump-ish can describe the flowers of the popular 'Annabelle', pinkish and obese may be better descriptors for 'Sonata'. Probably more red fuchsias, such as 'Beacon', are sold than any other, but flowers with more than one color are also popular. 'Mrs Lovell Swisher' is one of the many bicolored fuchsias, in this case white (sepals) and red (petals), and she is not alone in her abstract art. 'Checkerboard', with its narrow white sepals, and the larger-flowered 'Loveliness' are but two examples. A half-dozen variegated forms may be grown as well, and they can be striking or strikingly awful. I enjoy 'Golden Marinka' and especially 'Pink Veins', perhaps because it is more subdued than others.

Fuchsia ×hybrida 'Loveliness'

Fuchsia ×hybrida 'Pink Veins'

Fuchsia ×hybrida 'Koralle'

Fuchsia ×hybrida 'Gartenmeister Bonstedt', garden

A group of fuchsias that has become immensely popular in the last ten years are the triphylla, or three-leaf, hybrids. As the number of gardeners continues to expand, so do the boundaries of trial and error. Everyone wants to take the fuchsia they grew in Winnipeg or Santa Barbara and try it out in Atlanta or Dallas. Young gardeners see a fuchsia in the store and without a second thought, buy it, ignore it, and kill it. The triphyllas were trumpeted as possible help for this intolerance-of-heat-and-abuse problem, which gets in the way of two-thirds of the population enjoying these fine plants. Has the hype worked? The answer is a definite maybe. The triphyllas are more tolerant of abuse, but they are still fuchsias and still need attention to keep them looking good. Look for 'Thalia' and 'Koralle', both excellent performers in containers or the garden. The most

popular of this popular group is probably 'Gartenmeister Bonstedt', thankfully shortened to 'Gartenmeister'. Plants have enjoyed an excellent reputation for performance, and they are classically handsome in containers or complementing other annuals like ornamental tobacco. If you have all but given up on fuchsias, try this one. If it still does not make you happy, spend your money on wine, then look again.

All fuchsias need consistent water; if they dry out, they will seldom recover. They look fine planted in the garden just like other plants, and if you can find an upright standard, you will reduce the problems of drying out. If using baskets or containers, use as large a size as possible, cramping their style will only cramp yours. Fertilize with a liquid fertilizer two or three times a season. Cool weather is always preferred to heat, and afternoon shade will be appreciated.

Gaillardia

BLANKET FLOWER

Most people recognize the genus as a perennial; however, the main annual species (*Gaillardia pulchella*) flowers longer and provides more choice of color. Although they are native to the southern United States, the annual species are not easy to locate in the garden shop, but many and various cultivars of *G. pulchella* have arrived on the scene to add to our annual palette.

Many of the selections bear rounded double to semi-double flowers; some (but not all) cultivars may be unnamed. 'Yellow Plume' flowers profusely on 12–15" tall plants, and I consider 'Yellow Queen' equally beautiful, if not identical: they may in fact be the same thing under different names. The Lollipop series was a popular selection in the 1980s; however, it is a little tall and is knocked

Gaillardia pulchella cultivars

MORE ☞

down by rain or wind. The Sundance series is an improvement and provides a number of color choices; 'Sundance Bicolor' is quite wonderful, and more compact than the older forms. Grown easily from seed, and occasionally will reseed. Full sun.

In 1996, I happened across an unusual white-flowered gaillardia in Mercer Botanic Gardens in Humble, Texas. Plants were on the endangered list in Texas, but I was given permission to collect seeds and see what they did in Athens. The plant is *Gaillardia aestivalis*

Gaillardia pulchella 'Sundance Bicolor'

Gaillardia pulchella 'Yellow Plume'

Gaillardia aestivalis var. *winkleri*, Texas

Gaillardia pulchella Lollipop series

Gaillardia aestivalis var. *winkleri*, purple form, UGA Trial Gardens

Gaillardia pulchella 'Yellow Queen'

var. *winkleri*, otherwise called white firewheel. To make a long story short, they did extraordinarily well, provided rich shades of purple as well as white, and have been perennial in our zone 7b garden. They are beautiful in every way, and we are making selections with the seed that has formed. Plantsmen at Steven F. Austin State University in Nacogdoches, Texas, are also working on domesticating the plant, and with a little luck, seed of selected cultivars will be available through seed companies in the near future. Full sun, sandy soils.

Gazania

TREASURE FLOWER

These South African plants sport some of the most beautiful and wonderfully detailed flowers among all the daisies.

MORE ☞

Gaillardia aestivalis var. *winkleri*, purple and white forms, UGA Trial Gardens

Gazania rigens has been sold for years as a bedding plant and exceptional colors have been developed. In many areas of the country, however, the heat and humidity of normal summers take their toll, and plants often melt out by July. While this continues to be the case in warmer areas, gazanias are becoming a little tougher. Hybridization with other species has helped. Their flowers are so beautiful, it is difficult to walk by a well-grown specimen in the garden center

Gazania rigens 'Ministar White'

Gazania rigens 'Sundance Yellow'

Gazania rigens 'Chansonette Yellow'

Gazania rigens 'Chansonette Pink'

Gazania rigens 'Daybreak Bronze'

Gazania rigens 'Daybreak Red Striped'

Gazania 'Double Yellow'

without wanting to take it home and plunk it in the garden.

The breeders have been busy, providing a number of series, each one supporting numerous color choices and often handsome gray-green foliage. The Sundance series was one of the earlier ones, 'Sundance Yellow' providing gardeners an insight of the potential the genus held. The Chansonette series lent 'Chansonette Yellow' and 'Chansonette Pink' to the garden palette, and Daybreak series came along with even more colors, and somewhat shorter plants. 'Daybreak Bronze' and Daybreak Red

Gazania rigens Klondyke series

Gazania 'Variegated Orange'

Gazania 'Orange Beauty'

Gazania linearis

MORE ☞

Striped' became quite popular. One of the problems with many of these selections was that they were a little too tall, and rain or wind could wreak havoc in the garden. They already had problems with heat and humidity, so shorter selections were called for. The Ministar

Gazania 'Waterlily'

Gazania linearis 'Peggy's Pet'

series, such as 'Ministar White', and the Klondyke series have provided some of the shortening needed.

But numerous other hybrids, incorporating the linear-leaf gazania, *Gazania linearis*, and other species, have also been developed, often with more handsome foliage and shorter stature. 'Double Yellow' provides a double-flowered selection, while 'Orange Beauty' allows for clean yellow flowers on short plants. Even variegated foliage is available, as found in 'Variegated Orange'; such variegated plants will become more readily available in the future but probably as vegetative material only. 'Waterlily' is an outstanding white-flowered gazania; flowers were bred in Australia, I am not sure if it is available in North America.

I mentioned that *Gazania linearis* was incorporated into the hybrids. This low-growing prolific flowerer is an outstanding plant on its own, but perhaps the more abusive climates on this continent have kept it out of our stores, because I never see it offered. Selections of this fine plant include 'Peggy's Pet', a mounding cultivar with silvery foliage

and handsome orange flowers. Full sun to afternoon shade. Well-drained soils a must.

Gerbera jamesonii

TRANSVAAL DAISY

Gerbera jamesonii has come a long way from its humble beginnings as a South African daisy. Gerberas have been bred to within an inch of their lives in Europe and have become major cut flowers for florists and designers all over the world. And they are beautiful! Grown in the sensual conditions of a heated greenhouse, they are cut, wrapped, and shipped without a blemish to enjoy some neighborly camaraderie with other flowers in the vase. Mixes like Gigi provide long stems and dazzling colors.

Outdoors, however, they are not quite as impressive, suffering from heavy rain, heat, and humidity, which are common to most of our gardens. Breeders have concentrated most of their efforts on cut flower varieties, but several dwarf forms suitable for the landscape have been developed. One of the first successful introductions was 'Happipot', which provided white, yellow, and red flowers, looked good in a container, and only grew about 18" tall. Similar flowers were seen in 'Mardi Gras' and other old cultivars. The brighter colors were (and still are) all the rage, but flowers in Masquerade Pastel Mix provided soft pastels pinks, salmons, and whites. The Masquerade series was bred for outdoor performance and has looked quite good, particularly the bright colors of 'Masquerade Scarlet'. Recently the Festival series appeared with 3" wide flowers on 10–12" tall plants. Beautiful in the pot, but like most others, they decline if the weather becomes abusive in the garden. Breeding of new landscape cultivars has slowed down, mainly because efforts

Gerbera jamesonii 'Happipot'

Gerbera jamesonii 'Mardi Gras'

Gerbera jamesonii 'Masquerade Pastel White', *G. j.* 'Masquerade Pastel Pink'

Gerbera jamesonii 'Masquerade Scarlet'

Gerbera jamesonii Festival series

Gerbera jamesonii Wolfpack Country series

have been concentrated on breeding more lucrative cut flower types; however, series like Wolfpack Country pop up every now and then and brighten the landscape one more time. Regardless of the color or name, all gerberas make excellent long-lasting cut flowers and are useful for entertaining.

Plants are better in containers than in the garden. Full sun to partial shade.

Gilia leptantha

Gilia capitata

Gilia

Native to California, gilias are wildflowers in the Sierra mountains but seldom seen in gardens, certainly not in the East. I have seen gilias here and there, but to grow them in the garden requires searching through seed catalogs and germinating your own plants. Two species are available from seed, and both sport handsome blue flowers on short plants.

Fine-leaf gilia, *Gilia leptantha*, has fine, almost filigreed leaves and wonderful light blue flowers, whereas globe gilia, *G. capitata*, bears much more rounded flowers and less divided leaves. They are most at home in open ground where drainage is excellent. Don't expect long-lasting performance in hot, humid gardens. Seeds of both may be found by consulting wildflower or meadow-flower catalogs online. Full sun.

Gladiolus

I have difficulty getting excited about gladioli as garden plants. They remind me of orchids: fabulous flowers, ugly plants. The hybrids (*Gladiolus ×hybridus*) are grown from corms, which are removed each fall to be replanted in the spring. The hybrids have been intensely bred but mostly for cut flower use, and one can see acres of flowers meant for florists and designers everywhere. As beautiful as many flowers are, the plants are often isolated and banished to the "cut flower" area of the garden, which is probably a good thing. A bucket of cut glads can bring a lot of joy to a lot of friends. Even in the overbred hybrids, a number of beautiful forms are available to discerning gardeners, and the dwarf forms can actually be incorporated into the garden. I have always loved the white flowers of 'The Bride', and it is hard not to get excited by cultivars such as the brilliant 'Robinetta'.

Gladiolus, cut flower field

Gladiolus, cut flowers

Gladiolus 'Robinetta'

MORE ☞

While the great bulk of glads fall into the cut flower hybrid category, a couple of species are well worth growing. I have always been impressed with the Byzantine gladiolus, *Gladiolus communis* subsp. *byzantinus*, because of the ease of growth and the wonderful electric-burgundy flower color. They are at home everywhere in the country, looking good in the garden as well as the flower vase.

Another marvelous plant to try is the Abyssinian glad, *G. callianthus* (aka *Acidanthera*), whose white flowers with a purple center also have a wonderful fragrance. The only cultivar available is 'Muralis', and corms are easy to find and easy to grow.

All glads should be planted as soon as frost is past, all can be cut when the first flower has opened. Corms should be dug and stored north of zones 8 to ensure perenniality. Full sun.

Glaucium

HORNED POPPY

When people see horned poppies, they are as impressed with the blue-gray foliage as they are with the flowers and the long, horned fruit. The foliage is as much a reason to try these plants in the garden as any, and in particular, the leaves of the red horned poppy (*Glaucium corniculatum*) and the yellow horned poppy (*G. flavum*) are every bit

Gladiolus 'The Bride'

Gladiolus communis subsp. *byzantinus*

Gladiolus communis subsp. *byzantinus*, garden

Gladiolus callianthus

Glaucium corniculatum

Glaucium corniculatum in snow

Glaucium flavum

as handsome as the ubiquitous dusty miller. A colleague of mine said I should explain that "it's not a *real* poppy," so people wouldn't look for it under P in a catalog. I replied, "Anybody that dumb wouldn't be reading this book." Don't look under P.

Plants are quite winter hardy and reseed prolifically in cool locations. I have seen plants of the red horned poppy absolutely ecstatic in the late snow of a Denver spring, and the red flowers, which emerge in May and June, are quite marvelous. Yellow horned poppies are more common on the eastern side of the country and have equally beautiful foliage and bright yellow flowers. The flowers of both are produced throughout the season, but flowering is heaviest in the spring. The long narrow fruit are responsible for the common name, and seeds can be gathered for next year's plants. Well worth a try in cooler climates. Full sun.

Gloriosa superba

GLORY LILY

The first time I saw this weird but spectacular plant, *Gloriosa superba*, I assumed that no one would grow it outside conservatories and home greenhouses. The fact that it is expensive, somewhat finicky, and dislikes being transplanted would also have something to do with its absence from gardens. However, it is for sale in many catalogs, I see it imprisoned in bulb bags at the local box store, and, sure as heck, people do grow it.

The deciduous climber comes from a tuber; if possible, start it indoors in a peat container three to four weeks prior to placing into a larger container outdoors. It can scramble through shrubs, but most people prefer to put it on a trellis in a protected area of the patio. Plants will not flower until mid to late summer, depending on heat, but what a dazzling show they provide.

MORE ☞

Gloriosa superba 'Rothschildiana'

Gloriosa superba 'Citrina'

The most common form is 'Roth-schildiana', an amazing combination of red and yellow on delightfully fashioned flowers. However, if you are not the gaudy sort, you might want to look for 'Citrina', a wonderful shade of yellow. Equally beautiful but without the flash. Full sun in the North, afternoon shade in the South. Bring in to a frost-free area after the first kiss of frost outdoors.

Gomphrena

"Want tough, try gomphrena!" That could make an advertisement on television to rival James Bond or Spiderman. Those guys have nothing on the globe amaranth (*Gomphrena globosa*). Starting out as a persistent weed in the tropics, it has been morphed into a bedding and landscape plant with few equals for perseverance. That does not mean that everyone likes it, or that it is the prettiest plant in the landscape, only that it spits out the heat of a southwestern summer, tolerates the rain in Portland, and thrives in the gardens of Boston. It is a common member in gardens, meandering through cosmos and other annuals, and it can fill in entire islands in busy downtown areas. Of course, any plant that is that tough will also be sought after as a cut flower, both fresh and dried, and in

Gomphrena globosa 'Buddy White'

combination with yellow craspedia and pink centaurea, it holds its own.

Gardeners can choose from low-growing forms such as the Buddy series, including 'Buddy White', or the Gnome series, such as 'Gnome Purple' and 'Gnome White', all of which stay around knee-high. One of the most popular forms for cut flowers and for landscapes is 'Strawberry Fields', possessing a brilliant strawberry color that does not fade throughout the summer. In the landscape or in a vase by itself, it is an outstanding choice. But numerous other choices are available, all of them tough

Gomphrena globosa, garden

Gomphrena globosa 'Gnome Purple'

Gomphrena globosa, landscape island

as nails. 'All Around Purple' is a bright choice for the garden whose opposite might be 'Lavender', far more subdued but an equal performer. One of my favorites was the recently developed 'Bicolor Rose', whose flowers are like the Energizer Bunny, they just keep going and going. As a garden plant or cut flower, it is tough to beat. Other species are occasionally found in garden centers, such as Haage's amaranth, *Gomphrena haageana*, but plants are generally so similar there is little reason to choose one over the other. Some of the cultivars are likely hybrids anyway, but one selection that has pleasantly stood out for me was 'Apricot'. It was sufficiently different in color and form that I

Gomphrena globosa 'Gnome White'

Gomphrena globosa, cut flowers

Gomphrena globosa 'Strawberry Fields'

Gomphrena globosa 'Strawberry Fields', cut flowers

Gomphrena globosa 'All Around Purple'

Gomphrena globosa 'Lavender'

wanted to try it. Not quite the vigor of many of the others but pleasant nevertheless. Full sun.

Graptophyllum pictum

CARICATURE PLANT

Another plant that was hidden for years in the bowels of conservatories and tropical greenhouses, *Graptophyllum pictum* has arisen from obscurity and become a popular plant for containers and gardens. Caricature plants are grown for their wonderful leathery foli-

Gomphrena globosa 'Bicolor Rose'

Graptophyllum pictum 'Chocolate'

Gomphrena haageana 'Apricot'

MORE ☞

age; flowers are not often formed except in the winter in heated greenhouses. For hot, humid, and drought-stricken gardens, this is the ticket.

The three main cultivars provide architectural interest and long-season enjoyment. The most popular is 'Chocolate', with dark purple leaves bisected with pink veins. An easy plant for combination plantings. 'Tricolor' is just that,

a kaleidoscope of colors, not harsh or brutal but easy on the eyes. And in keeping with the trend for dark purple and black in plants, 'Black Beauty' is perfect. All selections are upright and ridiculously easy to grow. They laugh

Graptophyllum pictum 'Chocolate', garden

Graptophyllum pictum 'Tricolor'

Graptophyllum pictum 'Tricolor', garden

at heat, look good wherever they are placed and then, like good annuals, fall apart when temperatures dip into the high 30s. Easily found in good garden shops. Full sun.

Hamelia patens

TEXAS FIREBUSH

The common name for *Hamelia patens* immediately tells us two things. If you guessed that the Texas part probably

means it loves heat and that the firebush has to do with the color, you would be right on. When I saw the plants thriving in the hellish August heat and brutal sun of San Antonio and then equally at home

MORE ☞

Graptophyllum pictum 'Black Beauty'

Hamelia patens, fall color

Hamelia patens, hedge, Texas

Hamelia patens, flowers

as a hedge in the Mercer Botanic Gardens outside Houston, I knew this would be a tough sell for the folks in Minot. However, as summers around the country heat up, the call for such colorful figures becomes stronger, but fair warning: they are not particularly vigorous until temperatures consistently remain above 80°F. Where they are happy, they make a brilliant showing of fire-red flowers and handsome green foliage, which will turn a brilliant burgundy in the fall.

Cultivars are not available; plants are generally raised from cuttings. For most gardeners in most of the country, they are best in containers by concrete, brick, or asphalt—that is, as brutal a location as possible. Full sun.

Helianthus
SUNFLOWER

How can there be so many different sunflowers? Van Gogh had it right when he painted the yellow kind, that is all there should be. But my oh my, how crowded the field has become. With all the bigger, brighter, bolder, dwarfer, larger, and seemingly better cultivars appearing

Helianthus annuus 'Ring of Fire'

Helianthus annuus 'Music Box'

Helianthus annuus, field

Helianthus annuus 'Sonya'

Helianthus annuus, dyed flowers

Helianthus annuus with lantana

Helianthus annuus 'Big Smile'

Helianthus annuus 'Crimson Thriller'

Helianthus annuus 'Chianti'

MORE ☞

every day, why is it that an old-fashioned field of sunflowers, grown for their seed, is still one of the prettiest sights on earth?

The sunflower (*Helianthus annuus*) has become the flower child for everything from coffee mugs to aprons and appears in vases in the sitting room and the boardroom. It has become a part of Americana, and a lovely one at that. Beats the heck out of the Confederate flag. As a cut flower, dozens of cultivars have been bred, ranging from 'Ring of Fire' to 'Sonya', and they are beautiful. However, there are always some people who feel that the natural colors need enhancing, and they vandalize the poor flower with gruesome dyes.

As garden plants, there is no end to what is out there, and one can find them standing off by themselves or mixed in with lantanas in the garden. They are all raised from seed, and the limiting factor as to what to grow is the availability of seed. I have seen well over eighty different cultivars of sunflowers, but I bet I couldn't lay my hands on more than a dozen. But what a wonderful dozen they would be.

The dwarf forms are becoming more popular, simply because they don't need staking and don't fall over. 'Music Box' is a handsome 2' form, and 'Big Smile' is even grown in containers, so that the large flowers can really be seen. The short and tall of it must include some of the big guys, and I figure if I am going to grow a 7' plant, it had better be impressive. The shimmering flowers of 'Crimson Thriller' are beautiful, and everybody can admire the flowers of 'Chianti',

Helianthus annuus 'Valentine'

Helianthus annuus 'Italian White'

Helianthus annuus 'Sun Goddess'

Helianthus annuus 'Sunbright'

if they are tall enough to see them. It is obvious that there is more than yellow to a sunflower, as attested by the pale yellow of 'Valentine' and the small white flowers of 'Italian White'.

But yellow is the dominant color, and there seem to be enough shades and shapes to keep everyone looking. 'Sun Goddess' and 'Sunbright' are attractive yellow flowers with large dark centers and look every bit the part of a sunflower. But if you don't pay attention, you may miss the double forms, two of which are 'Helios' and the beautiful 'Goldburst'. They hardly look like sunflowers, but people really love them.

All the previous cultivars belong to a single species of annual sunflower, but more is yet to come. I believe we will see more of the marvelous silver-leaf sunflower, *Helianthus argophyllus*. It is fabulous even when not in flower, the silvery leaves always an eye-grabber in the

MORE ☞

Helianthus annuus 'Helios'

Helianthus annuus 'Goldburst'

Helianthus argophyllus, container

Helianthus argophyllus, flowers

ground or in a container. The flowers are nothing to write home about, but they provide the classic sunflower look, and that is certainly not all bad. This is a sleeper, about to become a winner.

All sunflowers, especially *Helianthus annuus*, decline rapidly after flowering. The further South, the more rapid and the earlier the deterioration. Simply place another seed beside the plant when it begins to bud up, and as it begins to decline, the new plant will be attaining maturity. Pull out the old one, and voilà, you can enjoy them all over again. Full sun, lots of water.

Helichrysum

With the removal of the main flowering species into the genus *Bracteantha* (which see), this genus is left with a higgledy-piggledy potpourri of annual goodies. Many have been around for years, while others are only now starting to be grown in gardens.

One of the best known is the curry plant, *Helichrysum italicum*, with a fragrance remarkably similar to curry. The silver leaves look fine all season, and for me, the fragrance is far more pleasant than the taste of the real thing. The flowers are pleasant enough, although if it never flowered, it would still be a sought-after addition to the garden. Best in rock gardens or where drainage is excellent, but also fine in containers. Full sun, good drainage.

Most of the "helis" have silvery foliage and have been used to accent other plants in baskets and containers. One such plant that has been sold for many years is licorice plant, *Helichrysum petiolare*. The plant is grown strictly for the foliage, the flowers are nondescript and of little value. 'Limelight' is one of the best, complementing other plants in containers or poking out from the edge

Helichrysum italicum

Helichrysum italicum, rock garden

Helichrysum petiolare 'Limelight'

of the garden. For a different look, 'Variegatum' provides all sorts of interest, although it is perhaps not as complementary to other plants as 'Limelight'. Best in containers, hates wet feet.

The other two plants hanging about the fringes are silver everlasting, *Helichrysum splendidum*, and silver spike, *H. thianschanicum*. The former

has upright shoots, almost standing at attention, and bears lots of yellow daisy flowers in late summer. Grown for the foliage; flowers should be removed. The latter is a recent introduction, designed to be put in containers by itself, or as a complement to others. It is sold as 'Icicles' and 'Silver Spike'. Both behave poorly in wet soils and high humidity. Full sun.

Heliotropium

HELIOTROPE

Grown in far greater numbers in your grandmother's heyday than today, heliotrope is nonetheless making a comeback. Ask anyone why they include heliotrope (*Heliotropium arborescens*) in the garden and they will immediately

MORE ☞

Helichrysum petiolare 'Limelight' with geraniums and phormium

Helichrysum petiolare 'Variegatum'

Helichrysum splendidum

Helichrysum thianschanicum 'Silver Spike'

self, or in containers with verbena and pentas, the plant performs well, and putting it near a garden bench where one can lean over and sniff is a great idea. Full sun. Plants persist longer in the North than in the heat and humidity of the South.

Not all heliotropes are created equal, that is for sure. In fact, just emerging from the wild is one of our native forms, creeping heliotrope, *Heliotropium amplexicaule*. It is surely winter hardy to at least zone 7, perhaps 6, but it is being sold as an annual, and cold tolerance is simply a bonus. The main cultivar is 'Azure Skies', which is grown for its flowing habit out of baskets and containers, or sliding down the edges of beds. It flowers most of the summer, but there is one drawback. No pleasant fragrance caresses your nostrils; in fact, some people say that the odor assails their nostrils. As for me, it is neutral, but the plant is so prolific, I can forgive its lack of perfume. Certainly worth a try. Full sun, good drainage.

Hemigraphis repanda

WAFFLE PLANT

I am not sure where the common name arose, but for small areas, rock gardens, or containers, waffle plant (*Hemigraphis repanda*) is as unique-looking as its name. They are small plants, never rising more than 6" in height, but the colorful purple foliage and the lovely white to pink flowers are always pleasing to the eye. They can be useful, flanking a

Heliotropium amplexicaule 'Azure Skies', garden

Hemigraphis repanda

Heliotropium amplexicaule 'Azure Skies'

Hemigraphis repanda, garden

marker but never hiding it, or in combination with other plants in the garden. The only drawback is that plants are slow-growing and can be overtaken by more vigorous neighbors. An overlooked winner. Full sun to partial shade.

Hibiscus

MALLOW

Many of the hibiscus used in gardens today are the hardy hibiscus, *Hibiscus moscheutos*, and they are big and brilliant compared to many of the annual ones that are commonly grown outdoors. But times are changing, and tropical hibiscus, like many other plants of that ilk, are moving from the Florida nursery to the Michigan garden.

Perhaps the most common annual hibiscus of gardens is the red shield hibiscus, *Hibiscus acetosella*. Plants provide marvelous deep to rosy red foliage all season, occasionally peeking out with a small red flower or two before the frost knocks them down. They can grow 6–8' tall and are great architectural features or complements to other plants in the garden. 'Copper Leaf' is sometimes sold; it bears more subdued leaves of a coppery rather than red color. Regardless, the upright stature and vigorous habit make this hibiscus difficult to overlook.

The diversity of the genus is best shown by having your eye drift from the heights of the red shield to ground level, where the dwarf flower-of-an-hour, *Hibiscus trionum*, resides. With its white flowers and dark centers, the plants bloom continuously and sneer at heat and humidity. Never attaining more than 1' in height, plants enjoy a position in the front of the garden or in containers.

The ascent of the tropical hibiscus (*Hibiscus rosa-sinensis*) into mainstream gardens has been slow but steady. Always thought of as a Florida plant, gardeners in more northerly

Hibiscus acetosella

Hibiscus acetosella 'Copper Leaf'

Hibiscus rosa-sinensis 'Jakarta'

MORE ☞

Hibiscus trionum

Hibiscus trionum, flower

Hibiscus rosa-sinensis 'Kona'

locales would admire them on their southern holiday but ignore them at home. A number of breeders and sellers are working at trying to provide plants with more weather tolerance, so they will bloom as well on 70°F days as on 85°F days. The colors are undeniably beautiful, and the dark green foliage can be handsome when well grown, but it will turn yellow if under stress. Many cultivars are being introduced, and the only way to know which are the best is to try a couple. Cultivars show up locally; few are nationally recognized, so no telling what might be for sale. I have enjoyed 'Jakarta' and 'Kona', but handsome cultivars are sold everywhere. Full sun for all.

Hypoestes phyllostachya

POLKA DOT PLANT

The polka dot plant is still produced by American growers, but it is not as popular as it was only ten years ago. Nothing wrong with the plant, it is simply inevitable that as more plants are put in front of the North American gardener, others lose some of their appeal. Such is the case with *Hypoestes phyllostachya*.

Plants grown in the greenhouse are compact and brilliant when placed on the retail shelf, and once planted in the garden tend to expand and grow out of that habit. They make excellent container and groundcover candidates,

Hypoestes phyllostachya 'White Splash'

Hypoestes phyllostachya, greenhouse

Hypoestes phyllostachya 'Confetti Carmine Rose', *H. p.* 'Confetti White'

Hypoestes phyllostachya 'Pink Splash'

Hypoestes phyllostachya 'Confetti Carmine'

providing vigorous low growth with interesting spotted foliage. Flowers are forgettable and minor. We have trialed many cultivars, and I find those with white markings, such as 'White Splash', don't get lost when grown with other plants. 'Confetti White' is superior, and shows up even more when planted near 'Confetti Carmine Rose'. The darker-colored leaves, like those found on 'Pink Splash', are too busy for me, but the in-teresting tones of 'Confetti Carmine' are not too dark and show up reasonably well in the landscape. Full sun in the North, afternoon shade in the South.

Iberis

CANDYTUFT

This is another genus dominated by a perennial species, in this case perennial candytuft, *Iberis sempervirens*. How-ever, there is more to candytuft than one species, and some of the annual forms are much showier than the usual perennials.

The most common of these uncom-mon plants is the amazing rocket can-dytuft, *Iberis amara*. Plants look like they're on the launch pad at Cape Canaveral, noses pointed in the air.

MORE ☞

They look terrific in gardens with a few red dianthus keeping guard. A number of improved rockets are also sold, the most popular being 'White Pinnacle', a large-flowered rocket that can also be useful as a cut flower. Quite outstanding but perhaps a little too big. A shorter but no less handsome form is 'Iceberg Superior'; either one is fun to grow. They are not as weather-tolerant as I would like and may not look good in the middle of July, but so what?

A form that is much less of a rocket is common candytuft, *Iberis umbellata*, which has wonderful colors on low-growing plants, looking like an aggrega-

Iberis amara 'White Pinnacle'

Iberis amara 'Iceberg Superior'

Iberis gibraltarica

Iberis amara

Iberis umbellata 'Brilliant White'

Iberis umbellata 'Brilliant Rose'

Iberis linifolia

tion of candytuft and alyssum. The Brilliant series certainly works for me; I can't get enough of 'Brilliant White', which has a tinge of pink in the flowers, while the rosy pink flowers of 'Brilliant Rose' are outstanding.

A couple of other annual candytufts are floating around out there, with names like the Gibraltar candytuft and the narrow-leaf candytuft. The former (*Iberis gibraltarica*) is a low grower, not more than 6" tall, with light pink and white flowers. They grow rapidly and can fill in an area quickly. The latter (*I. linifolia*) is more upright, and while all the leaves of the annuals are narrow, these are the most so. Flowers are smaller and not as impressive as the others, but this species is perhaps worth a try if you find the seeds. All grown from seed; full sun, good drainage, cool temperatures.

Impatiens

From the balsam plant to busy lizzie, from jewelweed to impatiens, this genus has it all. From 6' tall weeds to the cheeky dwarf forms of the highly bred bedding plant to the brilliant flowers and foliage of the New Guinea plant, the

MORE ☞

Impatiens balfourii

Impatiens balsamina

Impatiens balsamina 'Tom Thumb'

Impatiens balsamina 'Blackberry Ice'

Impatiens balsamina 'Peach Ice'

Impatiens walleriana 'Variegata'

Impatiens glandulifera

Impatiens glandulifera, flowers

Impatiens walleriana, mix, UGA Trial Gardens

Impatiens walleriana 'Mini Variegated'

Impatiens walleriana 'Pixie Pink Border'

Impatiens walleriana 'Cheeky Spotted Orange'

Impatiens walleriana 'Fiesta Salmon with Blush'

MORE ☞

candy store is open and gardeners can choose their sweets. And choose they have been doing, making this genus the number-one-selling bedding plant in this country. Impatiens are without doubt the main choice for color in shady gardens. No other group of plants provides so much pizzazz for so long a time to so many shady areas.

However, there is more out there than simply the bedding impatiens or the New Guinea forms, albeit more is not always easy to find. Not that many years ago, one of the most common impatiens was rose balsam, *Impatiens balsamina.* It is slowly making a comeback but will likely not return to its former glory; the impatiens field is too crowded. However, the double-flowered species is easy to grow from seed and is readily available in seed packages. Often sold as "Camellia Flower," they are about 15" tall, but a dwarfer form, 'Tom Thumb', is also available. One of the best series I have grown is the Ice series, with double flowers and handsome variegated leaves. 'Blackberry Ice' has deeper rosy flowers, while 'Peach Ice' bears pastel pink blooms. They are outstanding for brightening up the shade.

While wandering around gardens here and there, one often finds the unusual among the plebeian. Such was the case when I first came across Balfour's impa-

Impatiens walleriana brightens a porch

Impatiens walleriana 'Dazzler Coral'

Impatiens walleriana, baskets

Impatiens walleriana 'Showstopper Picotee'

tiens, *Impatiens balfourii*, in a garden on Long Island. I have since grown it in Georgia and admired it in Vermont, but nobody seems to offer plants for sale. Plants attain about 18" and flower most of the season with pendulous white and pink blooms. Find it, grow it, enjoy it.

As beautiful as the genus is, many people consider some of the members awful weeds. Jewelweed and other tall forms inhabit moist areas and reseed themselves everywhere. They can be-come a bother, however. Policeman's hel-met, *Impatiens glandulifera*, is at least beautiful before it becomes a nuisance; plants grow 5' tall but have beautiful large flowers of light to deep rose-pink. They tower over others and are not as weedy as some, but expect them to appear in a different area the next year.

Of course, the Big Two dominate the impatiens market. They are bedding im-patiens, *Impatiens walleriana* (affection-ately known as busy lizzie), and New Guinea impatiens, *I. hawkeri*. They are everywhere, and deservedly so. We have trialed hundreds of cultivars in Athens, and I can honestly say there are no "dogs," only differences in color, habit, or form that might impress one person more than another. They look outstanding dripping out of baskets, in combination with bed-ding plants like red salvia, or as simple porch plants planted in old strawberry pots. While the mainstream colors and form are most common, variegated culti-

Impatiens walleriana with red salvia

Impatiens walleriana 'Showstopper Flair'

Impatiens walleriana 'Accent Bright Eyed'

Impatiens walleriana 'Impulse Appleblossom'

MORE ☞

vars are sometimes available but don't seem as popular when so much else is out there. However, two other areas of breeding continue to expand the range. One is the dwarfing of impatiens, resulting in plants with smaller leaves and small (but seemingly hundreds of) flowers. They go under names like Mini series, such as the bicolor flowers of 'Mini Variegated', the Pixies, like 'Pixie Pink Border', or the impish Cheeky, one of the best being 'Cheeky Spotted Orange'. Outstanding performers, with quite a different look. The second area outside the main avenue of impatiens is the renaissance in double-flowered forms. A few cultivars have always been available, but the ascent of the Fiesta series, shown off by 'Fiesta Salmon with Blush', has brought the doubles out of hiding. Additional fine series are now available to gardeners.

While the previous forms and sizes enhance the usefulness of impatiens, it is the mainstream bedding plant that fills the garden centers and brightens the shade. And there's so much to choose from, it seldom matters if you read the label. The Dazzler series, such as 'Dazzler Coral' has been a terrific choice, but 'Super Elfin Blue Pearl' has probably had as many fans as any impatiens recently bred. For bicolored flowers, it is hard to beat 'Showstopper Picotee', and 'Showstopper Flair' is impressive also. I could go on forever about the diversity of color, but ending with an excellent "eyed" form, as in 'Accent Bright Eyes', and a beautiful pastel form, as shown by 'Impulse Appleblossom', may be enough. It is not hard to see why bedding impatiens holds onto

Impatiens walleriana 'Super Elfin Blue Pearl'

Impatiens hawkeri 'Trinidad'

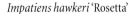

Impatiens hawkeri 'Rosetta'

Impatiens hawkeri 'Pure Beauty Melissa'

Impatiens hawkeri 'Celebrette Wild Plum'

Impatiens hawkeri 'Illusion'

Impatiens hawkeri 'Petticoat Fire'

Impatiens hawkeri Painted Paradise series

Impatiens hawkeri 'Aztec'

the number-one spot in sales.

The bedding group may be leading the race, but New Guinea impatiens are rapidly making up ground. In tubs in Atlanta, Georgia, or in public gardens in East Lansing, Michigan, New Guineas are doing just fine, thank you. They tolerate more sun than the bedding forms and are able to be used in more areas of the garden. As with bedding impatiens, there is no end to the number of choices being bred and sold at the garden center and box store today. From the light flowers of 'Rosetta' to 'Pure Beauty Melissa' (one of over twelve cultivars in the Pure Beauty series) to the dark iridescent color of 'Celebrette Wild Plum' and the incredibly bright 'Petticoat Fire', there is something for every color combination and every taste. And yes, there are other horses in the race, and some beautiful variegated foliage forms of New Guineas are reemerging. The old 'Aztec' has given way to the spectacular Painted Paradise series. Handsome leaves and good flowers, they will almost be impossible not to put in your shopping cart come spring.

All impatiens favor at least afternoon shade; only the bedding forms require shade most of the day. Lots of water.

Ipomoea

MORNING GLORY

This is probably one of the most confusing genera in the garden, being represented by such different-looking flowers as the Spanish flag and morning glory. Most members of the group love to climb or at least romp around, and few remain well behaved, especially where they are happy.

And happiness is not all that difficult to attain for this vigorous group of happy-go-lucky well-known plants.

MORE ☞

Interestingly enough, however, not all are as well known as they should be. People are fascinated by the twisted flower buds of moon vine (*Ipomoea alba*); they can hardly wait to plant it themselves so they can watch the flowers open in late afternoon and evening. Moon vine is particularly appealing climbing over brick or stone walls, and the flowers are perfect at dusk. A great excuse for a walk in the garden with a glass of wine. But don't be too late—like many big-flowered vines, the flowers persist but a day.

Other lesser-known vines also make fabulous houseguests, and your own houseguests will believe you to be a master gardener. One of the weirdest is Spanish flag, *Ipomoea lobata*, with its elongated red and yellow flowers. Perhaps the common name resulted from the fact that red and yellow are the colors on the Spanish flag, but this plant is native to Mexico. Go figure. Plants are vigorous and can easily attain 15' in a single year. And I am seeing the cypress vine (*I. quamoclit*) more and more and beginning to appreciate the beautiful fern-like appearance of the foliage. Another of our southwestern natives, but plants look

Ipomoea alba, flower bud

Ipomoea alba

Ipomoea alba, flowers

Ipomoea tricolor 'Heavenly Blue'

Ipomoea ×sloteri

Ipomoea lobata, flowers

Ipomoea quamoclit

Ipomoea quamoclit, flowers

Ipomoea lobata

Ipomoea tricolor 'Pearly Gates'

MORE ☞

outstanding twining around posts in the Allen Centennial Gardens in Madison, Wisconsin—those fire-engine-red flowers almost require the use of polarized sunglasses. A hybrid of this species, *I. ×sloteri*, combines the dazzling flowers with fabulous frilly leaves.

As many people curse morning glory vines (*Ipomoea tricolor*) as love them. They curse them for their reseeding tendencies and persistent weedlike growth years after the original vine was re- moved. That characteristic alone has turned many gardeners off these vines, but let's not throw the baby out with the bath water. Beautiful plants are out there, and they may well be worth the future weeding. Many are hybrids with other species, and probably the all-time favorite is 'Heavenly Blue', a winner everywhere it is planted. The color seems perfect for nearly everyone. For a white, I love 'Pearly Gates'; it reminds me of a daytime moon vine but far more floriferous. Darker flower colors are also available, including 'Magenta', which is somewhat on the red side, and the ghoulish 'Kniola's Black', with small but almost black flowers. I think only people with hidden pierced body parts enjoy this one. And morning glories keep surprising people with the changes in their makeup. Who would have thought that variegated vines would have appeal, but 'Cameo Elegance' started off the movement, and the worker bees at our gardens just loved the combination of variegated foliage and red flowers of 'Good Morning Red' and the lavender-blue of 'Good Morning Blue'. Plants were bred in

Ipomoea tricolor 'Good Morning Red'

Ipomoea batatas 'Black Heart'

Ipomoea batatas 'Margarita'

Ipomoea batatas 'Margarita', containers

Ipomoea tricolor 'Magenta'

Japan, and the Good Morning series is a translation of the original unpronounceable Japanese names. They do not climb as well (they will need some help in twining) nor are they as vigorous as their non-variegated counterparts.

If you asked gardeners a few years ago what they thought of sweet potatoes (*Ipomoea batatas*), they would opine about their love or dislike of the taste of the yellow tuber. Who would have thought that this vegetable would become so popular as a garden plant?

But it has, partly because the plants are almost indestructible, regardless of where in the country they are planted. 'Blackie' was one of the first introduced to the unsuspecting public, and it performed well in landscapes and baskets, spilling out of containers and adding a class of purple to the garden. 'Black Heart' (aka 'Ace of Spades') is similar in color but with heart-shaped leaves. It too looks great in containers, and between 'Black Heart' and 'Purple Majesty'

MORE ☞

Ipomoea tricolor 'Kniola's Black'

Ipomoea tricolor 'Good Morning Blue'

Ipomoea batatas 'Blackie'

Ipomoea tricolor 'Cameo Elegance'

Ipomoea batatas 'Pink Frost'

millet, containers are lush, full, and black as Mordor in Middle Earth. 'Pink Frost' adorns a few gardens as well, and although the rainbow colors are handsome, plants are far less vigorous (which is not necessarily a bad thing) than other cultivars on the market.

The all-time success story for this abused vegetable has to be the chartreuse 'Margarita', who can be found from Edmonton to Miami, brightening up landscapes and making gardeners feel like professionals. Whether falling out of beds in Athens or making cannas look even better in Niagara-on-the-Lake in Ontario, this is a no-brainer. And for even more fun, dig out the tubers in late fall—you will be amazed at the size of these things. Plant all ipomoeas in full sun, then get out of the way.

Iresine
BLOODLEAF

If we threw various types of iresine, coleus, acalypha, alternanthera, and amaranthus together and asked experts to properly identify them, there would be considerable head-scratching going on. While there are differences for those in the know, they all kind of look alike to the rest of us. *Iresine* has small flowers, similar to those acalyphas, and often painted foliage, like coleus and alternantheras. The beefsteak plant, *Iresine herbstii*, can attain 4–5' in the tropics but behaves more like a coleus in our gardens. There are a number of fine forms; unfortunately few are labeled, except as beefsteak plant. I love the upright rosy red form with dark red midribs and silvery veins, it seems to soften everything around it. For a dwarf selection, I have been most impressed with 'Purple Lady', a trailing dark purple form that has maintained the dark foliage and looked good all season. Well worth finding for baskets and containers. Full sun to afternoon shade.

Iresine herbstii

Kaempferia pulchra var. *mansonii*

Kaempferia, Cornukaempferia
PEACOCK GINGER

Perhaps because I reside in an area of the country that is neither "in the North" nor "in the South" as far as plantings are concerned, I see many tropicals growing beside temperate plants. Obviously

Iresine herbstii 'Purple Lady'

Athens is in the South, just walk by the beautiful antebellum homes on Milledge Avenue, but our relatively cold winter temperatures allow plantings of many temperate plants, while our hot summers invite more and more tropicals. That long introduction is my explanation of how hostas and peacock gingers came to be planted side by side in the shade garden at the University of Georgia. People from Florida and the Gulf Coast swear by the ornamental foliage and shade-loving characteristics of *Kaempferia*. They even call them southern hostas, since the true hosta does so poorly south of zone 7. And once I tried them at UGA, I fell in love with them and had to grow them in my shaded garden at home.

And they should be grown elsewhere.

If you are trying any tropicals in the garden, include this in your wish list. There are over fifty species, but most available plants will be hybrids of various species such as *Kaempferia pulchra* or *K. gilbertii*. Don't worry about the parentage, look for named hybrids, as they all behave the same. Flowers look like phlox flowers, although they have only four petals. In general, they are light blue to

Kaempferia 'Alva'

Kaempferia 'Grande'

Kaempferia 'Bronze Peacock'

Cornukaempferia aurantiflora 'Jungle Gold'

MORE ☞

almost white, appear in the leaf axils, and flower on and off most of the summer. All selections grow from compact rosettes and remain 1–2' tall.

Manson's peacock ginger (*Kaempferia pulchra* var. *mansonii*) is a vigorous grower that flowers well but doesn't have the prized foliage of many of the others. One of my favorites is 'Alva', with large patterned leaves and light blue flowers; this also appears to be the most cold-tolerant, having come back, at least in zone 7b. 'Silverspot' has the most silvering on the leaves and is equally beautiful. 'Grande' is bigger than the others, with large wide silvery spotted leaves—excellent where the budget allows only one or two plants to be purchased. And for the bronze lovers, 'Bronze Peacock' is truly remarkable, with dark foliage that is an excellent contrast to the lavender-blue flowers.

A close relative also known as the peacock ginger is *Cornukaempferia*. Plants behave identically to the kaempferias, but *Cornukaempferia aurantiflora*, the yellow peacock ginger, is even more beautiful, if that is possible. We have been growing 'Jungle Gold' for many years; the foliage is exquisitely patterned on the top and purple beneath. Add to that the bright golden yellow flowers, and this is pretty much a no-brainer.

These plants will not be easy to find through regular plant shops or normal catalogs. However they are being produced from tissue culture, and the only reason they are not more visible is that people don't ask for them. Like any member of the ginger family, they relish heat and are at their best in the hot, humid months. Place in deep shade (direct sun is a no-no), and wait until temperatures are consistently in the 50s before planting. Dig up after the first frost, and put in an area that doesn't freeze. They will emerge again when temperatures heat up. A heated cold frame works well, and the spring sun inside the frame will provide the extra heat needed to get them going again.

![Kaempferia 'Silverspot']

Kaempferia 'Silverspot'

Kochia scoparia 'Acapulco Silver'

Kochia scoparia

BURNING BUSH

The woody plant lovers have their burning bush, *Euonymus alatus*, and the herbaceous plant people have their kochia. There is no comparison—in most parts of the country, the woody one wins the brightly burning contest hands down. The popularity of burning bush (*Kochia scoparia*) has declined in the last decade or so, perhaps because of its lack of flowers, and impatience of gardeners who didn't want to wait until the fall to see the bush burn.

However, it has an understated elegance even when in its green clothing.

And it is a really neat plant; it can be used in containers or as small "trees" in mixed landscapes. I think the planting at the Butchart Gardens, in which heliotrope bathed the floor while bushes of kochia stood at attention, was a classic. Along with cosmos and verbena and geraniums, the kochias held their own.

Several cultivars have been selected; the best known is 'Acapulco Silver', in which the tips of the branches are tinged in silver. Quite distinctive—provides color for those who miss flowers and burns quite nicely in the fall.

Full sun in the North, afternoon shade in the South. Grown from seed.

Lablab purpureus

HYACINTH BEAN

217

Some plants have unpronounceable names, some have onomatopoeic names, others are simply fun to say. This great plant has one of those names you can drop at parties, as in "How is your lablab doing?" At best, somebody might engage you in conversation about this wonderful vine; at worst, they'll think you are stuttering about your dog.

Hyacinth bean (*Lablab purpureus*) will grow 10–15' in a single season, all the while producing wonderful flowers and great fruit. It can cover arbors, lathe houses, and entire sides of buildings when supplied with ample light and fertility. The "purpureus" comes from the fact that the plant sports purple leaves, deep pink flowers, and purple fruit. Fruit are edible, meaning you won't get violently ill, but far more tastier beans are out there.

MORE ☞

Kochia scoparia 'Acapulco Silver', fall color

Kochia scoparia with heliotrope

Lablab purpureus

Save the seeds in the fall in a dry cool area, then direct sow where you want them when the soil warms up. Full sun, feed heavily during the first three to four weeks of growth.

Lantana

Lantanas have become a hot item in ornamental horticulture circles. Gardeners can choose from low-growing forms, upright bushes, many flower colors, those with variegated foliage, and even those with ornamental fruit. When temperatures are hot and cruddy and humidity is so thick you can cut it with a knife, lantanas will be standing strong and proud while many of their brethren will be cowering on the ground. Few plants can stand up to weather abuse as well as lantanas, and in many parts of the country, there is sufficient abuse to justify entire lantana gardens. Even in Europe, lantanas are making a lot of noise, and several cultivars, like 'Professor Raoux', are often seen as standards. Gardeners in the North have been ignoring this plant, but other than snobbery, I can think of no good reason why. Those in the South who are tired of it perhaps will be interested in the diversity of color and form.

Lablab purpureus, flowers

Lablab purpureus, fruit

Most lantanas seen in landscapes tend to be low-growing, usually no more than 2' tall. An underused species in this country is weeping lantana, *Lantana montevidensis*, which at the height of bloom is absolutely choking with purple flowers. Plants are more visible in areas with moderate temperatures and low humidity; they are mainly grown in the West.

Most lantanas used in gardens in the rest of the country belong to a single species, common lantana, *Lantana camara,* yet the variety is quite amazing. Choices among the dozens of low-growers include the deep colors of 'Radiation' and the calming hues of 'Silver Mound'. Prob-ably the Patriot series contains the best diversity of lantanas, and seemingly dozens of varieties bear the Patriot name. I have been impressed with the orange-red hues of 'Patriot Firewagon', the mute yellow of 'Patriot Honeylove', the soft pink of 'Patriot Parasol', and the hot colors of 'Patriot Hot Country'. My guess as to the most popular low-grower is 'New Gold', whose golden flowers were so common between Athens and Atlanta during the 1996 Olympics that the passage between the two cities was known as "the pathway of gold." It flowers all season with absolutely no care and is still one of the leading sellers today. And like every other group of plants, a variegated form of lantana is also available, and this smart-looking one with yellow flowers and handsome foliage is 'Samantha'.

Not all lantanas are prostrate, weeping, or even low-growing. Tall-growing shrubs of common lantana are widely used in landscapes throughout the South and more and more in the North. The best known is 'Miss Huff', a plant that can grow 8' tall in a heartbeat and produces orange-yellow flowers all summer. She is probably the most cold hardy of all the lantanas, routinely coming back in the spring in zone 7, and often 6. However, two other upright forms have also shown

Lantana camara 'Professor Raoux'

Lantana camara 'Radiation'

Lantana montevidensis

Lantana camara 'Patriot Firewagon'

MORE ☞

Lantana camara 'Silver Mound'

Lantana camara 'Patriot Parasol'

Lantana camara 'Patriot Honeylove'

Lantana camara 'Patriot Hot Country'

Lantana camara 'Athens Rose'

Lantana camara 'Miss Huff'

considerable cold hardiness but have not been field tested for as long. 'Athens Rose' is about half the size of 'Miss Huff' and beautifully covered with rosy red flowers. Outstanding in gardens wherever it has been tested. A relative newcomer to the upright group is 'Deen Day Smith', with handsome pink flowers, larger than 'Athens Rose' but smaller than 'Miss Huff'. The plant recognizes a great lady and excellent gardener from Georgia.

Lantanas should always be functional, but who says we can't have a little fun as well? I named a particularly handsome hybrid, involving *Lantana trifolia*, 'Lavender Popcorn', and the moniker has stuck. The leaves are in threes and the small flowers are lavender. If that was all that could be said, I would have dismissed the plant as just another lantana; however, its true colors are shown around mid summer. At that time, small shiny balls of purple begin to appear; like an ear of corn, more and more "kernels" occur, and soon the long purple fruit are formed. At any one time, flowers and fruit are on the plant. Great fun, quite different. Plants are as tolerant of heat and humidity as all the others.

Any lantana can be cut back hard

Lantana camara 'New Gold'

Lantana camara 'Samantha'

Lantana 'Lavender Popcorn'

Lantana 'Lavender Popcorn', fruit

MORE ☞

during the growing season if it gets out of hand or needs a little shaping, but wait until spring to cut back dead limbs on perennial cultivars. Full sun.

Laurentia

ISOTOMA, PRATIA

The common name, isotoma, used to be the name of the genus, and people still tend to use the names interchangeably; the name pratia is also bandied about when discussing these plants. Not that any of the names are used that much, since plants are hardly known in North American gardens, an oversight that must be corrected.

The two species found in catalogs and garden centers are also confused. The

Lantana camara 'Deen Day Smith'

Laurentia axillaris

Laurentia axillaris 'Alba'

most common one is star flower, *Laurentia axillaris*, which bears somewhat prickly-looking foliage that gets covered up with handsome blue flowers in the shape of a star. Each arm of the star is long and narrow. Whether flowing out of baskets or brightening up a garden bed, plants are quite marvelous. The only cultivar I know is the white form, 'Alba'. We put it in a container with petunia and lantana and it held its own, but the blue is a better performer.

The second species, *Laurentia fluvi-atilis*, which is often sold under *Pratia*, is much smaller and lower to the ground. It bears many small light blue, almost white, flowers, which are also in the shape of a star but with much shorter arms. They are often used between rocks in rock walkways and can be shaped and trained to go where you want them. Both species have a milky sap and can cause skin irritation to sensitive people. Don't rub your eyes after handling the plants. Full sun to partial shade, excellent drainage.

Lavatera

TREE MALLOW

Lavateras became popular perennials with the introduction of 'Barnsley Pink' to North American gardeners. Others had been lurking in the shadow for years, including a few annual forms, but none has been particularly popular, at least in the east side of the country. The annual *Lavatera trimestris*, known simply as lavatera, is as beautiful as anything in the mallow family, and that is

Laurentia fluviatilis, rock work

Lavatera trimestris 'Tanagra'

Laurentia fluviatilis

Lavatera trimestris 'Loveliness'

MORE ☞

Limonium sinuatum 'Forever Gold'

Limonium suworowii, flowers

Limonium suworowii

flower or as part of a dried arrangement but believe that it, like milk, only comes from stores. Plants are generally obtained from seed; few retailers stock annual statice anymore, but if you enjoy cutting flowers from your garden, this is an easy plant to grow.

Not a great deal of choice is available, but you can't go too far wrong with the Fortress series, such as 'Fortress White' or 'Fortress Yellow', or the Forever series, like 'Forever Gold'. For fresh flowers, cut the stems when the first few flowers have opened (you can see the white centers, particularly in the darker colors), bunch them up, and enjoy their long vase life. If you are drying them, bunch up as before

Linaria maroccana 'Fantasy Sparkling Pink'

and hang them upside down in a dry warm room.

Occasionally, seeds of the rattail statice (*Limonium suworowii*, *Psylliostachys suworowii*) can be found in obscure seed catalogs, and if you enjoy cultivating the weird, give these a try. They produce long tails of light pink flowers and, common name aside, are really quite a delightful garden plant. An excellent cut flower, fresh or dried. Handle similarly to annual statice. Full sun, good drainage. All statice struggle in hot, humid summers.

Linaria

TOADFLAX

There must be something worth trying in this little-known genus, some of the species have such colorful common names. To be sure, many gardeners know the roadside flower, common toadflax, *Linaria vulgaris*, but few purposely plant it beside their roses. However, a number of annuals and reseeders are available to North American gardeners, some of which do well in the West and one or two in the East.

Probably *Linaria maroccana*, annual

Linaria maroccana, Sea Island, Georgia

toadflax (aka bunny rabbits), is the best known of the species. Native to North Africa, plants have escaped and are quite common in the western half of the United States. They are closely related to snapdragons and have similar cultural requirements, that is, cool temperatures and full sun. I was impressed with the compact 9–12" height of a mixed planting at the Missouri Botanical Garden; however, the same planting on Sea Island, Georgia, although equally colorful, was almost 18" tall. Such height differences are quite common, as plants tend to stretch a little more in response to warm temperatures. A number of cultivars have been bred, but my choice is Fantasy, a modern series with vigor and many appealing colors. The mixture is fine in a wild setting, but single colors are more appropriate for the garden; 'Fantasy Sparkling Pink' has to be one of my favorites.

Of the many species of toadflax, one of the prettiest is probably purple net toadflax, *Linaria reticulata*. As an early-season planting, 'Crown Jewels' more than holds its own, competing quite happily with poppies, snapdragons, and pinks.

MORE ☞

Linaria reticulata 'Crown Jewels'

Linaria triornithophora, flowers

Linaria triornithophora

When I read about a plant called three birds flying (*Linaria triornithophora*), I had to give it a try. I grew it and noted the spurs (the wings) at the base of the flowers, but when the first flowers opened, I noticed there were four birds flying at each flower node. The flowers expanded and grew taller, and soon entire flocks were flying around. Handsome colors, upright stems, and excellent cut flowers as well—the plant needs to be seen in more of our gardens. One of its limitations (as in the entire genus) is its dislike of heat and humidity, but what else is new? They can be considered early spring candidates, planted along with nasturtiums and calendulas. Full sun.

Lobelia

Lobelias are as American as apple pie, and our red cardinal flower, *Lobelia cardinalis*, is probably the best known of them all. Perennial lobelias have been the hot item in the last number of years, while the old 1960s standby, annual bedding lobelia (*L. erinus*), has been relegated to the background of mainstream gardening, at least in the East and South. Not that it is any less useful or less colorful, it is simply that there are so many other plants to choose from that weren't there in the 1960s.

The fact is, bedding lobelia is better than it has ever been, with brighter colors and even heat-resistant cultivars that persist longer into the season. Having said that, it is no secret that plants do much better in cooler-summer climates than in hot, humid ones. Growing up in Montreal, I remember lobelia edging every garden bed in the entire city. And hanging around

Lobelia erinus 'Palace Blue with Eye'

Lobelia erinus, edging

Lobelia erinus 'Cascade Blue'

Lobelia erinus 'Cascade White'

all summer as well. Boring, but effective with marigolds and alyssum. I grow lobelia in Georgia, but it must be put in early and, if grown as an edging, is probably best removed by late June. While I was in Auckland, New Zealand, where the thermometer seldom sees 85°F, the baskets of 'Cascade Blue' lobelia were among the best I had ever seen.

Most cultivars have flowers in blue or purple, but a few bicolors are available, such as 'Palace Blue with Eye', and even an occasional white form ('Cascade White'). They are difficult to maintain in baskets, but large patio containers suit them just fine, and plants persist far longer. The most heat-tolerant cultivar I have ever trialed in Athens was 'Periwinkle Blue', which mixed well with double impatiens and white bacopa. Plants looked great all the way to August. Full sun in the North, afternoon shade in the South.

Lobularia maritima

SWEET ALYSSUM

Sweet alyssum (*Lobularia maritima*) really is sweet: on a warm summer evening, the fragrance from the flowers

Lobularia maritima 'Wonderland White'

Lobularia maritima 'Wonderland Deep Purple'

Lobularia maritima Easter Bonnet Mix

Lobelia erinus 'Periwinkle Blue'

Lobularia maritima 'Snow Crystals'

MORE ☞

is unmistakable, not overwhelming like hyacinths, but ephemeral and less obnoxious. The flowers and plants have been a mainstay for years, used as edging and anywhere low-growing plants with lots of flowers were needed.

I wonder how many beds have been edged with the white flowers of 'Snow Crystals' or covered by the snowfall of 'Wonderland White' over the years? Everyone thinks that alyssum comes only in white, but 'Wonderland Deep Purple' quickly puts that myth to rest. And mixtures can also find a place in gardens; the best one I have seen is Easter Bonnet, made up of whites, purples, and pinks. My favorite single color is 'Easter Bonnet Deep Pink'. All alyssums need excellent drainage and are equally at home in containers or in the garden bed. Full sun in the North, afternoon shade in the South.

Lotus berthelotii

PARROT'S BEAK

When gardeners are asked what they think about lotus and lotus flowers, nine times out of ten they will talk about the water plant known as sacred lotus. But as beautiful as that plant is, it belongs to the genus *Nelumbo* (which see). Few people have grown or appreciated the beauty of parrot's beak, *Lotus berthelotii*, probably because it is so little known.

The foliage of parrot's beak is beautifully blue-gray, soft, and compact. Most of the time I see plants used as fillers in mixed containers, because in much of this country they seldom flower. In our Athens garden, the basket did little more than look ornamental, but the foliage was highly effective. However, when it does flower, look out. The cultivar 'Amazon Sunset' was flowering in coastal California in April, and people were gawking at all the red beaks. Actually it is a little much, and I prefer the subtle foli-

Lobularia maritima 'Easter Bonnet Deep Pink'   *Lotus berthelotii* 'Amazon Sunset'

Lotus berthelotii with torenia and lantana

Lotus berthelotii

age without the flowers. And for most of us, that's all we will get anyway. Full sun, best in containers.

Lychnis

CAMPION

The species that belong to this genus are both colorful and plentiful. Many are perennials, but a few of the more enjoyable ones happen to be used as annuals. The flowers are colorful, and many species are easy to grow.

The most colorful is a hybrid that goes under the name of Arkwright's campion, *Lychnis ×arkwrightii*. When it was first introduced, gardeners were told that it was a perennial, but plants have not shown a perennial tendency at all, perhaps hanging on for a second year but often succumbing after one season. However, the brilliance of their flowers is such that they cannot hide anywhere, regardless of the number of plants surrounding them. The main cultivar is 'Vesuvius', an apt name for its spectacular fleeting color, but what light it brings!

As much as I enjoy Arkwright's cam-

Lychnis ×arkwrightii 'Vesuvius'

Lychnis ×arkwrightii 'Vesuvius', flowers

Lychnis flos-cuculi

Lychnis flos-cuculi 'Rosea'

Lychnis flos-jovis, flowers

MORE ☞

Lychnis flos-cuculi 'Alba'

Lychnis flos-jovis

pion, it has frustrated me more often than not. That is not the case with one of my favorite little jump-ups, known to all as ragged robin, *Lychnis flos-cuculi*. It "jumps up" every spring, returning from seeds thrown off during the past summer. The petals seem to be all beat up, and ragged it does appear. But they are undemanding and unpretentious, flowering away all spring and well into the summer. Since all are grown from seed, a good deal of variability occurs, and flowers from white ('Alba') to deep rose ('Rosea') can occur. However, for most of us, the light pink flowers are sufficient, growing where they feel comfortable and soon finding their own space. Put in some plants this spring, and within three years, you will have lots to share with friends.

Another charmer, although not nearly as cooperative, is flower of jupiter, *Lychnis flos-jovis*. Plants are native to mountain areas, mostly the European Alps, and are not as happy in areas of warm temperatures and high humidity. However, they are colorful, particularly the rose-colored form. Plants grow no taller than 1' but are covered with flowers in early summer. Not recommended for southern gardeners, but that leaves many others, particularly in the Northwest and Canada. Full sun.

Lysimachia congestiflora

LOOSESTRIFE, GOLDEN GLOBES

Few annuals of loosestrife are grown; the big sellers are all perennials. However, if you have been told that gooseneck loosestrife or some other perennial form is worthy of consideration, it is time to meet golden globes, *Lysimachia congestiflora*.

Plants grow in anything, anywhere. I have seen them falling out of hanging baskets at a garden center in Strongsville, Ohio, as well as planted at the base of a lantana standard in Columbus. The most common cultivar, 'Eco Dark Satin', has a darker eye than the species and looks terrific as a container plant. The green foliage always contrasts well with the golden yellow flowers, which tend to stay in bloom almost all season. For even more contrast, try 'Variegata'; it does not flower as prolifically, but the variegated foliage is sufficiently handsome to give it some space in the garden anyway. Full sun.

Mandevilla sanderi

BRAZILIAN JASMINE

Every year I drive past a modest home in Athens, and every year I say to myself, "I have to do that." For years now, a beautiful rose-colored mandevilla (*Mandevilla sanderi*) flowers in the front yard by the sidewalk of the house, and every year I notice it around June. Plants twine around a pole of some kind, and although the glossy green leaves are pleasant enough, all I see are flowers, flowers, and more flowers. Finally, when the first hard

MORE ☞

Lysimachia congestiflora 'Variegata'

Lysimachia congestiflora, basket

Lysimachia congestiflora 'Eco Dark Satin'

Lysimachia congestiflora with lantana standard

frost comes, the plant crumples and goes to bed. Athens is in zone 7, yet this sucker comes back; that's all I need to know to become a believer in global warming.

But I see people in Michigan and Wisconsin putting plants in containers and letting them climb on their porches and patios. Cultivars have definitely left the tropics, and plants like 'Leah', with her blush-white flowers, and 'Janell', with rosy red blooms, are becoming more available. And why not? They grow perfectly well at 70–75°F, and while they won't grow as quickly as in Florida, they will provide months of pleasure nevertheless.

They are expensive, so after the first frost, cut them back and put them either in a cold frame or in a garage where temperatures stay above freezing.

Mandevilla sanderi 'Leah'

Mandevilla sanderi, Athens, Georgia

Mandevilla sanderi 'Janell'

Matthiola incana

STOCK

Stocks have so long been the domain of florists and cut flower growers, we seem to have forgotten that their origins were in the garden. Long admired for its fragrance and persistent vase life, stock (*Matthiola incana*) can more often be found by the acre in cut flower fields than by the plant in our gardens. As gardeners, we can never duplicate the job that cut flower producers do; we don't have the facilities or expertise, nor do we have access to cultivars specific to the cut flower trade. But that should not dissuade us from adding a few plants to the garden. Not to do so is a shame, because if part of the joy of having a garden is to cut flowers from it, then why not have a few plants of stocks to sweeten the arrangement?

Stocks can be bought as seed, and if put in the garden early enough, they will germinate and do well if you live in an area of cool summers. However, for the many of us who live where summer heats up rather quickly, started plants should be put in the ground as soon as possible after the last frost. The only forms you will find will be shorter than those grown commercially but can still be quite useful in the vase. 'Legacy Pink', at about 15" tall, is outstanding, while white forms, such as 'Column White', are standouts in the garden.

Dwarf forms have been all the rage, and perhaps they will catch on. While they are a little too short for my taste,

Matthiola incana, cut flower field

Matthiola incana 'Legacy Pink'

Matthiola incana 'Harmony Purple'

Matthiola incana 'Column White'

MORE ☞

others treat them as bedding plants and are quite content. The Cinderella series provides several colors, but 'Cinderella Lavender' is the hit. 'Harmony Purple' is but one of many colors available from the emerging midgets. One of the problems inherent in seed-propagated stocks is that a certain percentage will be single, such as with 'Midget Lavender', rather than the more favored double forms. All

cultivars are supposed to be double, but in some cases up to 40 percent may be single (10 percent is more common). The singles simply are not what stocks are supposed to look like, but there is little that a gardener can do to determine if the seedlings going into the garden will be single or double. Some people enjoy them just as much. Full sun, cool temperatures only. They will likely perish when temperatures remain above 75°F and humidity gets high.

Melampodium paludosum
MEDALLION FLOWER

It was around 1985 that I first received some seeds of medallion flower (*Melampodium paludosum*) and reluctantly put them in the trial garden. After all, we had already trialed enough yellow daisies, most of which wussed out after a few weeks of hot weather, so I was hardly primed to be impressed. Six

Matthiola incana 'Cinderella Lavender'

Melampodium paludosum 'Medaillon', lining stairs

Matthiola incana 'Midget Lavender'

Melampodium paludosum 'Medaillon', Texas

Melampodium paludosum, framing bench

months later, I was telling others they had to try this thing, it really worked.

I had received a cultivar called 'Medaillon', which we soon put all over the campus at the University of Georgia. In our trial garden, I was so impressed that we lined the stairs with these wonderful starry flowers. Why was I providing such high praise? Simply because they grew well, flowered constantly, and did not suffer from heat and humidity in the way usually seen with marigolds or rudbeckias. Soon plants were being

MORE ☞

Melampodium paludosum 'Million Stars' with celosia

Melampodium paludosum 'Million Stars'

Melampodium paludosum with salvia

Melampodium paludosum 'Lemon Delight'

combined with acalyphas along paths at the Mercer Botanic Gardens in Humble, Texas, and later I was tripping on it planted with celosias and alternantheras and all sorts of plants. Each time, however, the melampodium was the showstopper. As a combination with velvet sage, or by itself, used as a backdrop for a small, very uncomfortable bench, the plants looked good nearly all season. And if they got tired or overgrown, all they needed was a serious haircut, and they would be in flower two weeks later.

Other yellow cultivars have come along, mainly to reduce the problem of stretch that plants were prone to. 'Million Stars' is one such introduction and probably my first choice. The excitement about the plant has died down considerably, and even I was walking by without a second look, until we received some seeds of a gorgeous lighter yellow form called 'Lemon Delight'. It was different enough for me to exclaim, "You have to try this thing, it really works!"

Full sun. Plants can reseed and become a nuisance; cut back hard about mid July in the South.

Mimulus

MONKEY FLOWER

A good deal of effort has gone into turning this average-looking flower into a big-time bedding plant. The hybrids (*Mimulus ×hybridus*) consist of parents native to the West Coast and high elevations. That computes into plants that do well in northern Europe, northern states, and coastal areas but generally do rather poorly in hot, humid areas.

Flowers often have spots on their faces, as shown by 'Highland Orange', but breeders have also provided clear faces. I have seen beautiful window boxes of the Magic series, whose clear faces were unusually bright, in Ireland. The Mystic series was also well received; 'Mystic Wine' and 'Mystic Yellow' certainly were impressive, but they still have problems with heat and humidity. Additional cultivars have been bred to overcome some of the heat problems, and better times are ahead.

Mimulus ×hybridus 'Highland Orange'

Mimulus ×hybridus 'Mystic Wine'

Mimulus ×hybridus Magic series

The best of the recent material is probably the Jellybean series (do you think the people who name plants must be smoking something?). We dutifully trialed a number of them; they were better, but they have a long way to go before they will be as mainstream here as in Europe.

Mimulus are best planted in window boxes or containers where soil, fertility, and water can be better controlled. Full sun.

Mirabilis

FOUR O'CLOCK FLOWER

Yes, they do. The common name is not a lie—perhaps not Rolex-accurate but close enough to show the kids. Flowers don't open until mid afternoon during the summer and are usually closed in the morning. People still enjoy these plants but perhaps not as much as they used to. Plants like *Mirabilis jalapa* and portulaca (which see) have the annoying habit of sleeping when we are awake,

and plant breeders have been trying to add a few more hours to their day. And barely succeeding.

However, the plants are easy to grow from seed, and they form good-sized bushes in eight weeks or so, making sturdy garden plants with lots and lots of closed flowers (I guess I have never seen a four o'clock earlier than two o'clock, which may explain my frustration). However, some of the newer cultivars are full of flowers, which is obvious even at noon. 'Broken Colors' consists of

Mimulus ×*hybridus* 'Mystic Yellow'

Mirabilis longiflora

Mirabilis jalapa 'Tea Time Red'

Mirabilis jalapa 'Broken Colors'

MORE 👉

pastels of pink and off-white flowers; the Tea Time series (great name for this flower) is available in numerous colors, but I have been most impressed with 'Tea Time Red' and 'Tea Time Rose'.

Another species or two are also sold here and there; I tried long-tubed mirabilis, *Mirabilis longiflora,* which has long tubular white flowers and opens all day. Unfortunately, for me it was a waste of time and space, but its evening fragrance may entice you to try it. Full sun.

Moluccella laevis

BELLS OF IRELAND

A number of plants started their careers in the garden but found fame elsewhere, as an herb or a houseplant, or in this case as a cut flower. Does anybody grow bells of Ireland (*Moluccella laevis*) as a garden plant anymore? While it is not as colorful as impatiens—what green flowers are?—neither should it be shunned just because we can find it cleaned and packaged at the florist.

Bells of Ireland actually looks pretty neat in the garden, generally grown in the front so the unique flowers can be appreciated. Plants grow about 2–3' tall, and in mid summer they produce the wonderful lime-green bells. If the flower stems get a little heavy, prop a Y-shaped branch underneath, so you can admire them. If you wish to take them in, they can be enjoyed for weeks as a fresh cut stem, or you can hang them upside down in a dry airy place, after which they can be viewed for years. Seed packages can be purchased; try a few—green flowers are always in. Full sun.

Mirabilis jalapa 'Tea Time Rose'

Moluccella laevis

Moluccella laevis, flower

Monopsis

I include this little-known genus for no other reason than to share it with you, and predict that it may become reasonably common in the next five years. It is a relative of lobelia and has many of the same characteristics. That is, plants are low-growing, look best falling out of containers, and prefer cool-summer climates to warm, humid ones.

Some selections of *Monopsis campanulata* have hit the American gardening market, but the choices are few. The foliage is variable and looks a little like common yarrow. I have been pleased with the coppery tones of 'Bronze Beauty' because the color is somewhat unique; however, the best performer has been 'Blue Papillo', with its many dark blue flowers. Plants appear to be better suited to containers than to the garden bed, at least in warm-summer climates, and will probably be more in demand in the North than in the South. They are not going to replace bacopa or lobelia, but they may find a place on the North American gardening stage. Full sun in the North, afternoon shade in the South.

Musa, Ensete

BANANA

Bananas . . . If you are reading this and are not thinking, "This guy is nuts!", then you are an open-minded gardener, and we can drink beer together. After that, you probably will think, "This guy is nuts!"—but at least not because of bananas. Most of the world's banana production depends on plants from the genus *Musa*, but some of the ornamental forms are from *Ensete*. It really doesn't matter: none will produce fruit outdoors, and they are both used in the same way.

Monopsis campanulata 'Bronze Beauty'

Monopsis campanulata 'Blue Papillo'

Musa acuminata

Ensete ventricosum 'Maurelii'

MORE ☞

It is amazing how many gardeners in the North, let alone the South, are incorporating bananas as an architectural feature in the landscape. They are relatively easy to find in catalogs and online, and the ornamental forms are quite beautiful. Forget the fruit, enjoy the foliage.

I am no connoisseur of bananas; I am only just learning of the great diversity that is available. Go to a tropical plant catalog or type in "ornamental banana" online, and you too will be amazed. In our garden in Athens, we stuck my favorite species, Sumatran banana, *Musa sumatrana* (aka zebra banana), right in the middle of the petunia trials. Looked great, although a little wind-rocked. Leaves of this species have wonderful purple markings and always look exotic. I was impressed with myself, but heck, turns out people figured bananas are no big deal. In southern Germany, not exactly the tropics, I loved the short squat form of the purple-leaved Abyssinian banana, *Ensete ventricosum* 'Maurelii', erupting out of some yellow creeping zinnia. Outstanding. And green-leaved bananas (*M. acuminata*) flanked a path at the famous Palmengarten in Frankfurt; protected from the wind, the leaves were relatively unscathed, and vigorous. But that was Europe, you say—how about this country?

In Washington, D.C., the hotspot of all things weird, I came across another lovely form of *Ensete ventricosum* growing out of 'Camilla' coleus. Since this was Washington, it did not seem out of place. It was only when I made a September visit to Olbrich Botanical Gardens, however, that I truly crossed into the Twilight Zone. There, in Madison, Wisconsin, was my old favorite, *Musa sumatrana*, along with Japanese banana, *M. basjoo*, magnificent in its wavy green leaves. This is said to be the hardiest of the bananas, perhaps overwintering to as low as zone 5 with protection.

Of course, the problem is no longer how to get them; in fact, many companies even sell seeds for the banana lover. The problem is what to do with these 6–10' things when winter arrives. If you have no place to overwinter them, consider them a fun but expensive summer

Musa basjoo

Ensete ventricosum with coleus

Musa sumatrana

toy. If you wish to overwinter them, plant them in containers; that way they will not grow excessively and they can be taken in, with effort, to the garage or greenhouse. Plants can be cut down after the first frost, but if you wish to keep the plant intact, you must have heat and light. A dark garage may work for cut-back tubers but not for ornamental bananas. Regardless, have fun. Full sun.

Mussaenda

This spectacular plant is actually a shrub, regularly growing 10–15' in its homeland in tropical Africa and the Philippines. Over 300 species have been identified, but outside of south Florida and perhaps some of the Gulf States, a mussaenda in a North American garden is a rare sight indeed. And for good reason: availability is almost nonexistent, plants are woody and need some heat to mature, and while they are really neat and interesting the first year, they are at their best only after a few years and therefore overwintering must be accomplished somewhere for best success. Perhaps we will see more of these fascinating plants in botanical gardens and public gardens in the future, and slowly they may seep down to hard-core gardeners around the country.

I planted white mussaenda (*Mussaenda incana*) many years ago, with no idea of what to expect. At first I was intrigued with the small yellow flowers and then really beguiled by the large expanded bract-like white sepal. A single sepal on each flower was three to four times larger than the others, and as the plants matured, they seemed to be covered with fluttering white wings (I was definitely beguiled). Plants grew only about 2' tall, but that just made them easier to bring in for the winter.

MORE ☞

243

Mussaenda incana

Mussaenda incana, flowers

Mussaenda frondosa

Mussaenda frondosa, flowers

Three or four years later I finally came across another mussaenda, this time at the Ripley Garden in Washington, D.C. Although it had similar white sepals, the flowers were red, and it was even more beautiful than the one I was growing back in Athens. I saw the same species a year later at Landcraft Environments on Long Island. The botanical names are not particularly well documented for this genus, but it was likely red mussaenda, *Mussaenda frondosa*. Both

places had been growing the plants for a number of years and obviously had brought them in for the winter. They are easy to grow; there is no reason why they can't be grown in Minnesota or Calgary. It is just a matter of finding a source to get started. Plant in containers, full sun.

Nelumbo nucifera

SACRED LOTUS

Plants have been cultivated for over 5000 years, and is it not special to have such a

valued piece of history in our gardens? In the world of water gardens, the sacred lotus (*Nelumbo nucifera*) is probably king, sharing its kingdom with water lilies and a few ugly carp. It seems every sunny water garden has all three, but lotus dwarfs the others in beautiful leaves, classical flowers, and useful fruit. Not to mention size—this is not a plant for the small backyard barrel.

From the Chicago Botanic Garden to the Zurich Botanical Gardens, lotus are at home. The large rounded leaves and the beautiful white to pink-flushed flow-

Nelumbo nucifera, Chicago Botanic Garden

Nelumbo nucifera, fruit

Nelumbo nucifera, Zurich Botanical Gardens

Nelumbo nucifera 'Chawan Basu'

ers lend a calmness to any garden vista. And once the flowers are finished, the large fruit capsules dominate the scene, each one containing a dozen or so rock-hard seeds. Over time, the seeds are dispersed, and the capsule turns bronze and starts to shrivel. The immature capsules with the seeds can often be found at farmers' markets or craft stores, sold as dry flowers for the vestibule washstand.

Lotus has not been around for fifty centuries without some selection, natural or otherwise, taking place. Hundreds of cultivars have been named and are quite easy to find. Many are truly outstanding. I have enjoyed only a few, but they include those with changeable flower colors, often starting yellow ('Mrs. Perry D. Slocum'), double red flowers ('Momo Botan'), and white flowers edged in pink ('Chawan Basu'). It really does not matter if cultivars or the species itself resides in the pond—sacred lotus is the perfect addition to the water garden.

Plants will overwinter as long as the water does not freeze around the roots, and that depends on the depth of the water. Just let them stay where you have them if your pond won't freeze to the bottom; if you house them elsewhere, be sure they stay immersed in water and don't keep them so warm that they think it is spring. If you see some leaf dieback, cut them off close to the tuber, then leave the plant alone. Full sun.

Nelumbo nucifera 'Momo Botan'

Nelumbo nucifera 'Mrs. Perry D. Slocum'

246 *Nemesia strumosa*

I must admit, I never really had a lot of use for the nemesias I saw in retail centers or in neighborhood gardens. They were all a little washed out, rather leggy and did not show up particularly well. The flowers are relatively small, but to be fair, when plants are at their best, they produce dozens and dozens of them.

The new selections in the past few years have gone a long way to changing my opinion about *Nemesia strumosa*, and I can recommend a number of them to gardeners in the Midwest, northern states, and to most Canadian gardeners. They do far better during cool-weather times and may struggle when temperatures are hot and humid. The longer the hot, humid weather persists, the more they struggle. Even so, those I would recommend are a great deal better than most of what was out there ten years ago.

One of the older forms but still lovely is the bicolored 'Woodstock', with flowers of purple and yellow. Plants stay nicely upright, and flowering continues for many months. The best of the pinks is 'Shell Pink', growing about 15" tall and absolutely covered with light pink flowers. If I was to select a white for my daughters' gardens, I would tell them to look for 'Compact Innocence', which we have watched flower most of the season even in Georgia. 'Aromatica Lavender' is equally good and even overwinters in zone 7. A number of other selections have been bred and with a little search-

Nemesia strumosa 'Woodstock'

Nemesia strumosa 'Shell Pink'

Nemesia strumosa 'Compact Innocence'

Nemesia strumosa 'Aromatica Lavender'

ing, they are well worth trying. 'KLM' is a beautiful bicolor, from Dutch breeding, of course, and seems to cover itself with small gray-blue and white flowers. And for large flowers that look more like primroses than nemesias, I recently discovered Sundrops series, from an excellent American firm. I have not seen them outdoors, so cannot comment on their garden performance, but they sure catch the eye while in pots.

Full sun in the North, afternoon shade in the South.

Nemophila

Plants are native to California, and prefer moist soils and cool nights. They are not well known on the eastern side of the country, and even less known in the southern portion of that half. However, they make wonderful groundcover plants as one progresses north. Plants tend to flower heaviest in spring, and taper off significantly if conditions deteriorate. They are useful for naturalizing large areas, as they come back read-

ily from seed. They are fanciful little plants, as can be seen by their fanciful common names.

Baby-blue-eyes may be the nickname of your favorite friend or pet, but it also refers to the magnificent blue flowers of *Nemophila menziesii*. The flowers usually have a clean white center, which makes the outer blue of the flower even more spectacular. In some cases everything gets turned around; the center becomes purple and the outer edges are white, as is the case with 'Pennie Black'.

Nemesia strumosa 'KLM'

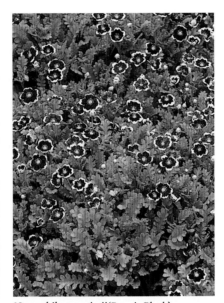

Nemophila menziesii 'Pennie Black'

Nemophila maculata

Nemesia strumosa Sundrops series

Nemophila menziesii

MORE ☞

Nicotiana

TOBACCO

Five spot refers to the five dark spots on the end of the petals of *Nemophila maculata.* The plants stand only about 12" tall and are a little leggy, but they can be covered with white flowers throughout the spring and into the summer if weather is not too hot and soils don't become too dry. Full sun if moisture is consistently available, partial shade if not.

I get a little upset whenever I read that global warming and air pollution are the result of "greenhouse gases." Even though it sounds unbelievable, many people out there now look at greenhouses suspiciously and feel they must be partly to blame for some of these problems. It would be laughable if not so ignorant. The same argument can be heard from anti-smoking zealots who want to plow under all tobacco plants, as if the plant itself was making them cough. Fortunately for us all, many plants in the tobacco family are terrific ornamentals. So if you find yourself in the same room with the anti-smoking and the anti-gas people, it may be wise not to mention that your favorite flowering tobacco plant was raised in a greenhouse.

At least three species of tobacco make great garden plants. One of them, *Nicotiana sylvestris,* looks ostensibly like a "real" Virginia Slim tobacco plant. But it

Nemophila maculata, flowers

Nicotiana sylvestris with pennisetum

Nicotiana sylvestris

is not, and would not smoke well. It is a large plant, and when it is growing vigorously, the wavy leaves look like big green paddles. Plants can stand alone or can be the main feature in a mixed bed of purple-leaved lobelias and pink impatiens. In Chicago, plants were growing in a small fenced corner, appearing to ward away the evil spirits of the pennisetum grass. The flowers are quite beautiful, seemingly exploding from the top of the plant, perhaps accounting for its common name, white shooting stars. However, all is not Camelot in the tobacco plot; if aphids are within a mile of the plant, they will find it. As long as you know this will happen, it is a nonproblem. When you see them, wash

Nicotiana sylvestris with aphids

Nicotiana langsdorffii

Nicotiana ×sanderae with conifers

Nicotiana sylvestris with lobelia and begonias

MORE ☞

them away with a garden hose. You can douse with chemicals if that is your thing, but that is seldom necessary if you inspect your plants every now and then.

The plant that all people seem to enjoy but often do not recognize as a tobacco is the lime tobacco, *Nicotiana langsdorffii.* In most plantings, the flowers are almost hazy, not really standing out from the surroundings. Maybe this is why it is so seldom used in mixed plantings. But where

plants are grown well, and when the dark green leaves contrast with the lime-green flowers, they are impossible to ignore. Lime tobacco has to be grown for a while to be appreciated; it is not going to be an impulse item at the corner garden store.

By far the most common plant in the

Nicotiana alata

Nicotiana ×sanderae 'Nikki Red'

Nicotiana ×sanderae 'Prelude Salmon'

Nicotiana ×sanderae 'Perfuma Lime'

ornamental tobacco family is the bedding form, the hybrid flowering tobacco, *Nicotiana ×sanderae*. They are unbelievably beautiful, and much of their beauty come from one of the main parents in the breeding, the winged tobacco, *N. alata*. Seldom seen for sale in containers anymore, winged tobacco is still available from seed. The plants are 3–4' tall, with numerous flowers of different colors, often red, and highly fragrant. In June Collin's garden in Portland, Oregon, the plant was reaching for the sky and perfuming all around it. Asked what she did to make it look so wonderful, she commented, "That old weed, I just threw it in there for the smell." Oh, to garden in Portland.

The hybrids are gorgeous, far shorter, and easier to grow. The color range is outstanding, but unfortunately, breeding for dwarfness resulted in the loss of fragrance. Such a shame, for now only the eyes can enjoy the planting. Oftentimes, plants won't even be labeled but can be seen from a football field away, flowering away in and among junipers and other plants in the garden. So many fascinating colors are available as well. A planting of Nikki Mix shows off many of the colors in the hybrids, and who

would have thought to put a specimen of 'Nikki Red' in a container on the step going up to the house? Salmon colors have been quite popular as well. The light salmon color of 'Prelude Salmon' is quite wonderful, whereas 'Avalon Salmon' provides a darker color and holds up even in hot summer temperatures.

But for me, there are two plantings I recall the most. One was when someone was complaining that they had to have the lime-green color found in lime tobacco but couldn't find that plant anywhere. I showed her the brilliant lime-green color of 'Perfuma Lime', and voilá, a perfect substitute was made. The other perfect use was at a perfect place, Banff, Alberta, where the cool mountain air made everything perfect. A simple container planting of lobelia and rudbeckia, topped with white flowering tobacco, was as wonderful as the scenery surrounding it. Who says simplicity is not the best thing? Full sun.

Nicotiana ×sanderae Nikki Mix

Nicotiana ×sanderae 'Avalon Salmon'

Nicotiana ×sanderae, white form, Banff

Nierembergia

CUPFLOWER

The cupflowers belong to the same family as petunia (Solanaceae) and have similar wide open flowers and spreading habit. Plants are much stringier and more woody than petunias, and a bit more temperamental. They can be used as edging, but well-drained soils, such as a rocky area, a raised bed, or a container, are necessary for best performance, particularly in southern climes.

All cupflowers are cold hardy to about zone 7 or 8, but most people treat them as annuals. The most cold hardy is probably whitecap, *Nierembergia repens*, often sold under the name *N. rivularis*. The flowers are large relative to the plant and can be used to line a driveway or just to provide some beautiful shiny white flowers. Not terribly common, but once established, they will reseed if they find an area to their liking.

I seldom see one of my favorites, tall cupflower, *Nierembergia scoparia*. I came across this plant many years ago,

and noticed that, unlike the more compact forms, this one liked to spread out more and grow a little taller. I also noticed that while some plants looked spectacular, too many others struggled. Inconsistent performance seems to be common, at least to my eyes, for many members of the genus. However, in areas where they have a little time to grow and overwinter, their second-year show is out of this world, with white flowers often blushed with lavender. If nierembergias do well in your area, this is a must-try plant.

Nierembergia repens

Nierembergia scoparia, flowers

Nierembergia scoparia

Nierembergia frutescens 'Purple Robe' with lotus and geraniums

The most common forms are two species that are inconsistently labeled and probably all mixed up. Both *Nierembergia frutescens* and *N. hippomanica* are called cupflower and are similar in appearance. The latter is less woody than the former and has shorter leaves and larger flowers. Both perform about the same and require similar conditions to do well, so it is not really all that important to know which one you are purchasing. 'Purple Robe' is the most common cultivar, and I have enjoyed it in a mixed container or by itself in a hanging basket. The deep color of a meandering planting of 'Purple Robe' was united with brightly colored florist hydrangeas in the conservatory at Longwood Gardens. A beautiful combination.

Plants sold as *Nierembergia hippomanica* var. *violacea* were perfect in the wonderful Old Westbury Gardens on Long Island, New York; this variety has some of the prettiest and largest flowers in the group. I most enjoy the white-flowered forms, such as 'White Star' or the even-better 'Mount Blanc'. Both have large clean white flowers and grow well if provided with well-drained conditions. If they overwinter, they will be some of the best and biggest plants in the spring garden, providing color to complement the pansies and violas. Full sun.

Nierembergia frutescens 'Purple Robe', basket

Nierembergia frutescens 'Purple Robe' with hydrangeas

Nierembergia hippomanica var. *violacea*

Nierembergia hippomanica 'Mount Blanc'

MORE ☞

Nierembergia hippomanica 'White Star'

Nierembergia hippomanica 'Mount Blanc', overwintered in Athens, Georgia

Nigella damascena, field for cut fruit

Nigella damascena, garden with fruit

Nigella

LOVE-IN-A-MIST

Between puffs and mists—loving must have enjoyed fascinating venues back when these names were first penned. When I look at love-in-a-mist (*Nigella damascena*), I see a nice blue-flowered plant with lacy leaves and interesting fruit, but I don't see love or the mist. Plant people will never be accused of being unimaginative.

This annual has been used for years as a simple and rather ordinary addition to

the garden. However, if you examine a flower, you will find the structure is anything but ordinary. At the base of the flowers can be seen the long thin leafy structures (involucres) that supposedly account for the "mist," and with the pistil and stamens sticking up above a full skirt of sepals and petals, the flower looks like it is growing upside down. Seed is often available in packages at the local garden store; a mixture of white and blue flowers may result, with the white flowers generally having only a single row of petals.

The most common form is 'Miss Jekyll', named after the famed English gardener and writer, with full lavender to blue flowers above fennel-like foliage. A number of good double white forms are available; 'Albion' is as good as any. If all that nigella did was produce flowers, that would be quite sufficient, but the fruit is as interesting as the blooms. Each flower gives rise to a strange pod that stands above the foliage in mid to late summer. They start green and essentially dry on the plant, turning to a dull bronze. If the summer

Nigella damascena 'Albion'

Nigella damascena, mix with single white flowers

Nigella damascena 'Miss Jekyll'

Nigella damascena, flower

Nigella hispanica 'Exotic'

Nigella hispanica, fruit

MORE ☞

is dry and not too hot, they stay quite ornamental for a long time. They are harvested by cut flower growers who sell them at farmers' markets and to wholesalers for dried arrangements for the home.

Certainly, common love-in-a-mist is the most popular form of nigella; however, some people like to try a few of the other oddballs. Fennel flower, *Nigella hispanica*, commonly available in the selection 'Exotic', is also handsome but

lacks the involucres and has single flowers only. But the finger-like appendages on the fruit make them even more bizarre than those of the common form. What better excuse to try some? Full sun.

Odontonema strictum

FIRESPIKE

This is not a plant for every gardener, especially impatient ones. In fact, I

would hazard that this is a plant only for those fortunate few with long autumns and calm dispositions. Firespike (*Odontonema strictum*) is cold hardy to about zone 7b, but a hard winter will take it out. Because it is a slow grower in the spring, it is best to buy started plants, even if you live in a moderately mild climate. For people in the Gulf States and those with hot, long summers, this is a no-brainer.

The glossy deep green leaves are outstanding, and for some people that is reason enough to have it in the garden. But most of us would like a flower or two as well, and therein lies the problem for the impatient gardener. Plants don't begin to flower until October, even in the South, and if snow is already falling, this plant is not for you. But when it flowers, the spikes truly are on fire, and if the plant is happy, half a dozen spikes may be flaming at once. A great plant to reverse the summer blahs and to rejuvenate the fall garden. A variegated form, 'Variegata', is also available; although the leaves are interesting, flowering is very sparse. Full sun.

Odontonema strictum, flowers

Odontonema strictum 'Variegata'

Odontonema strictum

Orthosiphon stamineus

CAT'S WHISKERS

I have never been much of a fan of cats, and at the risk of losing readers, I must admit I just don't get it. Independence is a great thing, but give me a tail-wagging, tongue-drooling, can't-wait-to-greet-me yellow lab any day. So when a cat-loving gardener introduced me to a plant called cat's whiskers (*Orthosiphon stamineus*), I wasn't as enthusiastic as I might have been. However, the plant is not half bad, and the name is indeed descriptive.

Cat's whiskers are whiskered, that is for sure, and the whiskers are the result of the long stamens protruding from the individual lavender flowers. The most

Orthosiphon stamineus

Orthosiphon stamineus 'Albus'

Orthosiphon stamineus 'Albus', flowers

common color, however, appears to be white, 'Albus', which is more floriferous than the lavender and contrasts better with the light green leaves. The opening flower spike is a beautiful study in plant function, the bottom flowers opening first, while the others patiently await their turn.

But two problems, other than the name, keep me from embracing this plant. Normally, only a few flowers appear at any one time, and the leaves always appear to be washed out and in need of fertilizer. When many flowers do open at once, however, they make a dramatic sight. Full sun.

Osteospermum

CAPE DAISY

Cape daisies, one of the many daisy flowers native to Cape province of South Africa, have been domesticated, bred, and morphed into an incredible number of colors and shapes. In their native setting, they receive cool weather in the winter and flower in the spring, then essentially are leafy plants during the hot summer. The same is true for the majority of the cultivars we see for sale in the spring on this continent: they flower profusely in the spring, then

Osteospermum, variegated form

MORE ☞

become little shrublets through most of the summer. That is not to say they are not beautiful or worthy of inclusion in the garden, it simply means that they are spring flowerers, and for most of us, they will provide very little color during the summer. The same can be said for *Argyranthemum* (which see). The many species may occasionally be found in botanic gardens, but gardeners have little choice except for the hybrids.

But are they beautiful! A planting at the Paul Ecke Ranch in Encinitas, California, is an incredible sight and makes you want to buy every one of them. Bred in Australia, Germany, and Scandi-navia, they are quite remarkable. A few variegated forms can be found, but they have a ways to go. Others cultivars, however, are striking. The whirligig pattern in the flowers of 'Nisinga Cream' is unique; the open daisy flowers of 'Seaside' and 'Brightside' provide a much calmer look. In western Washington state, the creamy flowers of 'Lubutu'

Osteospermum 'Nasinga Cream'

Osteospermum 'Seaside'

Osteospermum, California trials

Osteospermum 'Lubutu'

Osteospermum Passion Mix

Osteospermum 'Brightside'

Osteospermum 'White Flash' with bidens

Osteospermum 'Sparkler'

Osteospermum 'Lemon Symphony'

were also outstanding. In southern Germany, osteos are everywhere, and cultivars like 'White Flash' are routinely combined with other annuals like bidens. It might seem clear that most of the places where these blow-me-away plants are prettiest are areas where day and night temperatures hover between 50 and 75°F during the summer. However, those areas are simply where the plants will flower the longest; they can be attractive anywhere. At Longwood Gardens, a planting of 'Sparkler' looked lovely in May, and even at the Park Seed Company in warm South Carolina, the seed-propagated Passion Mix was outstanding in the spring. In our trials in Georgia, numerous cultivars have looked good in spring, such as the yellow 'Lemon Symphony', but flowering finished by early June.

Therefore, everyone can enjoy osteos, it is simply the expectations that disappoint some gardeners. Most of us will enjoy them in the spring; a few in the North, the mountains, or the West Coast can have them longer, perhaps even flowering through the summer.

The cultivars I have mentioned are but a small sampling of what is presently offered. There is far too much beauty not to try a few of them; buy them in flower and as large as the budget will allow. The foliage is quite handsome and at worse, you will end up with some nice little shrubs. Place them in well-drained areas of the garden or in large containers. Full sun.

Otacanthus caeruleus

BRAZILIAN SNAPDRAGON

If you can't get enough blue in the garden, Brazilian snapdragon (*Otacanthus caeruleus*) may be a plant worth considering. The leaves are clean, seldom attracting insects or diseases, and they grow reasonably vigorously, neither taking over the garden nor getting buried by a neighbor.

The lavender-blue flowers have a white eye, and three or four flowers are whorled around the end of the stem. Unfortunately, they don't begin to flower well until mid to late summer but, once in bloom, remain colorful for months.

They are excellent for cutting as well and will persist in the vase for a week to ten days. Full sun.

Papaver

POPPY

The annual forms of this popular genus are not nearly as common in the garden as the perennial Oriental poppy, but at least one of them, the Flanders poppy, is at least as well known. Most of the poppies are short-lived perennials or biennials, and they self-sow so readily that it is sometimes difficult to characterize their growth cycle. For example, the Iceland poppy is perennial in northern climates, but an annual or biennial in most other areas of the country. All of these, however, are marvelous garden plants and provide stunning color.

I can never look at a Flanders poppy, *Papaver rhoeas*, in a field or garden without thinking of the destruction of life and the ability of one poem to capture the carnage, futility, and sacrifices of war. As a result of John McCrae's poem, the poppy became the visible means for nations to remember the

Otacanthus caeruleus

Otacanthus caeruleus, flowers

Papaver rhoeas, roadside

Papaver rhoeas Shirley series

Papaver rhoeas, field, Belgium

Papaver somniferum, flower

Papaver somniferum, single and double flowers

Papaver somniferum 'Paeoniflorum'

MORE ☞

Papaver somniferum 'Double Pink'

Papaver somniferum 'Single Puce'

Papaver somniferum 'Fringed Red'

Papaver somniferum 'Album'

Papaver somniferum, fruit

Papaver nudicaule with pansies

price of freedom. Fortunately, the flowers we use for roadside plantings and in the garden are too beautiful for such sobering thoughts to linger in our minds, and now we can simply enjoy their fleeting color. The choices for color are few, however, with the exception of the poppies in the Shirley series. Most of the time, seeds will yield plants with flowers of intense red or scarlet. Plant a lot of seeds, and if you are lucky, the planting may bring to mind the field of poppies in Belgium that so inspired the young Canadian physician and poet.

Just as the Flanders poppy evokes stories in my head, I can't help but imagine Toto sleeping in the field of flowers whenever I see the beautiful opium poppy, *Papaver somniferum*. I much prefer to think of the girl and her dog than of the despair and misery that have

Papaver nudicaule, Palmerston North, New Zealand

Papaver nudicaule 'Champagne Bubbles'

Papaver nudicaule, Chicago Botanic Garden

MORE ☞

Papaver nudicaule 'Party Fun'

Papaver nudicaule Wonderland series

Papaver nudicaule Constance Finnis Group

Papaver nudicaule, double form

resulted from abuse of its by-products. And as with the Flanders poppy, the deep scarlet flowers are too beautiful not to enjoy: planting some seeds in the fall results in some beautiful forms and colors the next spring. The main forms of opium poppy are the single and doubles, which often grow side by side. The double form, called 'Paeoniflorum' for obvious reasons, is quite spectacular. But spectacular is not the only color in this great plant; a mix of seed may yield single puce and double pink and white flowers, a calming influence on the riot of scarlet. If outrageous is your shtick and for sheer immodesty, try a few plants of 'Fringed Red'; people may think you have been sampling the juice. The fruit capsule, which has been the root of so much misery, is also quite beautiful and is cut for dried arrangements in the house. Break open the capsule and gather the seeds for next year's show.

Papaver nudicaule, the Iceland poppy, evokes images of flowers rising from melting ice packs, but in truth, as a garden plant, it is seldom used as a perennial. It has gained popularity in many regions because of its tendency to flower in the early spring and is often seen in the company of pansies and nasturtiums. Plants can stay in the ground until night temperatures begin to remain in the 70s. There is no hard and fast rule; simply remove them when they look tired, or when you want the space for something else. I have seen wonderful plantings at the State Botanical Garden of Georgia in which the Iceland poppies were interspersed with blue and white pansies, and in Chicago, a mixed panorama greeted walkers in the botanic garden there. One thinks of exotic plants when one thinks of New Zealand, but a mixture of white and yellow Iceland poppies in July provided a magnificent vista at the Victoria Esplanade in Palmerston North. A vista may be a marvelous sight from a distance, but the flowers of Iceland poppies should be appreciated up

close; they are quite marvelous. Numerous cultivars have been bred, like 'Champagne Bubbles', 'Party Fun', and those in the Wonderland series. There are few differences between them, and all should do just fine. Occasionally, a single color may be available, as in the white poppies of the Constance Finnis Group, seen in England; and if you are a glutton for punishment, give the double forms a try. They are gruesome, the breeder should be imprisoned, but to each their own. Full sun, cool temperatures.

Passiflora

PASSION FLOWER

Passion flower vines and passion fruit were not even in my Canadian vocabulary as a boy growing up in Montreal. Much later, when I moved to the States, people would talk about what they called maypops as an obnoxious weed; I thought they were beautiful. I saw more passion flower vines in botanic gardens and conservatories, but they never seemed to get outside. In the last few years, however, I have admired the

Passiflora citrina

Passiflora coccinea

Passiflora violacea

MORE ☞

Passiflora serratifolia

Passiflora caerulea

Passiflora 'Sunburst'

Passiflora 'Amethyst'

Passiflora 'Little Orchid'

Passiflora 'Debbie'

yellow flowers of *Passiflora citrina* and the blue blossoms of *P. caerulea* in European gardens, and in this country, I reveled in a gorgeous planting of *P. violacea* at the Ripley Garden in Washington, D.C. Plantings are popping up further north as well, and other than the cost, there is no reason not to include them on an arbor or trellis.

Some of our better mail-order nurseries offer a wonderful variety of passion flower vines, including both species and named hybrids. The species are numerous, and easiest to think of by color; for example, the red flowers are brilliant in *Passiflora coccinea*. Marvelous small yellow flowers can be found on the hybrid 'Sunburst', hidden in the white-veined leaves. While multiple colors are the norm on passion flowers, blue and lavender is the most common combination. 'Amethyst' has beautiful blue flowers, while 'Little Orchid' provides some of the prettiest shades of orchid on any of the vines. Much of the beauty of passion flowers is due to the slender filament-like structure called the corona. They are particularly obvious in 'Debbie' and appear to be doubled in the flowers of *P. serratifolia*. All are wonderful; some flower more persistently than others, but all will transform your old trellis into something quite spectacular.

If placed in pots, plants can be cut back and brought into a heated garage to overwinter, or cuttings may be taken in the fall. Full sun.

Pavonia

Pavonias are known around the world, but American gardeners have not yet discovered them. Plants belong to the mallow family, the same as hibiscus, flowering maple, and cotton, and few members of that family do not have ornamental value.

The only species I can recommend is Brazilian firecracker, *Pavonia multiflora*, mainly because that is the only one most of us will have any chance of obtaining. Selection is under way, and this plant should be much more available to gardeners in a few years' time. Plants send up straight stems with leathery green leaves, and the unique blossoms are blood red. The weird flowers consist of thin bracts and red petals, which surround multicolored stamens protruding from within. Another weird thing is the alternative botanical name this plant sometimes goes under, *Triplochlamys*. Arguments have been made for both generic names, but until the dust settles, I vote to use the one I can pronounce.

Plants have been grown in conservatories and in tropical areas for years, and gardeners might want to try one or two in the patio container. Full sun.

Pelargonium

GERANIUM

The interest in geraniums rises and falls from one generation to the next, but they are always among the top five in annual sales of all flowers in North America. To the uninitiated, there does not seem to be all that much variety in geraniums; most of them are red, with a few whites and pinks thrown in every now and then. But, from my perspective, seeing what breeders have introduced to the greenhouse trade, there must be over three hundred different cultivars available, albeit many quite similar to each other. I have been studying, evaluating, and appreciating the beauty of geraniums for years. We had baskets by the front stairs in Guelph, Ontario, when my daughter Laura was six years old, and recently I trialed over 120 cultivars at the University of Georgia. Of those 120 geranium cultivars of all colors, probably no more than half a dozen existed more than three years ago. A lot of plants have

MORE ☞

Pavonia multiflora

Pavonia multiflora, flowers

Pelargonium ×hortorum, Guelph, Ontario

Pelargonium ×hortorum, UGA Trial Gardens

Pelargonium ×hortorum with verbena and pocketbook plant

gone under the bridge in the past twenty-five years, but not geraniums—they are as beloved as ever. Except perhaps by the people who have to maintain them. The constant deadheading is a long and tedious job. Still, it does not seem to matter what other flowers are on the market: landscapers and gardeners always want good old geraniums, and usually good old red geraniums.

In the garden, geraniums fall into two main categories, zonal geraniums (*Pelargonium ×hortorum*), by far the most common, and ivy-leaf geraniums (*P. peltatum*), always grown in hanging baskets. Martha Washington geraniums (*P. domesticum*) are only now starting to be seen again in garden containers, and few at that. Numerous other species geraniums, such as fancy-leaf forms and scented geraniums, can be found, but few of these find their way into outdoor gardens in this country.

I think most everybody knows what geraniums look like, so I will simply share a few creative settings and handsome cultivars. Red geraniums seem to make everything better, and mixed beds are the perfect setting for these colorful plants. The most beautiful use was at the

Pelargonium ×hortorum in a window box with bidens and Cape daisies

Pelargonium ×hortorum in a window box

Pelargonium ×hortorum with verbena and marigolds

Pelargonium ×hortorum with heliotrope

MORE ☞

Butchart Gardens in British Columbia, where the combination of red geraniums, lavender verbena, and pocketbook plant was the illustrated definition of awesome. Then I saw them combined with the same verbena but highlighted with yellow marigolds. The lowly marigold had never been in such exquisite company. And the bed of red geranium and 'Marine' heliotrope looked so good that I had to wait for about twenty minutes to take the picture because admiring people kept getting in the way!

Plantings don't have to be so grandiose or large to provide pleasure. Window boxes have always been an ideal setting for geraniums; a mixed box of light yellow Cape daisies, purple petunias, yellow bidens, and red geraniums made a wonderful scene in a mountain village. On paper, a mixed planting of rose and red geraniums sounds rather gruesome, but it sure worked for me.

Geraniums come in all Kodak hues, but approximately 80 percent of those sold are red; the next most popular color is pink. Heliotrope looks almost as good combined with pink geraniums as it did with red, and white alyssum has always been a good edging plant, helping to render the pink flowers even pinker. The next most sought-after color is white. In a combination setting or filling in an area between clipped yew hedges, white ('Pinto White') will always be popular. The zonal geraniums have it all, and it would be remiss of me not to add that orange, lavender, rose, salmon, and bicolor flowers can also be purchased. And just when I thought I had seen it all, I looked behind a solemn green bench, and there was a magnificent planting of 'Wilhelm Languth', arguably the best variegated geranium on the market. There is no doubt that zonal geranium performance is significantly enhanced in areas with cool nights.

In our trials in Athens, Georgia, we

Pelargonium ×*hortorum* with heliotrope

Pelargonium ×*hortorum* with sweet alyssum

Pelargonium ×*hortorum* 'Pinto White'

find that geraniums are one of the most time-consuming plants to maintain: spent flowers must be removed (deadheaded) or plants stop blooming and become susceptible to numerous fungal diseases, requiring constant attention. Maintenance is still a chore in the North, but not as much so. They are at their best in the North, Far West (where they are often perennial), and at higher elevations.

The ivy-leaf geranium is also highly popular and becoming even more so, for good reasons. The performance of the new cultivars is outstanding throughout the country. The preference for hanging baskets mirrors the trends to containers and smaller gardens, and many fine colors are now available to gardeners. They have handsome foliage and even when not in full flower, as in a container positioned on the stairs at Old Westbury Gardens on Long Island, the plants still looked good. Red is the dominant color in the ivies, and it was pretty difficult to argue with the large basket at the Montreal Botanical Garden. A basket of salmon-pink in Sydney, Australia, also looked magnificent, but we had only to step outside the door here at the University of Georgia to admire a mixed basket of rose and red ivies. Our baskets impressed and stopped people all summer, demonstrating another reason for the popularity of this group of geraniums: they tolerate heat and humidity better and deadheading is much less of an issue.

I am starting to see a few more Martha Washington geraniums, mostly in containers, in North American gardens. They still have problems with heat tolerance, so they are always going to be more popular in cooler areas. They can be grown in warm temperate areas, but

Pelargonium ×hortorum 'Wilhelm Languth'

Pelargonium peltatum, Old Westbury Gardens

Pelargonium peltatum, Montreal Botanical Garden

Pelargonium peltatum, Sydney

MORE ☞

Pelargonium domesticum 'My Choice'

Pelargonium domesticum 'Carnival'

Pelargonium peltatum, UGA Trial Gardens

Pelargonium domesticum 'Hollywood Lady'

much like osteospermums, they will seldom flower once night temperatures rise above 75°F. However, cultivars with flowers of red ('Carnival'), rose ('My Choice'), and white ('Hollywood Lady') might make any gardener with a little money decide to try a couple anyway. They are best in containers, they will do poorly in the ground.

All geraniums, except the Martha Washington types (partial shade), per-

form better in full sun; be careful of overwatering, particularly as temperatures rise.

Pennisetum

As a general rule, most ornamental grasses used by gardeners are perennial, and plants in this genus are no exception. However, at least three species

make excellent annuals, and they provide grasses that do go away, unlike some of the persistent, spreading perennial grasses out there.

The least common is feathertop, *Pennisetum villosum*, which is perennial in zone 7b and warmer, but for most of us, it is best used as an annual. It grows 2–3' tall and by late summer is topped with feathery plumes of flowers. They are excellent leaning over walkways or simply gently flowing with the wind. The foliage is handsome enough, but it is the flowers that gardeners enjoy.

For foliage, two excellent choices are available. The old-fashioned purple fountain grass, *Pennisetum setaceum* 'Rubrum', is used in containers which can be placed anywhere that purple color is needed, and the same plants, towering over begonias in Will Carlson's Michigan garden, showed that the flowers are as beautiful as the foliage.

Pennisetum villosum

Pennisetum setaceum 'Rubrum'

Pennisetum setaceum 'Rubrum' with pink begonias

Pennisetum glaucum 'Purple Majesty'

MORE ☞

Pennisetum glaucum 'Purple Majesty', stand

The nice thing about the grass is even when not in flower, it is a terrific plant.

The latest and perhaps the one that may be even more popular is ornamental millet, *Pennisetum glaucum.* No kidding, these are the seeds usually found in your birdfeeder mix, hardly something you would ponder in the plant center. We grew a beautiful purple-leaved, purple-flowered cultivar for years, even before it had a name, and so I can highly recommend 'Purple Majesty', the name it bears today. As the dominant feature in a container or as a dense planting, a wonderful show is assured. The flowers not only attract birds but also make fine persistent cut flowers. Some people find the malodorous aroma of the cut stems outweighs the vase life. Regardless, this is a must-have grass for the garden. All pennisetums perform best in full sun.

Pentas lanceolata 'Orchid Illusion'

Pentas lanceolata 'Nova', flowers

Pentas lanceolata

STAR FLOWER

Star flowers (*Pentas lanceolata*) have been sold as ornamental plants for many years, but it is only in the last decade or so that they have attracted gardeners around the country. That they are good flowerers is a given, but with more attention being paid to garden form, and better breeding material, they have simply caught on with more people. As well they should—excellent color choices are available, and once temperatures warm up, plants will flower the entire season.

For many years, pentas hung around garden centers and on the periphery of gardeners' thoughts, never really enjoying stellar popularity. The cultivars were pretty enough but did not display sufficient vigor or flower power. Selections like 'Orchid Illusion' and 'Pearl White' were difficult to locate and were disappointing in most areas of the country after a month or so in the garden. I had trialed a lot of star flowers, and the only one I considered worthy of being included in my daughters' gardens was

Pentas lanceolata Butterfly series

Pentas lanceolata 'Pearl White'

Pentas lanceolata 'Nova'

Pentas lanceolata 'New Look Pink'

Pentas lanceolata 'New Look Violet'

MORE ☞

'Nova', a vigorous grower with many rose-colored flowers on 2' tall plants. The individual stems carry exquisite flowers, which are useful as cuts for the house and patio.

But the late 1990s and early 2000s have seen the renaissance of pentas from a once-in-a-while plant to one that is in constant demand, particularly as summers seem to be warming up. The New Look series is a seed-propagated form with excellent flowering on dwarf 1½' tall plants. Its fine flower colors and good vigor (plants don't get too big, however) renewed interest in the plant. 'New Look Pink' and 'New Look Violet' are among the many colors available in the series. The vegetatively propagated Butterfly series came on the heels of New Look and provided bigger, even more vigorous plants with flowers in numerous colors. We found they all flowered well, but 'Butterfly Pink' and 'Butterfly Red' were even better than the others. Hot temperatures won't reduce their flowering or vigor, but under such conditions, they may need a haircut in mid summer. The most eye-catching of all the star flowers is 'Stars and Stripes', the first available variegated leaf form, which has spurred interest even further. Both the variegation and the flowers remain all season. And another wonderful characteristic: almost every publication about butterfly or hummingbird gardens suggests pentas as an attractant. Need I say more? Go get some and get dirty. Full sun.

Perilla frutescens

There is very little reason for including perilla (*Perilla frutescens*) as a garden annual; for many gardeners, it is nothing more than a green weed that reseeds everywhere. However, the purple-leaved form (var. *atropurpurea*) has benefitted from the interest in plants with purple foliage and is fairly common and easy to find. Its reseeding tendencies, its ease of growth, and the contrast it provides to green-leaved plants are a few good reasons to include it. Similar plants, like purple basil, seem to taste better, and purple coleus seems to perform better, but what do I know? A number of cultivars are available, including 'Nanking',

Pentas lanceolata 'Stars and Stripes'

Pentas lanceolata 'Butterfly Red', *P. l.* 'Butterfly Pink'

Perilla frutescens 'Nanking'

which goes well with white salvias and other light-colored plantings. But be careful: plants reseed with great abandon, and you may be inundated with little purple things for many years. Full sun.

Petunia

It is a toss-up to determine which bedding annual takes the most verbal abuse in gardening, the marigold or the petunia. There are always lots of garden snobs who would rather eat horse dung than actually have a petunia in their garden. However, every endeavor has its snobs, who need be given no more thought than one would extend to a balloon expelling gas.

Without doubt, petunias are one of the all-time great success stories in horticulture. In the 1980s, petunias were the number one seller in American horticulture, but as other plants became available they lost popularity, mostly because breeders rested on their laurels a little too long. That is not to say that older cultivars were not good; in fact,

many have been tweaked here and there and still are sold today. However, dozens more have been bred in the last ten years, revitalizing interest in this fine genus. At the UGA Trial Gardens, I am sure I have seen every one, row after row, after row, after row. I mean every last one of them! Of course, the interest by breeders simply reflects the interest of gardeners. While they have always been popular in gardens, today they are also poked and prodded into every available nook and cranny in containers across this country.

Perilla frutescens var. *atropurpurea*

Petunia 'Primetime Rose'

Petunia hybrids, UGA Trial Gardens

Petunia 'Surfina Rose Veined'

MORE ☞

Flower size differs from cultivar to cultivar; the large flowers, such as found in the Primetime series, are still common but not nearly as popular as they once were. The Surfinia series has been highly popular because of its better performance, cascading habit, and striking colors. 'Surfinia Rose Veined' is one of the brighter colors in the series; 'Surfinia White' is a clean white. Smaller-flowering forms have truly been the rage in recent years, because they are more weather-tolerant; when it rains, for example, flowers rebound more quickly. 'Supertunia Blushing Princess' provides handsome pastels. 'Carpet White' is part of the low-growing Carpet series, and the Fantasy series, such as 'Fantasy Ivory', has always been one of the best low-growing forms in our trials in Athens. However, even more compact forms, sometimes called petitunias or pocket petunias, are hitting the marketplace. Members of the Suncatcher series, such as 'Suncatcher Pink Vein', will be excellent additions to the garden, and 'Happy Dreams' and 'Bright Dreams' are outstanding and more in demand every year. It seems that of all the traditional bedding plant genera, petunias have held their place in the marketplace by constant renewal of cultivars that better reflect our need for good performance, not bigger flowers.

I suppose that it is impossible to suggest that one petunia is more important than another, but one series has nearly become a household name. The Wave series started with 'Purple Wave', which combined beautifully with everything,

Petunia hybrids, container

Petunia 'Surfina White'

Petunia 'Supertunia Blushing Princess'

Petunia 'Carpet White'

Petunia 'Fantasy Ivory'

Petunia 'Suncatcher Pink Vein'

Petunia 'Happy Dreams'

Petunia 'Bright Dreams'

Petunia 'Purple Wave' with coleus and sweet potato

Petunia 'Misty Lilac Wave'

Petunia 'Pink Wave'

MORE ☞

even plants like 'Amazon' coleus and 'Margarita' sweet potato. Its excellent performance all season long, everywhere in the country, soon spawned other colors in the series. 'Misty Lilac Wave' provides wonderful pastel flowers, and the lovely shade of 'Pink Wave' was not far behind. On the UGA campus they provided color from May to October. I thought I had seen all the pink I could stand until I discovered some small pots of 'Pink Wave Variegated' on a small patio table in Long Island. In

that setting, they were quite wonderful—in the garden, well, not my cup of tea. Once the Wave series caught on, it seems that a new wave is introduced every year. Double-flowered forms were only a matter of time, and sure enough, 'Double Misty Lilac Wave' and others appeared in the early 2000s. With all the breeding for smaller flowers, and smaller plants, who would have believed that a group of plants called hedgifloras would be created? But created they were, and the Tidal Waves were almost as big as a hedge, a small one anyway. Certainly impressive.

With all the hybrids out there, species petunias have essentially gone the way of the ivory-billed woodpecker, but occasionally gardeners can find seeds of *Petunia integrifolia,* whose small flowers, heat tolerance, and long cascading habit still have a place in today's hybridized garden. The white form 'Alba' is my favorite.

All petunias perform better in raised beds or containers and in full sun. If some cultivars get too leggy by mid summer, give them a bit of a haircut, but don't be abusive. Plants will reflower in about two weeks.

Petunia 'Tidal Wave Rose'

Petunia 'Double Misty Lilac Wave'

Petunia 'Pink Wave Variegated'

Petunia integrifolia 'Alba'

Phlox

These plants are everywhere in the perennial garden—tall stately garden phlox to low-growers like creeping phlox and woodland phlox. Some of the prettiest flowers in the genus, however, reside in the much overlooked annual phlox, Drummond's phlox, *Phlox drummondii*. That it is so seldom used is a shame, because when people see it in full bloom, they stop and ask about it, wondering why they hadn't seen it before. The prob-lem is that the plant is not particularly weather-resistant, breaking down under extremes of heat, humidity, and rain. Therefore I won't recommend that my daughters go out and buy half a dozen, but I can tell them to try one or two in a container. I have seen marvelous plantings in Calgary and Riverhead, Long Island; in Athens, they are marvelous only until mid June.

Traditional phlox flowers can be seen in Globe Mix, a mix of common colors on plants growing about 1' tall. I recall minding my own business in a Long Island garden, then being assailed with questions about an "unknown beauty" there. It was the annual phlox 'Phlox of Sheep', which, if for no other reason than the great name, should be more widely grown. I much prefer the single flowers over some of the other forms that the hand of man has obviously touched. I can put up with the star-shaped flowers of 'Petticoat Pink Shade' (they are cute and at least attractive), but I cannot

MORE ☞

Phlox drummondii Globe Mix

Phlox drummondii 'Promise Pink'

Phlox drummondii 'Phlox of Sheep'

Phlox drummondii 'Petticoat Pink Shade'

stomach the double flowers of some selections, such as 'Promise Pink'. Many people love them, I am simply not one of them. Full sun. Plants and seed may be found in the garden center.

Plectranthus

SWEDISH IVY

Here is a group of plants that has truly gone through a remarkable renaissance! To the interior landscaper, this was a mainstay plant, and basket after basket of Swedish ivy would hang in offices and malls. If someone said "Plectranthus" in a crowd, however, someone else might reply "Gesundheit," and if a gardener said he had plectranthus, others would wish him a speedy recovery and move away in an attempt not to catch it. Such was the depth of understanding of this group of plants.

Nearly all plectranthus are grown for their foliage. Some species have variegated or purple leaves and are quite handsome, but beware the odor: more than a few people have been turned off by the nasty smell of some of the species. The odor is only a problem if you get your nose too close, otherwise it's not an issue.

The other problem with this group of plants is, they look so much like other plants, such as coleus, perilla, and even basil, that often retailers are not even sure of the genus they are selling, let alone the species or cultivar. The number of common names provides a hint to the confusion. Flowering bush coleus, Chinese basil, prostrate coleus, country borage, French thyme, Indian mint, Mexican mint, soup mint, and Spanish thyme are only some of the names heard

Plectranthus forsteri 'Marginatus', Minnesota

Plectranthus forsteri 'Marginatus', Georgia

Plectranthus madagascariensis 'Variegatus'

Plectranthus ornatus

in a plectranthus discussion group. Smelling the leaves helps a lot in your identification sleuthing: basil smells like basil, coleus has no particular smell, and plectranthus, well, enough said.

Some of the old-fashioned forms have made a significant impact in the marketplace, such as *Plectranthus forsteri* 'Marginatus', whose white-margined, oval to rounded leaves make a nice show. When I saw the plants in Minnesota, they were rather small, but the margins were white and distinct; in Georgia plants were more robust, but the variegation was not the clean white it was in the North. A relatively hard-to-find plant is a beautiful small-leaved trailer, Madagascar variegated mintleaf, *P. madagascariensis* 'Variegatus'. Plants grow vigorously and are at their best bungee-jumping off a wall. Numerous other forms can be found, such as the green ornate mint, *P. ornatus*, although I am not sure there is a good reason to spend your money on it. I prefer to spend mine on the free-branching gray-leaved form, Cape mint, *P. oertendahlii*. The leaves are most unique, not flashy, but people often do a double take, especially when they are combined with purple-leaved plants, as here with purple shamrock. I have also been impressed with the potential of the low golden hybrid 'Troy's Gold', which seems to hold its color in abusive conditions. Nice in combination with darker foliage.

The most popular forms are probably those whose leaves mix well with other plants, such as silver plectranthus, *Plectranthus argentatus*, which is often used as a substitute for dusty miller. Plants grow too well at times and can be pruned at least once to provide a branched habit. Any variegated plant with a pleasant fragrance that can grow

Plectranthus oertendahlii

Plectranthus 'Troy's Gold'

Plectranthus argentatus

Plectranthus amboinicus 'Variegatus'

MORE ☞

Plectranthus amboinicus 'Athens Gem'

Plectranthus ciliatus 'Mona'

in all climates will have a great following. Such is the case with oregano mint, *P. amboinicus* 'Variegatus', whose white and green leaves are excellent garden companions to sedum and can also be found in baskets complementing red verbena. A closely related selection with similar oregano-like fragrance but with yellow and green foliage is 'Athens Gem'. Both are tough as nails and provide season-long pleasure.

The assortment of plectranthus just mentioned are grown for the foliage alone; the flowers, if any, are secondary. However, a couple of new plants are quite beautiful in the fall when the lavender-blue flowers appear. They belong to either *Plectranthus ciliatus* or *P. zuluensis*, and, of the several forms, 'Mona' and 'Zulu Wonder' are worth a second look The former I thought was all right, the latter was terrific. Both have dark green foliage, and quite truthfully, do very little to pay back the money you spent until the fall, perhaps late September or October. At that time plants of 'Zulu Wonder' (and to a lesser degree 'Mona') are transformed into eye-catching beauties by the lovely lavender-blue flowers, which continue until temperatures hit 40°F. All plectranthus flower as days get shorter, some require such a short daylength that they flower only in the winter greenhouse. 'Mona' and 'Zulu Wonder' are

Plectranthus ciliatus 'Zulu Wonder' in flower

Plectranthus amboinicus 'Variegatus' with verbena

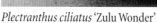

Plectranthus ciliatus 'Zulu Wonder'

excellent additions to the garden because the absolute length of day is not as critical as with other cultivars. The only recommendation I have for northern gardeners is to try only one or two to determine if plants flower sufficiently before cold weather sets in. Otherwise, I am excited by any flowering plant that spruces up the fall. Full sun, good drainage.

Plumbago auriculata

CAPE LEADWORT

A visitor from the Midwest traveling to south Texas or south Florida cannot help but be impressed with the number of plantings of Cape leadwort (*Plumbago auriculata*): it seems to be the Official Plant of the Gulf States. If one also adds the number of plants used in California and in other parts of the world, that same visitor can't help but wonder why so few of these handsome plants are available in his part of the world. If gardeners ever mention leadwort, they are usually referring to the common perennial, *Ceratostigma*. In the southern Gulf States, plumbago is a shrub, much like caryopteris and salvia when they are

MORE ☞

285

Plumbago auriculata, Australia

Plumbago auriculata 'Escapade White'

Plumbago auriculata, Germany

Plumbago auriculata 'Imperial Blue'

perennial; elsewhere it acts like a vigorous annual. The plants eat up heat and humidity and flower throughout the season once temperatures rise above 70°F. The flowers resemble those of phlox and are generally light to dark blue. Not only do they look good in Texas, but they shone in containers in southern Germany and were hedge-like in Perth, Australia. This is a plant for all places.

There is not a lot to choose from in plumbago, although a white form, 'Alba', has been around for years. 'Royal Cape' and 'Imperial Blue' both have more vibrant, darker flowers than the species and seem to be used interchangeably; both are propagated from cuttings and are quite easily available. The Escapade series, introduced from seed, has done well in trials across the country. The plumbagos can be highly recommended for containers, and particularly in areas where heat and humidity are becoming more of a problem. Full sun.

Polygonum

Some polygonums are awful weeds, always present in the garden, and obnoxious as can be. Of the dozens of species worthy of actually spending money on, nearly all are used as perennials. Wouldn't it be nice if there was a plant with vigorous growth and nice flowers that did not threaten to take over everything around it? A plant known as magic carpet, *Polygonum capitatum*, perfectly fills the bill.

Plants are produced from seed and are seen only occasionally at garden centers. That is unfortunate, as they are easily grown in almost any climate and provide small but handsome, round pink flowers and excellent dark green to bronze foliage. All this on a spreading plant no more than 6" tall. The small dark leaves have a distinctive red V-shape

pattern, which adds to the interest of the plant. In the summer, dozens of flowers form and continue to open throughout the season.

Magic carpet is well worth growing but is unlikely ever to be a mainstream item. It is difficult to talk people into an annual groundcover: after all, who wants to keep recovering the same ground year after year? However, as a short, vigorous garden plant, it really should be tried more often than it is. Plants may reseed in subsequent years, but that can't always be counted on. Full sun to afternoon shade.

Polygonum capitatum in flower with begonias

Polygonum capitatum

Portulaca
PURSLANE

I always marvel at the ability of plant breeders to take a genus of what most people consider weeds and create plants that are nothing short of beautiful. There are still plenty of weeds in this genus, but moss rose (*Portulaca grandiflora*) is not one of them. Over the years, a number of ornamental plants have been bred, including the Sunglow series, with half a dozen colors on low-growing plants. But the real breakthrough was with the Sundial series, which brought

Portulaca grandiflora 'Sundial Peppermint Stick'

Portulaca grandiflora 'Sundial Mango'

Portulaca grandiflora Sunglow series

Portulaca grandiflora 'Sundial Peach'

Portulaca grandiflora 'Sundial Mix'

MORE ☞

the moss rose out of the shadows and into the bright light of high demand.

A planting of some old 'Sundial Mix' shows off the many colors, but over the years the palette was widened. Some, like 'Sundial Peppermint Stick', were basically weird, but taste notwithstanding, there seemed to be a color for everyone. 'Sundial Mango' and 'Sundial Peach' were different and outstanding, 'Sundial Gold' was brilliant, and 'Sundial Fuchsia' was hot. Plants look good in the ground, in containers, or in baskets, but they are susceptible to a number of diseases that can cause problems in late summer. Be sure drainage is adequate, they do not like wet feet.

As much as I enjoy the colors of moss rose, I find them disappointing as temperature and humidity rise. However, I am seldom disappointed with ornamental purslane, *Portulaca oleracea*. Every

Portulaca grandiflora 'Sundial Gold'

Portulaca grandiflora 'Sundial Fuchsia'

Portulaca oleracea 'Yubi Rose'

Portulaca oleracea, UGA Trial Gardens

time I look at these plants, I cannot help but remember tearing purslane-the-weed from the lawn and even from cracks in the driveway; they were awful things that belonged in the rubbish. So what was I thinking when I said I would trial some purslane for a breeding company? It is good to keep an open mind, and in this case, I was so impressed that I became a big fan of this tough, colorful group of plants.

At Georgia, we evaluated rows of ornamental purslane, and I began to appreciate the color mix available. They can be used in baskets, in mixed containers, or as groundcovers. A number of cultivars are produced, including the Yubi series, which became the standard for ornamental purslane. Dark colors like 'Yubi Scarlet' and 'Yubi Rose' are impossible not to see from fifty yards away, but hot colors are not always appreciated in the middle of a sizzling summer. 'Yubi Light Pink' has always been my favorite; its soft colors and ability to combine with other plants keep it on my A list. For most gardeners, the way to use purslane is in mixed containers. The Summer Joy series also provides excellent colors, and we cram as many plants as possible into mixed containers. I am sure followers of the color wheel would disagree, but in our containers, it is a free-for-all, and, usually, the purslanes come out just fine. 'Summer Joy White' softens the verbena and ornamental grass in a container, and 'Summer Joy Scarlet' nicely complements some marguerite daisies and mussaenda in another mixed planting.

Portulaca oleracea, basket

Portulaca oleracea 'Yubi Scarlet'

Portulaca oleracea 'Yubi Light Pink'

Portulaca oleracea 'Summer Joy White'

MORE ☞

The recent addition of double forms really pushed the purslane envelope, and they were bred in the hopes that the flowers would stay open a little longer. The Fairytale series was developed, and even if the plants don't turn you on, the names would make Walt proud. Both 'Sleeping Beauty' (yellow, seen here with verbena) and 'Snow White' look good falling down the sides of patio pots, but the most interesting is probably 'Cinderella', with orange and red bicolor flowers. I said interesting, not necessarily beautiful. Look for other Fairytales coming your way, they are certainly different.

All is not perfect in the world of portulaca. The biggest complaint continues to be that flowers are closed early in the morning and after about 5:00 p.m. In this age, where the whole family is often out working or schooling during the day, being greeted by closed flowers entering and exiting the home does not do a great deal to endear these plants to gardeners. The double flowers of moss rose are better at staying open, and the purslanes are the worst; even the double forms are open only slightly longer than the singles. That is a bit of a bummer, so purchase with your eyes wide open, and enjoy them as you enjoy the rest of your garden: on the weekends. Full sun, good drainage.

Portulaca oleracea 'Summer Joy Scarlet'

Portulaca oleracea 'Sleeping Beauty'

Portulaca oleracea 'Snow White'

Portulaca oleracea 'Cinderella'

Pseuderanthemum

Here is yet another plant hardly anyone above the 30th parallel has ever heard of, but one that can provide excellent foliar color and reasonably good flower show with minimal effort. The hardest part will be to find the silly thing; be prepared for blank stares when you ask, "Do you have any pseuderanthemums?" One of the common names is chocolate soldier, which won't help much with the blank looks but will roll off your tongue a lot easier.

Chocolate soldier (*Pseuderanthemum alatum*) is grown for the Toblerone color of the leaves with their white-chocolate midveins. They grow vigorously, particularly as temperatures increase, and fill in areas of the garden rapidly. The pink flowers are a bonus, and are another reason for trying them, but it is the foliage and ease of maintenance that will make you come back for more. Plants are equally comfortable in full sun in the North or afternoon shade in the South.

Red pseuderanthemum (*Pseuderanthemum atropurpureum*), a relatively new addition to the garden palette, produces large, vigorous, shiny red-purple leaves. It is the sheen that makes it different from other upright purple-leaved plants. No flowers but quite a noticeable feature in the summer garden. Full sun everywhere.

Pseuderanthemum alatum

Pseuderanthemum atropurpureum

Reseda odorata

SWEET MIGNONETTE

Boy, trying to find some sweet mignonette anywhere in this country is a battle. It will be almost impossible to find plants for sale at your local garden center, and finding seeds is not that easy either. A quick search of the Internet yielded only a couple of companies selling mignonette seeds; there are others for sure, but suffice it to say, you really must want this plant in your garden.

And it is eminently want-able, particularly if you live in a cool climate, where summer temperatures of 80°F are uncommon. The green-tinged white blossoms are held like rockets, and plants flower for months at a time. This plant reeks of history, and yesterday's poets loved the plant. In the 1890s, in "The Old-Fashioned Garden," John Russell Hayes wrote what seems to be the

Reseda odorata

MORE ☞

precursor of "Where Have All the Flowers Gone?":

> *Foxgloves and marigolds and mignonette,*
> *Dahlias and lavender and damask rose.*
> *O dear old flowers, ye are blooming yet,*
> *Each year afresh your lovely radiance*
> *glows:*
> *But where are they who saw your beauty's*
> *dawn?*
> *Ah, with the flowers of other years they*
> *long ago have gone!*

Find some seeds. Plant them early.

Pick a few for the vase. Don't bore people with bad nineteenth-century American poetry. Place in full sun in the North, afternoon shade in the South.

Rhodochiton atrosanguineus

PURPLE BELL VINE

This handsome annual vine is not used to advantage in American gardens. Purple bell vine (*Rhodochiton atrosanguineus*) climbs by twining its long petioles around structures and carries wonderful pendulous purple flowers. The name comes from *rhodo* ("red") and *chiton* ("cloak"), a reference to the sepals, which envelop the flower like a cloak. They are beautiful and should be admired up close.

No cultivars are available, so find some started plants or purchase some seeds and sow them in the house about six weeks before you want to put them outside. Be sure you place them by a structure that allows plants to twine. Full sun.

Reseda odorata, mixed border

Rhodochiton atrosanguineus, flowers

Rhodochiton atrosanguineus

Ricinus communis

CASTOR OIL PLANT

This is the same plant whose oil was plied on unsuspecting children growing up in the 1940s and '50s for stomach and bowel problems. It was vile stuff and is still obtainable at the local pharmacist. *Ricinus communis* also yields the deadly toxin ricin, used by terrorists and murderers. However, the plants from which the oil and toxin are derived are among the "in" plants used by designers for architectural interest—that is, they are big and bold, and usually with burgundy- to bronze-colored leaves. In warm climates, plants can easily grow 6' tall in a single season; elsewhere, 2–3' may be all that is reached.

Their garden popularity comes from the colored foliage. 'Carmencita', the

Ricinus communis 'Carmencita'

Ricinus communis 'Scarlet Queen'

Ricinus communis 'Impala'

MORE ☞

most popular of the bronze-leaved forms, may be used as a great big solitary feature in the garden or combined with the riotous colors of red lobelias and orange Mexican sunflowers. 'Scarlet Queen' (aka 'Carmineus') is similar, and I particularly enjoyed them in France, where pink dahlias and yellow statice offset the bronze foliage. 'Impala' has a flush of red in the leaves but is not as colored as either of the aforementioned cultivars. Plants with bronze leaves will continue to be the most popular; however, some green forms are also part of the castor oil plant family. 'Gibsonii' has green foliage when young but bronzes as

Ricinus communis 'Carmencita' with lobelias and Mexican sunflowers

Ricinus communis 'Gibsonii'

Ricinus communis var. *cambodgensis*

Ricinus communis, fruit

it ages. It grows to only 4'. It is much prettier than another "in" form, var. *cambodgensis*, which bears large dark green foliage.

The prickly seed pods may be deep red to pink and contain beautiful gold, silver, and black seeds. However, admire them from a distance. As Karen Neill of North Carolina State University states, "These temptingly attractive seeds are quite poisonous, so you must be sure to keep them away from children and unknowing adults. Three seeds are sufficient to kill an adult. One seed may be fatal to a child." Plants will often reseed, and once planted may be in the garden year after year. Full sun.

Rudbeckia hirta

BLACK-EYED SUSAN

I have always loved black-eyed susans. The old-fashioned daisies (*Rudbeckia hirta*) are still available from seed packages in garden centers and are often part of a meadow-flower mix. There is absolutely nothing wrong with these "old" plants, and they are still a favorite for North American gardeners. Two of the best named varieties in the mid 1980s were 'Rustic Colors', with their multicolored flowers, and the unassuming 'Marmalade', as simple as the spread for which it is named. Both are still available today. Annual rudbeckias essentially disappeared from the radar screen with the blitzkrieg of perennial forms like *R. fulgida* var. *sullivantii* 'Goldsturm', but in the mid 1990s and early 2000s, a number of exciting new cultivars emerged from breeding programs.

Rudbeckia hirta 'Rustic Colors'

Rudbeckia hirta 'Marmalade'

Rudbeckia hirta 'Gloriosa Double Gold'

Rudbeckia hirta 'Goldilocks'

MORE ☞

Today we can choose from tall forms and dwarf ones, and many beautiful colors as well. I have fallen in love with these plants all over again.

How can so many cultivars be developed when the colors don't really change that much? To my eyes, regardless of whether there is red or green in the flower, the dominant color is nearly always yellow. No blues, no whites, no purples, but they seldom disappoint. Cut flower growers and gardeners who enjoy cutting can still find 'Gloriosa Double Gold', a 2–3' tall large-flowered double form. For those who cannot grow dahlias well, these look sufficiently similar to yellow dahlias in the vase that your non-plant friends may not know. If the full-bodied look is your cup of tea, you might still be able to find 'Goldilocks', a semi-double that has long been a favorite. However, the newest of the doubles

Rudbeckia hirta 'Cherokee Sunset'

Rudbeckia hirta Becky Mix

Rudbeckia hirta 'Sonora'

Rudbeckia hirta 'Cordoba'

is 'Cherokee Sunset', with beautiful bi-colored flowers. In the early 1990s, the single-flowered Becky Mix became a favorite because of the excellent outdoor performance, and landscapers opted for her above other single yellow forms.

Shorter than many cultivars, she became increasingly popular because plants do not fall over with rain or wind as badly as the taller forms.

The centers of the flowers are generally black or bronze, but large red cen-

ters have become in vogue. 'Sonora' gets my vote for the most outstanding bi-color, and while she led the way for flowers with large red centers, at least two others recently appeared. 'Cordoba' and 'Spotlight' can also light up the garden,

Rudbeckia hirta 'Prairie Sun'

Rudbeckia hirta 'Indian Summer'

Rudbeckia hirta 'Indian Summer', flowers

Rudbeckia hirta 'Toto'

MORE ☞

and if you have a chance to grow any of these, you cannot go too far wrong. In the world of the dwarf daisy, 'Toto' has become the benchmark for yellow forms of black-eyed susans.

Black centers, bronze centers, even large red centers are not uncommon, but 'Irish Eyes' become phenomenally popular because of its green eye. Its instant success spawned the latest of the green-eyed forms, 'Prairie Sun', with two shades of yellow around the green eye. It per-

Rudbeckia hirta 'Spotlight'

formed so well that it was an All-America Selection in 2002. However, the cultivar that spurred the annual rudbeckia market the most was not fancy, or double, and had no particularly weird center. It was simply an excellent performer with a short habit and large flowers. 'Indian Summer' was the hands-down favorite for the All-America Selection medal in 1995 and is still among the most popular daisies in the garden today. Not only that, it was voted best fresh cut flower for the year 2000 by the Association of Specialty Cut Flower Growers. When you walk by a handsome planting of simple black-eyed susans, perhaps beside some red petunias, you are probably admiring a superstar.

The beauty of black-eyed susans is obvious; however, do not believe that they will look as good as the magazine photos all season. As the temperature and humidity rise, the quality of the plants declines. The warmer the summer, the faster the plants are pulled. In Athens, we usually replace the rudbeckias by mid July, although they can stumble through the entire season. To have the trials look as good as the images, we reseed more susans beside the original plants while they still look good, so that when we take them up, the new ones

aren't far from flowering. The further north, the longer it takes to get an outstanding show, but the longer the plants will persist. Full sun.

Ruellia

I have been working with herbaceous plants for a good while, and living in the North didn't prepare me for some of the plants that were routinely used in warmer climates. When we looked at photos of plants like taro, peacock ginger, and Mexican petunia, gardeners in Montreal knew that, like Mickey and Donald, they were fictional characters. Boy, have times ever changed. The comic books have come to life, and those plants are real.

When I saw ruellia growing in Texas and Florida, I was not sure if they could grow in northern climes. While they are slowly creeping northward, heat is required to provide a season long show, and Cincinnati may be their northern limit. They are becoming much more available, and only time will tell if northern gardeners discover these neat plants.

The biggest one among them is Texas petunia (*Ruellia brittoniana*), which, where happy, can easily grow 5' tall and

Rudbeckia hirta 'Irish Eyes'

Ruellia brittoniana 'Alba'

4' wide in a single season. It is cold hardy to zone 7b, perhaps to 7. In the North, 3' will be more common, but the handsome blue flowers are produced all summer. Each flower persists but one day, but the black stems and the disease and insect resistance are great positives. They are better as annuals than perennials, because they can be invasive in warm climates and will self-seed everywhere. If the species is too big, try a few of the cultivars. 'Alba' is a little smaller and has white flowers; 'Chi Chi' is about half the size of the species and bears beautiful pink flowers. 'Katie's Dwarf' is really an outstanding cultivar, growing only 6–9" tall and bearing large blue flowers like the species. Plants are hardy to zone 7, but as perennials, at least in their northern range, they tend to flower sparsely. Grow as annuals.

Another fine addition to the field is the hybrid 'Groundhugger', which can make a reasonable groundcover but is better used in pots or baskets. Plants grow about 12" tall and send out long stems that hug the ground or dangle from containers. Blue flowers occur along the stems. Of all the ruellias, this one probably needs the most heat to sustain persistent flowering. Light blue flowers occur on *Ruellia humilis*, and I have seen it reseed all over the place, in gardens as far north as the Missouri Botanical Garden. However, if blue is getting a little tiresome, the red ruellia 'Ragin' Cajun' is

Ruellia brittoniana

Ruellia brittoniana 'Chi Chi'

Ruellia brittoniana 'Chi Chi', flowers

Ruellia brittoniana 'Katie's Dwarf'

MORE ☞

outstanding. Also only about 12" tall, this dwarf selection of the red Mexican petunia (*R. elegans*) flowers all season with bright fire-engine-red flowers.

Plants are not as restless as other forms and tend to stay where they are planted.

All in all, any ruellias that can be found are worth a try, first in containers (if they overwinter, they may not be worth keeping), then in the garden.

Beware of self-seeding tendencies, particularly in the species; if insufficient heat is available, plants will be fine but flowering will be limited. Full sun.

Russelia

CORAL PLANT

Coral plant has been residing in obscurity in most of the country for many years. It is a shrub in its native habitat of Mexico and southern California but seldom attains shrub-like proportions in other parts of the country. The most common form is the fountain plant, *Russelia equisetiformis*, in which the foliage resembles horsetails. I have seen them as shrubs at Leu Gardens in Orlando, Florida, but even in Long Island they were interesting when mixed in containers with parrot's beak. Not as big but still worth planting. The coral tubular flowers begin when temperatures consistently get above 75°F and will flower on and off all season. I personally don't have much use for it, but Alan

Ruellia 'Groundhugger'

Ruellia elegans 'Ragin' Cajun'

Ruellia humilis

Russelia equisetiformis, Leu Gardens

Russelia hybrid

Russelia equisetiformis with parrot's beak

Shapiro in Gainesville, Florida, grows it in his garden and loves it, and I never disagree with Alan. Hybrids involving running russelia, *R. sarmentosa*, have much more "normal" foliage and excellent flowers as well. It is unlikely the hybrids will ever be readily available outside of the Gulf States or California, but if you happen to find one, the beautiful shade of flowers and its disdain of heat and humidity may be worth a few dollars. Full sun.

Salpiglossis

PAINTED TONGUE

You are far more likely to see this plant in a conservatory or public greenhouse than you are in home gardens. In conservatories, these spectacular plants show off their flowers to the public for a few weeks, then are put back in the dusty corner. However, if you live in the mountains or on the northern edges of either coast, then perhaps you will also get to enjoy them for a few weeks in the garden or in containers. They are useless in the heat, humidity is not to their liking, they fall over with rain, and wind is not much good either. That is not to say you shouldn't try them, it is simply better if the public gardens waste their

Salpiglossis 'Splash Ivory'

MORE ☞

Salpiglossis 'Casino Royale'

money rather than you wasting yours. If their poor performance in any kind of inclement weather isn't enough to turn you off, then consider the common name. Enough said.

Of course, the fact that they are so fickle and wimpy means they must be gorgeous, and they are! Mixtures such as 'Casino Royale' and the Splash series bring many large petunia-like flowers in different shades to the table, and people, including myself, can't get enough of them. In spite of my less-than-enthusiastic recommendation, I still try a few every other year or so, even though I will only get to enjoy them for a heartbeat or two at most. They are better in containers than in the ground; if they flower for more than a month, buy every one of them. Seed is available from seed catalogs; have fun. Full sun in the North, afternoon shade in the South.

Salpiglossis 'Splash Purple'

Salpiglossis 'Splash Pale Yellow'

Salvia

SAGE

Having gone through the Salvia Stage of Life and survived, I can be both an advocate for and opponent against certain forms of this great genus. Many ornamental salvias, as well as the culinary sage, are perennials; however, the genus also sports many annuals. Salvias can be wonderful or just plain terrible, and the nice thing about the annual selections: if they do terribly, they will be put out of their misery over the winter.

I freely admit to confusion as to what species should be included in an annual book, because *Salvia*, as much as any genus, does not lend itself to being cubbyholed. Rather than spend time figuring out that it may live in zone 6b or 7a, I used this standard: if it is doubtful that

Salvia splendens, Michigan State University

Salvia splendens 'Carabiniere White'

Salvia splendens 'Hotline Red'

someone in Oberlin, Ohio, can grow it as a perennial, I include it here. That leaves many fine forms, from the red bedding plants that paint the landscape to hybrids that are only now becoming available to salvia fanatics.

Let's start with the much maligned bedding salvia, *Salvia splendens.* Like most bedding, it is overused, overweight, and sometimes over the top. Gardens like the one at Michigan State University trial dozens of cultivars—very bright, but, after a while, they become, well, a

Salvia coccinea 'Snow Nymph'

Salvia splendens 'Sangria'

Salvia 'Faye Chapel'

Salvia darcyi

Salvia coccinea 'Lady in Red'

Salvia coccinea 'Hummingbird Forest'

Salvia coccinea 'Coral Nymph'

Salvia farinacea 'Victoria'

Salvia farinacea 'Argent'

Salvia farinacea 'Reference'

Salvia patens 'White Trophy'

Salvia farinacea 'Rhea'

Salvia greggii, Ireland

MORE ☞

Salvia patens

Salvia patens 'Cambridge Blue'

Salvia greggii 'Navajo Bright Pink'

Salvia greggii 'Coral'

Salvia greggii 'Desert Blaze'

Salvia 'Cherry Queen'

little boring. However, let's be honest, they work, and the planting of 'Hotline Red' looks as nice as any planting you will see in a landscape. Red is surely the dominant color of bedding salvia, but let's not forget the white flowers found on 'Carabiniere White', or the purple ones on 'Cleopatra Violet', to name just a couple of alternate colors. To make the point that there is no such thing as bad taste when it comes to breeding flowers, 'Sangria' is available to gardeners as well. Call it interesting, and leave it at that. A naturally occurring tall variant of bedding salvia is Van Houtt's salvia,

Salvia leucantha

Salvia leucantha 'Santa Barbara'

Salvia leucantha 'Midnight'

Salvia rutilans, unpruned

Salvia involucrata, flowers

MORE ☞

'Van-Houttei', which is normally a burgundy color, but I really enjoy its bright red sport, 'Faye Chapel', which flowers all season.

The red that dominates the genus is personified in Darcy's salvia, *Salvia darcyi* (*S. oresbia*). I saw some lovely plantings at the exquisite Chanticleer Garden, in Wayne, Pennsylvania, where plants had reseeded among the rocks around a pond. The bloody sage (*S. coccinea*) is aptly named; the blood-red flowers are reflected in its most famous cultivar,

'Lady in Red'. An even brighter red, if that is possible, is found in 'Hummingbird Forest', and yes, these red salvias really do attract hummingbirds, and butterflies and bees. But not all the bloody salvias are bloody, and selections such as 'Coral Nymph' and 'Snow Nymph' are some of the prettier forms of the species.

Blues, violets, and purples are the next most common shades, after red. The sage most often associated with this range is the mealy-cup sage, *Salvia farinacea*. Of all the mealy-cups you will pass by, the most common by far is 'Victoria', a handsome mid-blue form

with time-tested excellence. 'Rhea', a darker form, was flowering in the Royal Botanical Gardens in Ontario at the same time as the snapdragons. Silver flowers are not uncommon in this species; the most common cultivar is 'Argent', which provides dozens of narrow silvery flowers most of the season. Not to be outdone by 'Sangria', the blue and white bicolored 'Reference' should be planted, perhaps in places where others can't see it. Lots of people love these bicolor salvias, but then lots of people love cats. Other blues in the genus include the gentian sage, *S.*

Salvia rutilans, pruned

Salvia 'Anthony Parker'

Salvia involucrata

Salvia regla

patens. The flowers are among the largest in the genus, but unfortunately, flowering is sparse most of the time. There are a few selections; 'Cambridge Blue' is probably the best known, and white-flowered forms, like 'White Trophy', can occasionally be found.

The Texas sage, *Salvia greggii*, has become quite popular, and with good reason. It does well in all conditions, and, although native to Texas, it flourishes in faraway places like Mount Usher Gardens in Ireland as well. The selections are reasonably short and, in the case of the Navajo series, also come in a number of colors. I have been most impressed with 'Navajo Scarlet' and 'Navajo Bright Pink'. Simple colors like 'Coral' are also easy on the eyes. A variegated-leaf form, 'Desert Blaze', has looked surprisingly good in trials, although it needs significant pruning if it grows too tall. Numerous hybrids with Texas sage have been bred. The best by far is 'Cherry Queen', which flowers the entire season and handles pruning well; the only maintenance sometimes required is a haircut. Texas sage is cold hardy to at least zone 7 and over a few years becomes quite shrubby.

A number of sages flower only in the fall. One of these is a tall vigorous blue-flowered species, known as velvet sage, *Salvia leucantha*. Hardy to about zone 7, it is being seen more and more throughout the country. The species itself, which has flowers of purple and white, is as good as any of the cultivars. Plants grow 4–5' tall and can be overwhelming, so a dwarf cousin, 'Santa Barbara', was selected as a better choice for smaller gardens. The most impressive cultivar, however, is 'Midnight', which bears totally purple flowers. Stunning from a distance, impressive close-up. A favorite red is pineapple sage, *S. rutilans*, whose leaves really do smell like pineapple and whose flowers are fire-engine red. Plants stand at least 4' tall and flower only in the fall, but they are worth waiting for. If not pruned in early summer, plants will produce only a few tall blooms; a hard pruning results in dozens of flowers. 'Anthony Parker' is a hybrid of velvet sage and pineapple sage. It is tall and interesting, but not as interesting as either of its parents. Another fall flowerer is the big, leggy, and altogether unmanageable rose-cup sage, *S. involucrata*. But the flowers are outstanding. The deep pink hue and the weird shape of the flowers, particularly the uppermost one, which

Salvia viridis 'Blue Bird'

Salvia viridis 'Rosea'

Salvia mexicana 'Limelight'

MORE ☞

Salvia viridis 'Rubra'

looks like a ball-peen hammer, keep people coming back for more. And finally, for the fall, if you can find the Hildago sage, *S. regla*, run out and buy it. The orange-scarlet flowers smother the plant and stop people in their tracks. The drawback to all these fall flowers is that the farther north one gardens, the more one worries that frost will take out the plants before the flowers have made a show. You take your chances, but the reward is worth the worry.

And to finish up, a couple of fun but unique salvias. Green sage, *Salvia viridis* (*S. horminum*), is not green but rather is distinguished by its colorful bracts. Pink ('Rosea'), purple ('Blue Bird'), and rose-colored bracts ('Rubra') make you look twice to determine that it really is a sage. Plants grow only 2' tall. If green is truly desired in the garden, you must try 'Limelight', a selection of Mexican sage,

S. mexicana. Lots of flowers, mostly in the fall; people will hardly notice until you point them out, but then stand back for the chorus of enthusiasm. All salvias prefer full sun and reasonably good drainage. They are all fond of being cut back when needed.

Sanvitalia procumbens

CREEPING ZINNIA

Sanvitalia procumbens is an old-fashioned plant that has not changed a great deal since Victorian times. Plants do well in most areas of the country but become tired by mid summer in places where summers are hot and humid. Flowers really do look like zinnias but are smaller and occur in yellow and

orange shades only. Plants are useful for edging and as a shiny groundcover, inserted among other annuals and perennials.

The most common form is 'Mandarin Orange', which can be used as a ground-cover skirting blue salvias and crawling over rocks. People can't help but take any low-growing plant and make an edging plant out of it; creeping zinnia is no exception. However, most selections, are sufficiently well behaved to handle the edging duty well; here, 'Orange Sprite' holds back bamboo and heliotrope. Orange is probably the more popular color, but I also like the yellows, particularly when they can be incorporated among other plants. 'Yellow Sprite' can be used along with zinnias and marigolds to soften the edges on a brick walkway, while the combination of 'Yellow Carpet' with purple verbena

Sanvitalia procumbens 'Yellow Sprite'

Sanvitalia procumbens 'Yellow Carpet'

MORE ☞

Sanvitalia procumbens 'Mandarin Orange'

Sanvitalia procumbens 'Orange Sprite'

and black-eyed susans at the Butchart Gardens had cameras clicking and people stopping.

Full sun in the North, afternoon shade in the South.

Scabiosa

SCABIOUS

When one mentions scabiosa, most gardeners immediately think of the perennial forms that have become so popular, but annual pincushion flowers (*Scabiosa atropurpurea*) have always been around—they just haven't been able to compete with petunias or begonias for greenhouse or retail space. Plants are easily grown from seed and are sometimes used in a meadow-mix, and unless a cultivar is specified, it will likely consist of a mixture of colors including rose and scarlet flowers.

Scabiosa atropurpurea

Scabiosa atropurpurea 'Ace of Spades'

Scabiosa atropurpurea 'Chile Black'

Some purple forms have captured the imagination of gardeners. The most common, 'Ace of Spades', has become more widely available; plants grow about 18" tall and can be used as a black spot in the garden or brought in for the vase. A similar form but shorter and more compact is 'Chile Black', which I believe is going to be an excellent plant for North American gardeners. Full sun, good drainage.

Scaevola aemula

FAN FLOWER

Fan flower (*Scaevola aemula*) is one of the success stories in which a new plant became a garden favorite not because of marketing or promotion, but simply because it performed so well in gardens. Its fame spread by word of mouth, and soon various cultivars of fan flower were available in retail stores. Plants are native to Australia and are tolerant of heat but do just fine in temperate climates as well.

Many cultivars have emerged, most in the blue-lavender color range. They all look good in baskets, particularly 'Sapphire Blue', and are equally attractive in the garden. 'Mauve Clusters', an old-fashioned form, has small flowers

Scaevola aemula 'Outback Purple Fan'

MORE ☞

Scaevola aemula 'Outback White Fan'   *Scaevola aemula* 'Sapphire Blue'

Scaevola aemula 'Mauve Clusters'   *Scaevola aemula* 'Blue Flash'

Scaevola aemula 'Blue Ice'   *Scaevola aemula* 'Zigzag'

but is absolutely covered with them. Larger flower forms have since emerged, but many cultivars are essentially the same in appearance. The Outback series, especially 'Outback Purple Fan', has always been an excellent performer in our trials. 'Blue Flash' and 'Blue Ice' are both marvelous selections too, and oftentimes the choice is based solely on availability.

Blue-lavender is not the only color in this species, and breeders have been developing whites and bicolors. Whites are fairly common, and you can't go too far wrong with 'Outback White Fan'; many other whites and bicolors will soon be available, and I like the bicolor 'Zigzag' simply because it performs well and provides a little extra pizzazz. All fan flowers are excellent in patio containers, where they can be combined with other annuals. One thing I should add: whenever I talk about scaevola, at least one person in the audience tells me how much the rabbits enjoy it. If rabbits are a problem, you probably don't want to waste too much of your money. Full sun.

Senecio

The genus has over 10,000 members, and the vast majority are not particularly ornamental. In fact, most are shrubs, and few have been domesticated. There is a spattering of herbaceous species, but only one is a common denizen of gardens. The popular gray-leaved *Senecio cineraria*, dusty miller, is used as edging and in container plantings; other dusty millers are sometimes placed in the genus *Artemisia*.

Senecio cineraria is a beautiful plant,

Senecio cineraria with pansies

Senecio cineraria 'Cirrus' with red salvia

Senecio cineraria 'Cirrus' with purple salvia

Senecio cineraria 'White Diamond'

MORE ☞

and because of its ease of production and soft silver-gray color, it was probably overused in many landscapes. They were planted as solid sheets and after a while became quite tedious. However, let's give them their due: when they are combined with other flowers, they enhance everything around them. Even in containers, the pansies look brighter because of dusty miller's silvery foliage. The form I like best is 'Cirrus', whose deeply cut leaves on vigorous plants are outstanding. I love them combined with red salvia (together, both plants look better), and later when I noticed some plants among purple salvia, I was again taken with the contrast. Not only are the leaves terrific, very few flowers are produced, and this is a good thing. Lack of flowers is not a characteristic of all cultivars. 'White Diamond' has handsome oblong fluted leaves and performs just fine, but the flowers that form in mid summer do nothing for its appearance; this cultivar reminds me of another gray plant, lamb's ear, whose purple flowers also detract from what it is supposed to do.

Senecio viravira, also known as dusty miller, bears beautiful gray cut leaves. Plants fill in well and exhibit significantly more cold hardiness than the

Senecio viravira

Senecio confusus

Senecio confusus with sweet potato

Senecio confusus, flowers

common dusty miller. In this species, the flowers are also unremarkable. Full sun. Cut back in mid to late summer if they look tired.

While there are many plants in this diverse genus, one doesn't expect to come across a vine. I first saw the orangeglow vine (*Senecio confusus*) in the conservatory at Longwood Gardens, and while I really enjoyed it and made copious notes, I put it down as a greenhouse plant, and that was the end of that. When I visited one of my favorite nurseries, The Planters Palette in Winfield, Illinois, and saw it there, with its flowers artfully poking out of 'Margarita' sweet potato, I told myself that I had to get some. Unfortunately, all the

visitors in the garden bought them while I was telling them how wonderful it was. Then on a chilly fall day, what did I walk under at Chanticleer Garden in Wayne, Pennsylvania, but two arbors of orangeglow. My friends all thought I was crazy as I traced and retraced my steps under the fiery orange daisies that complemented the plant. Even at that time of year, it was pretty darn neat. It may not be for everybody, but what is? How many daisies do you know that climb up trellises?

Some authorities have changed the botanical name to *Pseudogynoxys chenopodioides*. That's too confusing for me, and I'll keep it here until they all agree. Full sun.

Setcreasea pallida

PURPLE HEART

I can't help but chuckle when I see purple heart (*Setcreasea pallida*) growing proudly in the landscape. After all, this "dormitory plant," originally known as purple wandering jew, was purchased by students with the best of intentions to cozy up their dorm room. After a month or so, it would end up as one long decrepit stem, begging to be put out of its misery. Now it is favored by landscapers as if they just discovered it.

It is a terrific low-maintenance plant and can even take the abuse of University of Georgia students, who dangle their feet in it as if they were poolside.

Setcreasea pallida with cannas and lantana

But as effective as it is as a monotone, it is even better when combined with plants like lantana and 'Bengal Tiger' canna lilies. It seems that it is only a plant for the South, but don't tell that to William Hoyt at the Allen Centennial Gardens at the University of Wisconsin. I visited this exceptional garden in September; Hoyt had combined purple heart with 'Aurora' coleus, and it was happily scampering over a few white petunias while still sporting colorful pink flowers. This is a plant that is in its glory anywhere in the country, and whether in containers or in the ground will not disappoint. Full sun.

Solanum

NIGHTSHADE

Plants that reside in this group are like Jekyll and Hyde: some are gentle and beautiful, while others are armed with sharp spines and dare you to grow them. Of course, give any gardener a dare, and that plant will be soon be in his garden.

Solanums are among the most sought-after plants these days. One of the most fashionable, which I hope is only a fad, is one of the most devious, purple solanum, *Solanum atropurpureum*. The green foliage is attractive, and the purple stems are handsome, if you can see them. I quickly found out that enthusiastically pulling apart the foliage to find the stems is not a good idea, as the stems are armed with sharp black thorns. However, after I pulled on thick gloves, I discovered the small orange fruit within, tasty but hardly worth the effort. Many of the solanums have excellent edible fruit, and some of these tropical vegetables are beginning to reside in our gardens. An example is naranjilla, *S. quitoense*, cultivated for fruit and juice production in South and Central America and now appearing in public gardens in Georgia and Washington, D.C. This plant is also ready for battle, but the foliage is really handsome, and the bright orange fruit are quite edible. Easy to grow from seed. Numerous little-known species are being grown only by solanum fanatics, including sticky nightshade, *S. sisymbriifolium*, grown for the prickly white flowers, cut leaves, and yellow fruit.

While thinking of fruit, I can't help but remark on the beautiful hanging baskets in a wonderful garden of Weihenstephan in southern Germany. The baskets were overflowing with fruit of

Setcreasea pallida, University of Georgia

Setcreasea pallida, University of Wisconsin

Solanum atropurpureum

Solanum atropurpureum, fruit

Solanum quitoense

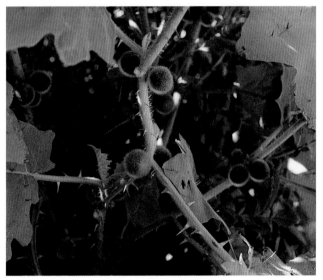

Solanum quitoense, fruit

Solanum muricatum 'Pepino Gold'

Solanum sisymbriifolium

Solanum melongena 'Lavender Touch'

MORE ☞

pepino plant, *Solanum muricatum* 'Pepino Gold', and it was all we could do not to climb a ladder and pick them. From ornamental kale to ornamental sweet potato, vegetables will always have a place in the garden. If we can accept

ornamental okra, then we surely will embrace ornamental eggplant, *S. melongena*. A number have been selected; I enjoy the handsome large leaves, purple flowers, and purple fruit of 'Lavender Touch'. Edible as well, if you are an eggplant person.

While most solanums are not overly

large, they can certainly become so if properly grown or trained. Purple nightshade, *Solanum rantonnetii*, is a shrub that may not have sufficient time to grow and flower well in American gardens. However, if trained as a standard—as it was in the Royal Botanical Gardens in Ontario, behind some 'Illumination'

Solanum rantonnetii with amaranthus

Solanum rantonnetii, Zurich Botanical Gardens

Solanum wendlandii

amaranthus, and in the Zurich Botanical Gardens near a concession stand—these can be knockouts. The dark blue flowers are beautiful and open most of the summer. Growing and training your own standards may not be something you want to do, but they are occasionally sold, and if you can afford one, give it a try. Full sun.

Thorns, veggies, shrubs . . . there seems to be everything in this genus, including vines. It is difficult to include these vines in an annuals discourse, because unless they attain some maturity they will not produce a great number of flowers, and they are not hardy north of zone 7 or 8. However, I include them

here so we can enjoy a few flowers if we get them. The easiest to find is the white form of the potato vine, *Solanum jasminoides*, which produces white tomato-like flowers on vigorous plants. This is a popular vine on the West Coast and in the Southeast, where it often overwinters. As an annual, it can be grown in a container and will still attain 5–6' the first year. Or, just let it roam over the ground, where it acts as a white ground-cover. Flowers will be sparse the first year. Another vine that is worth a search is paradise flower, *S. wendlandii*, with beautiful large blue flowers on armed plants. Might be more appropriate to the conservatory than to the garden, but it is

a beauty. Check your friendly Google-button for a source or two. Full sun.

Stachytarpheta

SNAKEWEED, FALSE VERVAIN

Too bad some of these botanical names are such a mouthful. People won't buy what they can't pronounce, and they certainly won't lay money down for anything that has "weed" in its common name. That is a shame, for while this is never going to be a mainstream plant, it has some interesting attributes. Plants in the genus should probably be called

Solanum jasminoides

Stachytarpheta jamaicensis, flowers

Stachytarpheta mutabilis

MORE ☞

the tease plant, because so few flowers open at any one time. The main species, *Stachytarpheta jamaicensis*, has blue-purple flowers and makes a wonderful plant in heat and humidity, but only three or four flowers open a day, until the entire length of the fifty or so flowers eventually opens. It is a long, painful process, but on the other hand, the flowers certainly continue blooming for a long period of time!

Pink snakeweed (*Stachytarpheta mutabilis*) is taller and lankier than its purple counterpart but is a much prettier color. It is another Mae West, teasing all the time, but the color is so nice, it doesn't seem to matter as much. Full sun.

Stachytarpheta jamaicensis

Stictocardia beraviensis

Stictocardia beraviensis

A plant that will be found only at the best of establishments; don't expect to find it at a box store but maybe at a specialty grower like GardenSmith, a wonderful, weird, and wacky place close to my home. The owner, Denise Smith, is the personification of her nursery, and between the two of us, we see who can surprise the other the most. She always wins. Like the time she gave me this marvelous vine, *Stictocardia beraviensis*, which we called braveheart vine. It grows about 3' a day, and has the most wonderful felty gray heart-shaped leaves and pleasant tropical orange flowers. It is useful as a screen for the side of a porch or to cover unsightly areas, like my garden. It's also a fun plant to simply watch grow.

The flowers are quite beautiful, but don't expect to see them unless you stick your face into the leaves; they are held close to the stems, and there are not that many anyway. Perhaps you have someone like Denise in your area; if so, try one. It is native to western Africa, and even though it looks like the next kudzu, it will not take serious frost.

Strobilanthes dyerianus

PERSIAN SHIELD

What a remarkable plant. Persian shield (*Strobilanthes dyerianus*) can be grown in almost any environment, in almost any part of the country. The bronze-purple coloring of the large leaves has been enjoyed in gardens for a long time, and when grown well, it is truly an architectural feature in the garden.

Plants can grow to 4' high and equally wide, even in a midwestern summer. They are as perfectly at home in the

Strobilanthes dyerianus

Strobilanthes dyerianus with verbena and purslane

garden bed as they are in a large container. This is a large plant, so a small container simply will not do. We plant them intermingled with white petunias and nicotiana, or pink 'Aztec' verbena and purslane. Plants are easy to find at any decent retailer, but do not put plants out too early, or they may start forming flowers. The flowers are boring at best but worse than that, once flowering starts, the plant stops growing. Persian shield can handle afternoon shade, particularly in the South, where midday sun can cause premature wilting of the large leaves. Otherwise full sun.

Sutera

BACOPA

When these small-flowering, trailing plants were first introduced, they were simply known as bacopa, both botanically and as a common name. The genus *Bacopa* consists of aquatic plants, somewhat similar in flower and more compact in habit. The bacopa of gardens is *Sutera grandiflora* or hybrids of the genus. That really doesn't matter a great deal, because wherever these are sold, they will be called bacopa, and that is that.

Strobilanthes dyerianus with verbena

Sutera 'Lavender Storm'

MORE ☞

Bacopas do not make particularly good garden plants, North or South, but are well suited to baskets and containers. We planted 'Lavender Storm', a well-known cultivar, among argyranthemum, purslane, and mussaenda, and the small flowers helped to fill out the container. I also enjoyed 'Snowflake' in our baskets, where they made a nice simple show. However, plants that remain in the greenhouse for a long time can really be impressive when they are placed in the garden. At the Missouri Botanical Garden, a basket of 'Snowstorm' essentially took over the entire corner of the garden, as well as the purple petunias trying to survive. Numerous cultivars have been bred, and differences are often slight, perhaps a little bigger flower here, or slightly different color there. Blues and lavenders are not uncommon, and 'Mauve Mist' is perhaps the best of them, with excellent color and rather large flower size. 'Lavender Showers' sports a large flower; 'Blue Showers' has flowers equally large and a bit more blue. I didn't think I would like the variegated form, 'Olympic Gold', but it mixed well with various plants and tumbled nicely out of the container. A genus closely related to bacopa is *Jamesbrittenia*, found as 'Penny Candy Violet' and 'Penny Candy Pink', which have flowers similar to bacopa but whose foliage is much more lacy and incised. Plants of *Jamesbrittenia* are not as vigorous as bacopa, at least in the heat, but still may appear under the bacopa name. They are sufficiently poorer in performance that it makes sense to check the leaves when buying.

Plants are much more vigorous in the North than in the South and outstanding in the West. In the South, they are more likely to struggle in the heat and humidity of July and August. Afternoon shade everywhere.

Sutera 'Snowflake'

Sutera 'Snowstorm'

Sutera 'Mauve Mist'

Sutera 'Lavender Showers'

Sutera 'Olympic Gold'

Jamesbrittenia 'Penny Candy Violet'

Jamesbrittenia 'Penny Candy Pink'

Tagetes erecta 'Voyager Orange'

Tagetes

MARIGOLD

Comments about garden snobbery and the preferred diet of said snobs were mentioned under petunia, and similar comments could be made here. No doubt, the popularity of many bedding plants has faded with the introduction of so much new material to the gardener, and the marigold is certainly not as popular as it once was. Of all the bedding plants I work with, I believe I prefer marigolds the least, but part of that's because whenever I handle them, I start sneezing. Not a good plant for one who suffers from allergies. But my biases aside, they are highly functional plants.

Marigolds come in an assortment of sizes and colors; they are not all yellow. Many have been shown to provide nematode suppression and have been used in vegetable gardens as companion plants for years. For the gardener, there is no lack of choice.

The tallest forms, which at one time were referred to as hedge marigolds, are the African marigolds, *Tagetes erecta*. Standing 3–4' tall, they were the most popular in the heyday of bedding, in the 1960s through the 1980s. Cultivars like 'Orange Crush' would tower over plant-

Tagetes erecta Inca series

Tagetes erecta 'Discovery Yellow'

MORE ☞

Tagetes erecta 'Disco Flame'

Tagetes 'Golden Gate'

Tagetes erecta 'Disco Marietta'

Tagetes tenuifolia 'Lemon Gem'

Tagetes tenuifolia 'Golden Gem'

Tagetes tenuifolia 'Lulu', flowers

ings of dianthus and other annuals. The tall forms were always popular, but when it rained or the wind blew hard, stems would invariably snap or plants would fall over. Newer, stronger African forms, such as 'Voyager Orange', were bred with large flowers on strong stems. The Inca series, in yellow and orange, remains one of the best for strength of stem, compact height, and persistent flowering. However, gardeners and landscapers still complained that plants were too tall, and as a result, the Discovery series was introduced. Compared to other African forms, it was far shorter and more weather-tolerant. African marigolds are easily found in retail stores; they are almost always yellow or orange and have round double flowers on reasonably sturdy plants.

While the African forms were always popular, the French marigold, *Tagetes patula*, was equally successful. Plants were shorter and better branched but had much smaller flowers. More diversity in flower color was available, and they were more weather-tolerant. French marigolds became the dominant form of marigold. Numerous cultivars appeared, classic double-flowered styles like 'Little Hero Yellow' or those with handsome

Tagetes patula 'Little Hero Yellow'

Tagetes erecta 'Durango Flame'

Tagetes tenuifolia 'Lulu'

MORE ☞

bicolored flowers, such as 'Durango Flame' and 'Disco Flame'. Single flowers also became available, cultivars like 'Disco Marietta', which were, and still are, quite popular. Many, many named varieties await you at the garden center. The genetic differences between the two species are significant, yet breeders found a way to bridge that gap and produced some exceptional hybrids. My favorite was 'Golden Gate', with excellent vigor and better disease tolerance, yet still compact. Other hybrids were bred, but difficulties in seed production have diminished the hybridization efforts and have made these increasingly difficult to obtain.

There is little doubt that when you walk into the garden center looking for marigolds, your choice will usually be limited to African or French forms. Hybrids may be available occasionally but are probably not labeled as such. However, approximately fifty species of marigolds are known, and a few of these may pop up every now and then at your favorite retail outlet.

The signet marigold, *Tagetes tenuifolia*, is my recommendation. The mounded habit, the fern-like leaves, and the small but numerous flowers provide welcome relief from the stiff upright forms of other marigolds, and breeders have provided us with some gardenworthy forms as well. The Gem series, including 'Lemon Gem' and 'Golden Gem', has been available for a number of years and stood the test of time. I also enjoy the look of 'Lulu', whose relaxed habit and persistent flowering allow it to combine well with petunias, amaranths, and zinnias. Excellent habit and flowering, even up close. 'Ursula' has also demonstrated excellent garden performance. There are parts of the country where other species may surface, such as *T. lemmonii*, native to Mt. Lemmon in Tucson, Arizona. Excellent for heat but rarely available. Fun to have as a native species but will do poorly in humidity and rain.

Marigolds have lost some of their luster in the gardening community for good reason. Among annuals, they are extremely high-maintenance, at least on my list. To ensure attractiveness, they must be deadheaded, a job that my nose and I detest, and they are susceptible to many insects, such as spider mites, leafhoppers, and thrips. For warm areas of the country, I recommend that they be planted early, removed in mid summer, and replanted in late summer for fall flowering. Seeds are cheap and germination is easy. Full sun.

Tagetes tenuifolia 'Ursula'

Tagetes lemmonii

Tecomaria

CAPE HONEYSUCKLE

I never am sure whether this genus should be placed under annuals, perennials, or shrubs, and I hesitate to get too enamored with it. I have tried Cape honeysuckle (*Tecomaria capensis*) several

Tecomaria capensis 'Scarlet'

Tecomaria capensis 'Apricot'

times over the years in our gardens at Athens; one year I think it is terrific, the next it dies. To many people, it is perennial to zone 8, occasionally coming down to zone 7 territory as well.

I have seen them listed under various flower colors, including 'Scarlet' and 'Apricot', and they make handsome plants throughout the season; but, at least for us, they put out few flowers until the fall. In general, I have no problem with fall-flowerers; however, I was not pleased with the flower power of the plants. To be honest, I have seen some

impressive specimens further south or in a greenhouse setting, but most of those have been perennial. I am not sure that the northern gardener would have sufficient growing time to enjoy ample flowering. However, if it is for sale, it is certainly worth a try; the plants are tough and not bothered by insects or diseases, and the flowers are gorgeous. Full sun.

Thunbergia

This genus is full of surprises. All but one of its members have struggled in relative obscurity, but there is so much more fun yet to be had with the plants found within. Most are vines and require some support to climb, but once they start to grow, they can provide immense pleasure.

The best known is the black-eyed susan vine, *Thunbergia alata*, which has been decorating trellises for centuries. The most common black-eyed susans are orange with a black eye, which is what will result from the seed package you buy. They will be reasonably vigorous and can be trained around posts (tie some thick strands of rope from

Thunbergia alata 'Susie Orange'

Thunbergia alata 'White with Dark Eye'

MORE ☞

nails to allow the stems to twist around). They also are available in named cultivars, and the vigorous 'Susie Orange' would have climbed all over our pergola had we let it. I enjoy other colors as well; I loved the basket of white flowers with black eyes and the subtle hue of 'Red Shades'. These are often labeled by flower color only and can be obtained from seed catalogs. A vegetative form, the Sunny series, was bred with electric colors of lemon and orange. The tremendous growth displayed at Michigan State University gardens gives an indication of the vigor of 'Sunny Orange'.

Other lesser-known vines are equally beautiful. I can't get enough of sky vine, *Thunbergia grandiflora,* and grow it every year in our gardens at Athens. The dark green glossy leaves are themselves handsome, but the beautiful light blue flowers are to die for. Unfortunately, the flowers don't appear until late summer,

Thunbergia alata 'Sunny Orange', Michigan State University

Thunbergia alata 'Red Shades'

Thunbergia alata 'Sunny Lemon Star'

Thunbergia alata 'Sunny Orange', *T. a.* 'Sunny Lemon Star'

but then they continue to frost. They are winter hardy to about zone 7b. I first came across clock vine, *T. gregorii*, in Europe and was immediately taken with the vibrant orange flowers. I have had trouble locating the vine in this country but will continue to try, as it is worth the hunt. The previous two vines are somewhat uncommon, but when I saw Nilgari vine, *T. mysorensis*, in New Zealand, I about flipped out. It was so amazing that I asked for some seeds, ready to introduce the next great vine to America. Then a few months later, on a visit to Denise Smith, of GardenSmith Greenhouses, not forty minutes away, I saw the same vine in her greenhouse! Since Denise is always on the forefront of change, I knew I had a winner. Time will tell. All thunbergia vines need something that the stems can twine around. Large posts are too thick, wire and string may be too thin. A wire net on a fence works well. Full sun.

Not all species are vines, and bush thunbergia, *Thunbergia battiscombei*, wants to grow along the ground, yet will

Thunbergia grandiflora

Thunbergia gregorii

Thunbergia grandiflora, flowers

Thunbergia battiscombei

MORE ☞

Tibouchina

also clamber over other plants in its way. It does not seem to know whether it wants to climb up, climb over, or simply be a bush. Regardless, the deep blue flowers with their orange eyes and white backs are quite beautiful. They may not put on a lot of flowers, but a few peeking out from the leathery foliage are common. They perform well in containers. Full sun.

Glory bush or princess flower, *Tibouchina urvilleana,* is not uncommon in south Florida and the Gulf States, where it makes a stately shrub or small tree. It is only recently, however, that the attributes of the plants are being recognized in other parts of the country. The most common form, if tibouchina can ever be called common, is the large-flowered var. *grandiflora,* brought to the United

States in 1985 from New Zealand. Plants were subsequently introduced as 'Athens Blue' and have been propagated for many years. They may or may not be called by that name any more, but the large blue to purple flowers and handsome disease-resistant, insect-resistant foliage are characteristic of the cultivar. They look terrific in containers or the garden; they start flowering in mid summer and continue on and off all season. They can carry dozens of flowers, but

Thunbergia mysorensis

Tibouchina urvilleana 'Jewel'

Thunbergia battiscombei, clambering

Tibouchina longiflora

four to six at a time is more common, depending on plant size. Plants will reach 3–4' in height, depending on locale, and become quite woody. They will often overwinter to zone 7b. Other forms of this species include the handsome but less vigorous smaller-flowered 'Jewel'.

The large-leaved tibouchina, *Tibouchina grandifolia*, has burst onto the landscape scene, at least in the southern states. This is one impressive plant, sporting huge velvety leaves on a 3–5' tall plant. It does not flower until late summer or fall, but even when not in flower, it adds that architectural feature to the garden. The purple flowers are smaller than 'Athens Blue' and are held in long inflorescences at the top of the plant. Truly a spectacular plant in and out of flower.

These two species are the best of the bunch, but others occasionally surface. I have grown long-flowered tibouchina, *Tibouchina longiflora*, but was disappointed with the lack of vigor and few flowers. This was a fall-flowerer only, and not really worth the wait. Full sun.

333

Tithonia rotundifolia

MEXICAN SUNFLOWER

This is a large, highly visible plant. It is amazing that such a small seed can produce such a colorful, giant plant in a single season. I see Mexican sunflower

MORE ☞

Tibouchina urvilleana var. *grandiflora* 'Athens Blue'

Tibouchina urvilleana var. *grandiflora* 'Athens Blue', flowers

Tibouchina grandifolia

Tibouchina grandifolia, flowers

(*Tithonia rotundifolia*) in many botanic gardens as well as private gardens, but it is usually too big for city lots. Most often I see it standing by itself, but when 'Torch' was combined with red dahlias, they made quite a sight. Even the fire-engine red of those dahlias was lost among the riot of orange in the bed. The most common of the Mexican sunflowers is 'Goldfinger', which can grow 6' tall in areas of warm summers and 3–4' tall elsewhere. The cultivar name is a little misleading, as the 2½" wide flowers are more orange than gold.

The best cultivar for smaller gardens is 'Fiesta del Sol', which grows about 3'

Tithonia rotundifolia 'Goldfinger'

Tithonia rotundifolia 'Goldfinger', flowers

Tithonia rotundifolia 'Fiesta del Sol'

Tithonia rotundifolia 'Torch' with dahlias

tall and equally wide. Its compact habit is a welcome sight after the bigger forms, which can get tall and leggy and snap off at various places. 'Fiesta del Sol' is not without problems; it tends to take a little longer to start flowering, but the shortness more than makes up for its laziness to flower. Full sun.

Torenia

WISHBONE FLOWER

I always enjoy teaching this genus in my herbaceous class, because I know it will always be readily identified (though perhaps not spelled correctly) as soon as the student looks inside the flower. There, two fused stamens look just like the wishbone from the Thanksgiving turkey. Simple stuff, this ID class.

The wishbone flower (*Torenia fournieri*) has historically been grown from seed and bred in many colors. Over the years, as the vigor improved and more cultivars became available, plants have become more visible, both indoors as houseplants and out. In the garden, I enjoy the Clown series, which offers many colors, including my favorite,

'Clown Blue'. The garden performance is excellent in spring and early summer but declines as hot temperatures occur. Plants persist longer in the North than in the South. Better in containers than in the garden bed.

A breakthrough in torenia breeding occurred with the appearance of 'Summer Wave Blue', a vegetatively propagated form. It has been an outstanding selection, and although flowering declines a little in the summer, the plant remains healthy. The flower color is excellent, and I highly recommend this flowering plant. 'Summer Wave

Torenia fournieri 'Clown Violet'

Torenia fournieri, wishbone

Torenia fournieri 'Clown Blue and White'

Torenia fournieri 'Clown Burgundy'

MORE ☞

Amethyst' followed that success and provided an additional color, then the Moon series came along, adding 'Blue Moon' and 'Pink Moon'.

Some people have tired of wishbone flower and even find it pedestrian. If this should happen to you, try the very different yellow wishbone flower, *Torenia flava* 'Suzie Wong'. She has bright yellow flowers with a deep throat. Mysterious and beautiful. The yellow wishbone has less vigor than the cultivars above, but it is fun to have her in the garden, even if that time is fleeting. All torenias do well in patio containers. Afternoon shade.

Torenia fournieri 'Pink Moon'

Torenia flava 'Suzie Wong'

Torenia fournieri 'Clown Blue'

Torenia fournieri 'Summer Wave Blue'

Torenia fournieri 'Summer Wave Amethyst'

Torenia fournieri 'Blue Moon'

Trachelium caeruleum 'Purple Umbrella'

Trachelium caeruleum 'Purple Umbrella', flower head

Trachelium caeruleum 'White Umbrella'

Tropaeolum speciosum

Trachelium caeruleum

THROATWORT

This annual is far more common in florists' shops and in vases than it is in the garden. Throatwort (*Trachelium caeruleum*) is usually produced in greenhouses and fields, and I have seen rows upon rows of these plants, which were thought to assuage ailments of the throat, ready for harvest. Flowers persist for well over a week in the vase. The flower head is beautiful, but it is not until you look at it closely that you realize it consists of hundreds of small individual flowers.

Although plants are usually greenhouse-grown, I have been asked to trial throatwort a number of times outdoors, but I can't say I have seen any breakthroughs for garden performance. In most gardens, they struggle in conditions of high heat and humidity, and heavy rain does not do them a lot of good either. Certainly they look better in the Northwest, Northeast, or in the mountains. Only purple flowers ('Purple Umbrella') and white ('White Umbrella') are available, and only occasionally at that. My feeling is that we will see a lot more throatworts in the vase, and few in the nursery. Full sun.

Tropaeolum

NASTURTIUM

The genus has been in gardens for centuries and takes on many faces. In the British Isles, hedges are often festooned with the flame nasturtium, *Tropaeolum speciosum*, which may succeed in half a

MORE ☞

dozen gardens in this country, but not yours or mine. Other species are absolutely fabulous, and equally difficult to grow, such as canary creeper, *T. peregrinum*, or the beautiful *T. polyphyllum* with blue-green leaves and vibrant yellow flowers. If you are really adventurous, try to find the vining multicolored nasturtium, *T. tricolorum*, purchased as a corm and trained in conservatories. All these magical plants can be found through diligent searching, all can be placed in the summer garden, all will be costly, and none will perform as well here as they do in England or Vancouver. But as long as the garden juices flow, we will always try plants the books tell us we can't grow. Just save a little money for the children's college fund.

The plant we are most familiar with is good old-fashioned *Tropaeolum majus*, and while these nasturtiums are kind of boring compared to the species just described, they have one characteristic that the others do not: they work! As many times as I have seen nasturtiums, I can't walk by these colorful plants as they flow out of window boxes or patio containers without admiring them. Perhaps nasturtiums have been superseded by newer introductions or other plants have better ad agencies—whatever, I don't really see a lot of nasturtiums anymore. Then again, maybe I am looking in the wrong gardens. All nasturtiums love cool temperatures; they are generally planted for the spring season and often removed as summer temperatures rise, for more heat-tolerant plants. That does not bother me at all—it is the lot of cool lovers like

Tropaeolum polyphyllum

Tropaeolum tricolorum

Tropaeolum peregrinum 'Canary Bird'

Tropaeolum majus Jewel series

calendula and viola, and they each have their place.

Nasturtiums come in many colors, and purchasing seeds will allow good selection. The Jewel series is a popular bright mixture of colors; 'Red Jewel' is particularly colorful. They are fine in the garden bed and useful in containers, and can be trained to climb as well. Orange and red are common, but lovely yellows like 'Moonlight' are worth seeking out. Many people are enamored with the variegated foliage forms, most often available in 'Alaska', which may bear yellow or orange flower. They are particularly handsome in containers. Fascina-

Tropaeolum majus 'Moonlight'

Tropaeolum tuberosum 'Ken Aslett'

Tropaeolum majus

Tropaeolum majus 'Red Jewel'

Tropaeolum majus 'Alaska'

Tropaeolum majus 'Darjean Gold'

MORE ☞

tion with variegation is one thing, yet when I heard about the double-flowered forms, I was definitely not interested. But when I saw 'Darjean Gold', I thought it was pretty neat, even if the flower color was not outstanding. However, I must have been fifty feet away when 'Hermine Grashoff' came into view. She had not yet reached her mature size, but she was already a 55-mph plant. The doubles are usually grown from cuttings and may not be all that easy to locate. Lastly, even harder to locate and more temperamental is the tuberous nasturtium, *Tropaeolum tuberosum,* which vines up walls with little effort. The only

named cultivar I am aware of is 'Ken Aslett'. This is a teaser, don't get mad at me when Ken doesn't make it. All nasturtiums decline in the heat, so get them in early. Full sun.

Turnera

One of my colleagues and friends in horticulture is Alan Shapiro, the owner of San Felasco Nurseries in Gainesville, Florida. I believe he feels that someone has to educate this poor foreigner, and he has taken on that difficult task himself. Whenever we talk plants, he always shows me species I have never heard of and helps me in spite of myself. A won-

derful nursery, a great plantsman. It was Alan who introduced me to turneras, in particular to the buttercup flower, *Turnera ulmifolia.* To Floridians and Texans, this is a fairly common plant, reseeding and often becoming somewhat weedlike, but to the rest of the country, it is unknown.

'Eldorado' is a selection that is available nationally, and time will tell if it succeeds above the 30th parallel. However, with its beautiful yellow flowers, handsome dark green foliage, and disdain of heat and humidity, this should be tried in Dubuque and Moose Bay as well as in Baton Rouge and Biloxi.

The genus is only now being trialed around the country, and another species that may have potential is *Turnera subulata,* with wonderful white flowers with a yellow eye. Plants are weedy, but selection is presently under way to improve the garden characteristics. Full sun.

Tweedia caerulea

Any plant with a name like tweedia can't be all bad, and I figured if I could get my hands on a few, I should surely like to try some. I did and I tried, and I found the ultimate in the color blue. *Tweedia caerulea* is surely not a common plant in retail stores, although more progressive growers may have some. It is also available through mail order and the Internet. So what's the deal? The flower color has been said to be the finest blue in the plant kingdom, and I cannot dispute that claim. Plants can be grown in containers or in the bed and have been used as cut flowers, the blue proving popular for weddings and corsages. When planting, put them where they will have protection from the wind and, if possible, from driving rain. They belong to the same family as milkweed, and they produce long narrow milkweed-like pods, which can get messy by the end of the season.

Tropaeolum majus 'Hermine Grashoff'

Turnera ulmifolia 'Eldorado', flowers

Turnera subulata

Turnera ulmifolia 'Eldorado'

Tweedia caerulea

Tweedia caerulea, flowers

While people sometimes gush over the plant, they must also remember that rain can disfigure the flowers. And the plants themselves, well, they don't smell very good. Personally I love these things, but they are not particularly easy to grow, they set lots of messy fruit, and they have a disagreeable odor. Given those characteristics, and the enthusiasm of North American gardeners, I expect tweedia to become a bestseller. Full sun.

Verbena

VERVAIN

I am often asked what group of plants has seen the greatest explosion in the shortest amount of time. It is a good question to ponder and I have no absolute answer, but I would put verbenas close to the top, along with pansies, coleus, and sunflowers. As late as 1989, most annual verbena (*Verbena ×hybrida*) were seed-propagated, like the Olympia series, and although they were pretty, they lacked the vigor to withstand landscape rigors in many parts of the country. Good grounds-keepers, like those at the University of Georgia, realized they needed some-

Verbena ×hybrida Olympia series

thing better and began to plant large beds of the pink Canadian verbena, *Verbena canadensis*. The perennial tall verbena did look much better with a dense planting of pink verbena at its feet, but landscapers needed additional choices. A few vegetative cultivars had always been kicking around, and in the late 1980s 'Homestead Purple' was introduced and enjoyed explosive popularity. It provided persistent flowering, excellent color, and exceptional vigor, and often overwintered in mild winters. Plants are still popular.

Armed with the knowledge that peo-

Verbena 'Fire King'

ple would purchase verbena in large numbers, plant breeders got busy, and within five years, dozens of hybrid cultivars were introduced or simply reintroduced to fill the demand. At Athens, we tested dozens, trying to come up with reasons to recommend some over others. As of this writing, I bet there are over fifty cultivars vying for the gardener's dollar; some are fabulous, some are just good, but all are improvements over the old-fashioned seed items sold years ago. Some of the best include the cutleaf Tapien series, such as the beautiful

MORE ☞

'Tapien Pink' planted in a boxwood container by the side of a pool. Another excellent series is Temari, and 'Temari Bright Red' is indeed just that. Red-rose has always been a popular color in verbenas, and 'Fire King' proved to be an exceptionally good performer as well. 'Blue Princess' provided a nice lavender-blue color, and 'Denim Blue' also had many fans when it hit the retail stores.

We do a lot of verbena trialing in containers, and they combine well with anything. I love the terrific introductions in the Wildfire series. 'Wildfire Purple' is

Verbena canadensis with tall verbena

Verbena 'Blue Princess'

Verbena 'Homestead Purple'

Verbena 'Denim Blue'

Verbena, UGA Trial Gardens

Verbena 'Tapien Pink'

Verbena 'Temari Bright Red'

Verbena 'Wildfire Purple'

Verbena 'Wildfire Blush'

Verbena 'Tortuga Peach', *V.* 'Tortuga Red'

Verbena 'Ron Deal'

MORE ☞

certainly vigorous, but I didn't really mind that it ate up almost everything in the container except some white purslane. 'Wildfire Blush' provides outstanding but more subtle color as well. 'Tortuga Peach' and 'Tortuga Red' have large flowers and happily coexist with purslane and mussaenda. 'Aztec Red', but one of many colors of the Aztec series, flowered all summer in the containers and the garden. 'Turkana Scarlet' is one of the new generation of bright colorful verbenas, and I was also pleased with the Twilight series, such as 'Twilight Blue with Eye'. One of the brightest new verbe-

Verbena ×hybrida 'Peaches and Cream'

Verbena 'Aztec Red'

Verbena 'Turkana Scarlet'

Verbena 'Twilight Blue with Eye'

Verbena ×hybrida 'Sandy Rose'

Verbena ×hybrida Quartz series

nas is 'Ron Deal', with electric violet flowers and fine heat and humidity tolerance.

One of the best things that all this breeding did was make the seed-propagated cultivars of *Verbena ×hybrida* better, because seed breeders realized that they had to instill additional colors and vigor if people were going to use their cultivars. In a European garden, I noticed 'Peaches and Cream' used at the front of a large planting of marigolds and ageratum. It was handsome, but summer weather there is not as abusive as it is in the Midwest. Newer seed strains such as the Sandy series performed well, and many colors in the Quartz series have been developed. One of the seed series that was most popular before the onslaught of the vegetative forms was the Romance series, and even it has been improved for gardeners. 'Romance Violet with Eye' is one of the more vigorous colors.

The hybrids of these colorful verbenas dominate the annual verbena market, but our native cutleaf verbena, *Verbena tenuisecta*, is also a marvelous plant. It can be grown in all its purple glory as a groundcover, and it will flower from May to frost. Its white coun-

MORE ☞

Verbena rigida 'Polaris'

Verbena tenuisecta

Verbena ×hybrida 'Romance Violet with Eye'

Verbena tenuisecta var. *alba*

Verbena rigida 'Lilacina'

terpart, var. *alba*, is almost as good and equally vigorous. These plants have also been the backbone of some of the cultivars listed previously. The rigid verbena, *V. rigida*, is considered more of a perennial than annual, but it is often used as an annual in the Midwest or Northeast, where it will likely not overwinter. A common form is 'Lilacina', with purple flowers, but by far the most handsome selection is 'Polaris', with light mauve flowers used to perfection in a combination planting with red geraniums and yellow bidens. Full sun.

Vigna

Whenever you eat bean sprouts in a sandwich or at a Chinese restaurant, you are eating sprouts from this genus. Moth bean, adzuki bean, mung bean, and cowpea are all important crops in India, Indonesia, and South and Central America. Gardeners are little interested in such facts but are fascinated with one of the members of this genus, the snail vine, *Vigna caracalla*.

Snail vines are easily grown from seed and consist of hairy leaflets and vigorous stems. They can grow 8–10' in a single season. However, it is not the leaves but the flowers that are unique, looking like pink to rose-colored snails' shells as they form later in the season. There are bigger vines, better vines, and more colorful vines, but none that will have people exclaiming as quickly as this one. Full sun.

Viola

PANSY, VIOLET

Many of the literally hundreds of species of violets may be obnoxious weeds in your garden, but there are at least a bazillion well-behaved pansies and vio-

Vigna caracalla

Viola ×*wittrockiana*, UGA Trial Gardens

las out there, waiting to be planted in early spring in the Midwest and North and in the fall in the South and Far West. Having resided in the South for the last twenty years, where pansies and violas are a landscape staple in winter and spring, I have been inundated with these plants and have trialed most of that bazillion. I have watched the trickle of cultivars become a torrent in a very short time. It has been a blast!

Pansies are not as popular in northern areas, where they are not normally planted out in the fall, but they are more cold hardy than many landscapers and gardeners give them credit for. They can be planted in early fall most anywhere, and if salt doesn't get them, they will flower at the first hint of spring. In areas of cool summers, they can remain in the ground the entire season. However, most pansies and violas are treated as winter annuals in the South (pulled out with the kale and Iceland poppies to make way for summer annuals) and as spring annuals in the North (removed with the nasturtiums for the same reason).

The pansies and violas sold in the garden center are referred to as *Viola ×wittrockiana*. In 1990, I was asked to help evaluate literally thousands of pansies in

Pansies with tulips and sign

Pansies, containers

Pansies high and low

Viola 'Medallion Yellow with Blotch' (pansy)

MORE ☞

trial fields in California; it was a daunting sight and, after the first fifty or so, an incredibly boring task. You would have thought I learned my lesson, but we were still doing the same thing in Georgia into the twenty-first century. And cultivars have evolved, not only in number but also in quality. I believe I can say there are no dogs out there anymore—buy the color you like, and it will more than likely perform just fine in your garden.

Pansies improve outdoor signage, fill baskets and containers high and low, and add early spring color to formal

Pansies in boxwood garden

Viola 'Accord Banner Yellow with Red Blotch' (pansy)

Viola 'Dancer Beaconsfield' (pansy)

Viola 'Maxim Marina' (pansy)

Viola 'Imperial Frosty Rose' (pansy)

Viola 'Ultima Yellow Beacon' (pansy)

Viola 'Atlas Blue' (pansy)

boxwood gardens, giving people an excuse to spend more than thirty seconds looking at boxwood gardens. Pansies come in two main color patterns, those with "faces" and those without. In the case of the former, the patterns are really quite fantastic. Those with big purple blotches are the most common, as in 'Medallion Yellow with Blotch', but blotches come in different colors, such as in 'Accord Banner Yellow with Red Blotch'. (Obviously, breeders' creativity in naming flowers died when they hit *Viola*!) Blues and purples combined with white also became popular. The

Viola 'Melody Red' (pansy)

Viola 'Padparaja' (pansy)

Viola 'Halloween' (pansy)

Viola 'Sorbet Coconut Swirl' (viola)

MORE ☞

purple color of 'Dancer Beaconsfield' is in sharp contrast to the more subtle blue in 'Maxim Marina'. One of the cultivars I thought was outstanding in our gardens was 'Imperial Frosty Rose', a color nearly everyone stopped to admire. When you walk into a garden center and see all these faces staring back at you, give one or two a home. However, landscapers realized that clear-face forms have the greatest visibility, and breeding those with clear faces (like 'Ultima Yellow Beacon'), which could be seen from a longer distance, became immensely popular. Blue will always have a place in gardens, and 'Atlas Blue' was a favorite to contrast with yellows. Reds are also reasonably popular; 'Melody Red' always showed up well in the landscape. Perhaps breeders got a little bored and went to work on eye-poppers and novelties. When the vibrant orange of 'Padparaja' was introduced, everybody did a double take; unfortunately it was a poor greenhouse performer and may be difficult to find these days. While that color was strikingly bright, black continues enormously popular. Black pansies like 'Halloween' are sold in the fall and must get gardeners into a ghostly spirit—how else can you explain such phenomenal popularity? To be honest, they are fascinating, and like them or not, isn't it great to have such a choice?

Viola 'Princess Deep Purple' (viola)

Viola 'Jewel Blue' (viola)

Viola Sorbet series (viola), container

Viola 'Penny Azure Wing' (viola)

Viola 'Wink Purple and White' (viola)

A major trend in flower breeding in the '90s was to reduce flower size but increase flower number on big-ticket items like petunia, impatiens, and pansies. A viola is nothing more than a small-flowered version of the pansy. While there are numerous similarities, there are also numerous differences. Our data suggest that for best weather tolerance against snow, wind, and rain, violas rebound more quickly and are better garden performers—a generality but one that our trials have borne out. And breeders have not been sitting on their hands. The Sorbet series, a fabulous group of plants, is one of the most popular, showing up in gardens and in containers that welcome people to the front door. Containers of 'Princess Deep Purple' offer that deep color so desired by gardeners today, but I prefer calmer waters, such as those of 'Jewel Blue'. Violas also provide unique colors; 'Penny Azure Wing' is subtle and engaging, while the small flowers of 'Wink Purple and White' earned it many fans when we planted it in 2002. But my favorite of all the violas I have seen has to be 'Bilbo Baggins', part of the Hobbit series. Hundreds of small colorful flowers on 9" tall plants—J.R. would be proud.

The modern pansies and violas are difficult not to admire, but we should not forget one of the plants that made this happen, that is the good old johnny-jump-up, *Viola tricolor*. Jumping up everywhere, they became one of the main parents in the breeding revolution of this genus. It is always fun to have some of the old folks around, it puts things in perspective. Some of the johnnies also became transformed, and it is difficult to know where the violas leave off and the jump-ups begin. Of course, it does not matter, and if you can locate 'Irish Molly' or 'Penny Wood', two old-fashioned but handsome cultivars, your garden will be even richer.

Full sun. In the South, plant in October, fertilize heavily in February. In the North, plant in September or as soon as the melting snow in spring allows; fertilize when warm weather is forecast for three days in a row.

351

Viola 'Bilbo Baggins'

Viola 'Irish Molly'

Viola tricolor

Viola 'Penny Wood'

Xanthosoma

TANNIA

I had never even heard of *Xanthosoma* until a few years ago, when I was at a plant seminar and trade show. I was walking the floor when one of my plant friends asked, "Allan, what do you think of that golden xanthosoma?" I didn't have a clue what he was talking about, so I replied, "I must not have seen it yet, I don't recall it." "But it's right beside you, you were just looking at it." "Oh, that xanthosoma." So much for the expert.

Xanthosoma sagittifolium (tannia) is second only to *Colocasia* (eddo, taro) as a food crop; its edible corms are a staple carbohydrate throughout the tropics. Several ornamental forms of tannia have found their way into the garden, but unless somebody is giving you hints, you are unlikely to tell *Xanthosoma*, *Alocasia*, and *Colocasia* apart at first glance. I certainly did not (see *Alocasia*). While *Alocasia* and *Colocasia* have been gaining a foothold in gardeners' consciousnesses, *Xanthosoma* is a relative rookie to North American gardens.

In general, they are large plants, growing 4–5' tall and equally wide in a single season. They are not grown for their jack-in-the-pulpit type flowers but rather for their large foliage and architectural dominance. A couple of cultivars exist, and their foliar qualities are the only reason to grow this rather than the less expensive colocasias. The biggest is blue tannia, *Xanthosoma violaceum*, with deep green to purple-tinged foliage. My favorite is golden tannia, var. *muffafa*, whose lighter-colored leaves are outstanding. I have also seen this plant, or something very similar, labeled as 'Chartreuse Giant'. Regardless of the name, it can make a significant landscape feature. All require heat to get going, but they are more tolerant of drought and lower temperatures than their tropical cousins. All require a cold frame or greenhouse for overwintering. I have no doubt that as the tropical movement continues to grow, this group of plants will also grow in popularity. Full sun.

Xanthosoma violaceum

Xanthosoma violaceum var. *muffafa*

Xanthosoma violaceum 'Chartreuse Giant'

Xeranthemum annuum 'Lilac Stars'

Zea mays 'Bars and Stripes'

Xeranthemum

IMMORTELLE

Immortelle is one of the many plants known as everlastings, including relatives like strawflowers, *Bracteantha*. I have grown xeranthemums on a few occasions; they are easy to germinate from seed and grow well in the spring and early summer but decline with warm temperatures, high humidity, and summer rainfall. They are South African in origin and prefer hot, dry climates with excellent drainage. They are fun to grow and pick for the everlasting vase or for potpourri. *Xeranthemum annuum* 'Lilac Stars' is an available mixture, growing about 12–15" tall and providing handsome color early in the season. They can also be planted around mid to late summer, and they will flower well into the fall. Full sun.

Zea

CORN

I should not be surprised by anything I see in gardens anymore. Not by weird and

Zea mays 'Tiger Cub'

worthless garden art, not by reflective mirrors, not by trains chugging back and forth, and certainly not by ornamental vegetables. In this book alone, I have described ornamental okra, kale, sweet potato, pepper, and eggplant, to name just a few, and so when I was told about some new cultivars of ornamental corn (*Zea mays*), I was somewhat prepared for the plants, which are now hitting the North

American marketplace. After all, some of the prettiest sweet corn has white and yellow kernels, and Indian corn has always been pretty, but I was not prepared for the beauty of the plants themselves.

There have been many attempts at making corn more ornamental, but the two I saw at the Parks Seed trials in South Carolina were the best yet. The

MORE ☞

dwarfer form, 'Tiger Cub', has white bands running down the leaves and only stands about 3' tall. It was beautiful, and I was impressed. However, I was floored when I saw 'Bars and Stripes' around the corner; plants were 5' tall and had similar white markings on the foliage, but the stems and the fruit were purple. I did not taste the ears—I suspect there are tastier cobs out there—but their beauty was unsurpassed. Seed is being multiplied, so there will be enough to offer in 2004 or 2005. If you cultivate this in the middle of your garden, your vegetable gardening friends might finally consider you a "real" gardener after all. Full sun.

Zinnia

Johann Gottfried Zinn (1727–1759), a professor of botany at Göttingen, Germany, would have long faded from horticultural history had Linnaeus, the father of modern botany, not named a small daisy to commemorate his friend. Zinnias have been part of our gardens for as long as there have been gardens, and from that small daisy, many cultivars have been developed along the way. They have always been enjoyed by gardeners, and they have also been harvested for ages as cut flowers, complementing other cuts like statice, melampodium, and ornamental grasses. There are approximately twenty species, but only two or three contain most of the plants we garden with.

The most common and colorful group of plants belongs to the common zinnia, *Zinnia elegans*. These were probably a mainstay of your mother's garden and

Zinnia elegans 'Cherry Ruffles'

Zinnia elegans, Butchart Gardens

355

Zinnia elegans 'Big Top'

Zinnia elegans 'Silver Sun'

Zinnia elegans Dreamland series

Zinnia 'Profusion White'

Zinnia elegans 'Oklahoma Mix'

Zinnia 'Profusion Orange'

MORE ☞

her mother's garden before her. They are easy to germinate, easy to grow, and easy to love. They are used as colorful companions to a winding path at the Butchart Gardens, as a bold planting on the University of Georgia campus, as with 'Cherry Ruffles' here—in almost every conceivable situation. Zinnias first became popular as tall cut flower types;

selections like 'Big Top' were used at the back of the bed so that their disease-ridden leaves would be hidden from the world. The tall cultivars were shortened a little, and much more garden-friendly forms, such as the Dreamland series, evolved. They are still 3' tall, with large flowers, but less needy of constant maintenance. Many other large-flowered tall cultivars have been bred. Oklahoma series was selected as the 2000 Cut Flower

of the Year by the Association of Specialty Cut Flower Growers; 'Oklahoma Mix', growing 2–4' tall, is an excellent cut flower and handsome garden plant. I have always enjoyed the Sun series, particularly 'Silver Sun', as well as the 3' tall plants common in the Dahlia series, such as 'Dahlia Royal Purple'. Shorter upright forms are also available; Blue Point Mix provides many vibrant colors in a compact package. Foliar diseases are the

Zinnia, arrangement with statice, melampodium, and ornamental grass

Zinnia elegans 'Dahlia Royal Purple'

Zinnia elegans Blue Point Mix

Zinnia 'Profusion Cherry'

biggest problems with all cultivars of common zinnia, and if you eventually see enough plants shriveling up or leaves turning white or brown, the passion for zinnia lessens. To be sure, some cultivars are less susceptible than others, and if you are fortunate enough to be able to grow picture-perfect zinnias all season, go for it. If not, all is not lost. Some people resow seeds at the base of existing plants in June or July and lift the old plants as they tire, allowing the youngsters to mature in late summer and fall.

Another increasingly popular choice is to choose cultivars derived from more disease-resistant species. The Profusion series is a hybrid with common zinnia and other species and is the best zinnia for good performance, low maintenance, and color choice. 'Profusion Cherry' and 'Profusion White' were named All-America Selections in 1999 and 2001, respectively; 'Profusion Orange' is just as good.

Gardeners have long recognized the low-maintenance attributes of narrow-leaf zinnia, *Zinnia angustifolia*. Plants grow only about 8–12" tall, but they flower and flower, normally in yellows and oranges; if they get a little leggy, simply cut them back. The Crystal series has performed very well in trials across the country, and both 'Crystal Orange' and 'Crystal White' provide months of color with few disease problems. That is not to say that disease will not rear its ugly head with these forms, but it will be far less obvious. Other low-growing forms include 'Persian Carpet', a selection of *Z. haageana*, with bicolored flowers and medium-grade maintenance.

All zinnias benefit from deadheading. Proper cultivar selection and ample spacing between plants reduces disease problems. Full sun.

Zinnia angustifolia

Zinnia 'Crystal Orange'

Zinnia 'Crystal White'

Zinnia haageana 'Persian Carpet'

PART TWO
Selected Plants
for Specific Characteristics
or Purposes

The following lists are for readers' convenience only, meant as guidelines for determining what plants fit what function. The plants are, for the most part, listed by genus only; the specific species or cultivar fitting the heading should be self-evident when reading that section.

FALL INTEREST
Many annuals provide outstanding interest in the fall, by virtue of their late flowers or fall leaf color. Plants that produce fruit in the fall are included under "Fruit."

Barleria (flowers)
Cuphea micropetala (flowers)
Kochia (foliage)
Odontonema (flowers)
Otacanthus (flowers)
Salvia (flowers)
Tecomaria (flowers)

SHADE
Some afternoon shade is necessary; most will tolerate filtered sun all day. Only *Cornukaempferia*, *Impatiens*, and *Kaempferia* tolerate deep shade.

Alternanthera
Begonia
Caladium
Coleus
Cornukaempferia
Impatiens
Kaempferia
Phlox

COOL SEASON
These plants perform best in the spring or fall, and do poorly in areas of hot summers and high humidity. Some are routinely used as winter annuals in the South.

Antirrhinum
Argyranthemum
Bellis
Brassica
Calendula
Clarkia
Consolida

Coreopsis
Dianthus
Erysimum
Felicia
Fuchsia
Heliotropium
Linaria
Lobelia
Matthiola
Osteospermum
Papaver
Pelargonium domesticum
Reseda
Salpiglossis
Viola
Xeranthemum

WINTER ANNUALS
These plants are usually planted in the fall and are often green during early winter, but flower or provide outstanding foliage in late winter and early spring.

Antirrhinum
Bellis
Brassica
Dianthus
Papaver
Viola

UNIQUE FLOWER OR FRUIT
Asclepias (fruit)
Bracteantha (flower)
Clerodendrum (fruit)
Lantana trifolia (fruit)
Nelumbo (fruit)
Nigella (fruit)
Ricinus (fruit)
Xeranthemum (flower)

EDIBLE PLANTS
These may not be on the menu of five-star restaurants, but each is enjoyed as a food crop somewhere in the world.

Abelmoschus esculentus
Abelmoschus manihot
Alocasia
Basella
Capsicum
Colocasia

Ipomoea batatas
Solanum

ARCHITECTURAL FEATURES
A nice way of saying that these are big plants that, when grown well, can dominate the garden.

Alocasia
Angelica
Basella
Brugmansia
Canna
Colocasia
Curcuma
Graptophyllum
Hibiscus acetosella
Leonotis
Musa
Mussaenda
Nelumbo
Solanum
Strobilanthes
Tibouchina
Tithonia
Xanthosoma

PRICKLY PLANTS
For the plant masochist, or lover of pain.

Argemone
Cirsium
Datura (fruit)
Duranta
Ricinus (fruit)
Solanum

FOR NATURALIZING
The following plants are often chosen for their ability to reseed and are tough enough to look good with minimal maintenance. Not all work as well as others, and plants must be chosen based on locale.

Coreopsis
Cosmos
Eschscholzia
Linaria
Lychnis
Nemophila
Polygonum

Portulaca
Rudbeckia
Sanvitalia
Scabiosa
Verbena

FOR FLORAL DESIGNS

These are plants for outdoor floral designs, such as floral clocks and formal floral settings. Essentially they are short, compact, and grown for their foliage, not their flowers.

Alternanthera
Begonia
Hemigraphis
Laurentia fluviatilis
Lobelia

FOR CONTAINERS AND BASKETS

Nearly all plants in this book perform well in containers or garden beds. This list contains those that, in general, perform better in containers than in the garden bed.

Abutilon
Acalypha
Alternanthera
Antirrhinum (trailing forms)
Asystasia
Ballota pseudodictamnus
Begonia (rex and tuberous groups)
Bidens ferulifolia
Brachycome
Calibrachoa
Cerinthe
Clerodendrum ugandense
Clerodendrum speciosissimum
Coleus
Dianella
Evolvulus
Gerbera
Heliotropium
Hemigraphis
Impatiens (doubles)
Iresine
Lobelia
Lotus
Mimulus
Monopsis

Musa
Mussaenda
Nierembergia
Pavonia
Pelargonium peltatum
Phlox
Portulaca
Scaevola
Sutera
Torenia
Verbena

FOR EDGING

These plants are generally short and provide season-long flowering.

Ageratum
Alternanthera
Begonia
Bellis
Calendula
Catharanthus
Erysimum
Evolvulus
Hemigraphis
Lobelia
Nierembergia
Sanvitalia
Verbena

FOLIAGE

Nearly all genera have a variegated member or two, but this list includes cultivars whose major ornamental asset is their foliage, either color, texture, or fragrance. Flowers may occur but are often secondary.

Abutilon
Acalypha
Alocasia
Alpinia
Alternanthera
Ballota
Basella
Begonia (rex group)
Breynia
Canna
Coleus
Colocasia
Curcuma
Euphorbia marginata

Graptophyllum
Helichrysum
Hypoestes
Impatiens (New Guinea)
Ipomoea batatas
Lotus
Pennisetum glaucum
Perilla
Plectranthus
Pseuderanthemum
Xanthosoma
Zea

FRAGRANCE

Fragrance is in the nose of the beholder, and not all of these are considered "bath-oil" fresh. However, they are fun to sniff.

Agastache
Cosmos
Datura
Helichrysum
Heliotropium
Lobularia
Nicotiana
Plectranthus
Reseda
Salvia
Tweedia
Viola

BIENNIALS

Some members of these genera require two years to flower, then either reseed or die.

Alcea
Angelica
Dianthus
Echium
Erysimum
Euphorbia
Glaucium

FRUIT

All of these provide fruit during the season, often quite ornamental.

Asclepias
Canavalia
Cardiospermum
Clerodendrum

Fruit, continued

Dianella
Duranta
Euphorbia lathyris
Lablab
Lantana trifolia
Nelumbo
Solanum
Tweedia
Zea

HERBAL PLANTS
Some medicinal, culinary, or fragrance use is contained in this group of plants.

Agastache
Acmella
Alocasia
Basella
Colocasia
Plectranthus
Salvia

NATIVES
Some members of these genera are native to North America.

Bidens
Centaurea
Coreopsis
Cosmos
Eustoma
Gaillardia
Gilia
Heliotropium
Ipomoea
Nemophila
Rudbeckia
Russelia
Salvia
Tagetes
Verbena

VINES
An absolute wonderful diversity of vines awaits the bold gardener.

Asarina
Basella
Canavalia
Cardiospermum

Clitoria
Cobaea
Gloriosa
Ipomoea
Lablab
Mandevilla
Passiflora
Rhodochiton
Solanum
Stictocardia
Thunbergia
Tropaeolum
Tweedia
Vigna

LOVE THE HEAT
Plants perform best when temperatures remain consistently above 75°F, and tolerate high humidity and heat well into the 90s. While they tolerate such abusive conditions, many perform well in moderate climates as well.

Alocasia
Alpinia
Catharanthus
Colocasia
Curcuma
Graptophyllum
Hibiscus
Lantana
Pentas
Plumbago
Ruellia
Russelia
Scaevola
Xanthosoma

LOVE THE WATER
These may do fine in regular garden beds, but they thrive in boggy soil or in garden ponds.

Canna
Colocasia
Nelumbo

BULBOUS ROOTS AND GRASSES
Alocasia
Caladium
Colocasia

Dahlia
Gloriosa
Ipomoea batatas
Pennisetum (grass)

POISONOUS
Be as smart as your dog, don't eat these things.

Alocasia
Brugmansia
Colocasia
Datura
Ricinus

CUT FLOWERS
Nearly all plants can be used as cut flowers, especially if vase life is not a consideration. This list contains an assortment of plants routinely used by florists, designers, and amateur flower arrangers.

Agastache
Ageratum
Antirrhinum
Bracteantha
Callistephus
Caryopteris
Celosia
Centaurea
Cirsium
Clarkia
Consolida
Curcuma
Dianthus barbatus
Euphorbia marginata
Eustoma
Gerbera
Limonium
Linaria
Moluccella
Nelumbo (fruit)
Nigella (fruit)
Otacanthus
Pennisetum glaucum
Pentas
Rudbeckia
Salvia
Scabiosa
Trachelium
Tweedia
Zinnia

U.S.D.A. Hardiness Zone Map

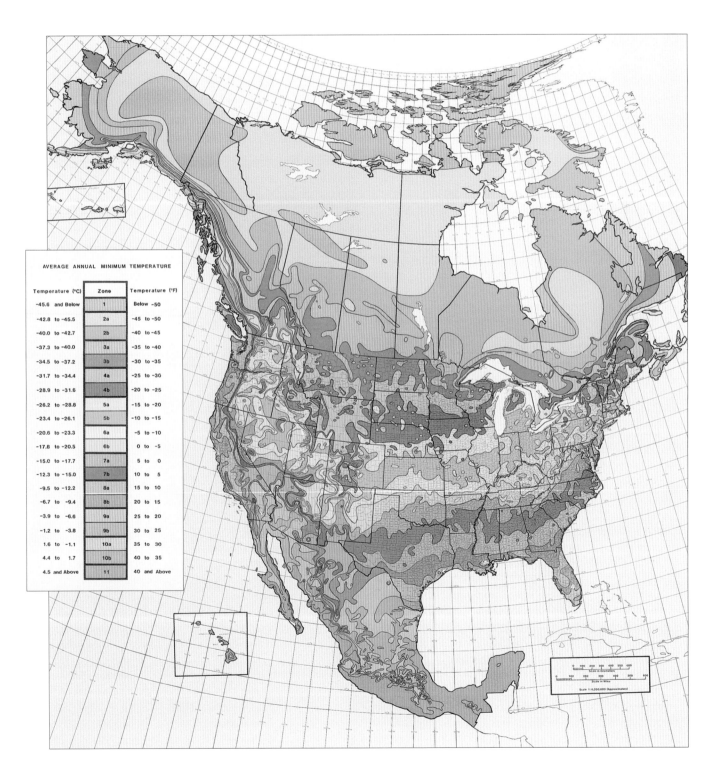

AVERAGE ANNUAL MINIMUM TEMPERATURE

Temperature (°C)	Zone	Temperature (°F)
-45.6 and Below	1	Below -50
-42.8 to -45.5	2a	-45 to -50
-40.0 to -42.7	2b	-40 to -45
-37.3 to -40.0	3a	-35 to -40
-34.5 to -37.2	3b	-30 to -35
-31.7 to -34.4	4a	-25 to -30
-28.9 to -31.6	4b	-20 to -25
-26.2 to -28.8	5a	-15 to -20
-23.4 to -26.1	5b	-10 to -15
-20.6 to -23.3	6a	-5 to -10
-17.8 to -20.5	6b	0 to -5
-15.0 to -17.7	7a	5 to 0
-12.3 to -15.0	7b	10 to 5
-9.5 to -12.2	8a	15 to 10
-6.7 to -9.4	8b	20 to 15
-3.9 to -6.6	9a	25 to 20
-1.2 to -3.8	9b	30 to 25
1.6 to -1.1	10a	35 to 30
4.4 to 1.7	10b	40 to 35
4.5 and Above	11	40 and Above

Index of Botanical Names

Index of Common Names